The Age
of Revelation

THE AGE OF REVELATION.

OR

THE AGE OF REASON

SHEWN TO BE

AN AGE OF INFIDELITY.

BY ELIAS BOUDINOT, L. L. D.
AND DIRECTOR OF THE MINT OF THE UNITED STATES.

" CHRISTIAN is the highest style of man,
" And is there, who the blessed cross wipes off,
" As a foul blot, from his dishonoured brow?
" If angles tremble, 'tis at such a sight.
" Wrong not the Christian; think not reason yours;
" 'Tis reason our great Master holds so dear;
" Believe, and shew the reason of a man:
" Believe, and taste the pleasure of a God;
" Believe, and look with triumph on the tomb."

YOUNG.

PHILADELPHIA:
PUBLISHED BY ASBURY DICKINS, OPPOSITE CHRIST-CHURCH.
HUGH MAXWELL, PRINTER, COLUMBIA-HOUSE.

1801.

THE AGE OF REVELATION

or

The Age of Reason Shewen to Be an Age of Infidelity

BY ELIAS BOUDINOT, L.L.D.
AND DIRECTOR OF THE MINT OF THE UNITED STATES

"CHRISTIAN is the highest style of man,
"And is there, who the blessed cross wipes off,
"As a foul blot, from his dishonored brow!
"If angels tremble. 'tis at such a sight.
"Wrong not the Christian; think not reason yours;
"'Tis reason our great Master holds so dear:
"Believe, and shew the reason of a man:
"Believe, and taste the pleasure of a God;
"Believe, and look with triumph on the tomb."
—YOUNG.

AMERICAN VISION PRESS
POWDER SPRINGS, GEORGIA

THE AGE OF REVELATION

or The Age of Reason Shewen to Be an Age of Infidelity

by Elias Boudinot, L.L.D.

Originally published by
"Asbury Dickins, opposite Christ-Church.
Hugh Maxwell, Printer, Columbus-House, 1801."

Produced by:
   The American Vision, Inc.
   3150 Florence Road
   Powder Springs, Georgia 30127-5385
   www.AmericanVision.org
   1-800-628-9460
   mail@AmericanVision.org

Printed in The United States of America

Cover design by Luis D. Lovelace
Typesetting by Adam Stiles

ISBN13: 978-0-9840641-7-5

CONTENTS

FOREWORD BY GARY DEMAR   vii

DEDICATION   xv

PREFACE   xxv

1   Age of Revelation   1

2   The Author of The Age of Reason's Introduction to His Work; Shewn to Be Without Proof or Argument   7

3   The Virgin Mary   15

4   The Divine Mission of Jesus Christ   31

5   The Christian Theory Misrepresented   43

6   Particular Notes on This Subject   71

7   The Character of Christ   85

8   Resurrection & Ascension of Christ   95

9   Authenticity of the Books of the New Testament   129

10   Objections to the Old Testament Considered   147

Foreword
by Gary DeMar

Elias Boudinot (1740–1821) was a lawyer who served three congressional terms representing New Jersey (1789–1795). He was a delegate to the Continental Congress, served as commissary general of prisoners at the request of George Washington, and was President of the Continental Congress from 1782 to 1783, making him the chief executive officer of the United States. Boudinot signed the Treaty of Paris in 1783 that ended the War for Independence, and while he did not participate directly in the drafting of the new Constitution in 1787, he "looked on approvingly at the events."[1] He helped design the Great Seal of the United States and served as Director of the United States Mint from 1795 until 1805. After his retirement from politics, Boudinot was a trustee of what is now Princeton University where he founded the natural history department in 1805. He was an early opponent of slavery.[2] This led him to found the American Bible Society in 1816 of which he served as its first president until his death in 1821. In accepting the position, Boudinot stated the following:

> I am so convinced that the whole of this business is the work of God himself, by his Holy Spirit, that even hoping against hope I am encouraged to press on through good report and evil report, to accomplish his will on earth as it is in heaven. So apparent is the hand of God in this disposing the hearts of so many men, so diversified in their sentiments as to religious matters of minor importance, and uniting them as a band of brothers in this grand object that even infidels are compelled to say, "It is the work of the Lord, and it is wonderful in our eyes!" Having this confidence, let us go on and we shall prosper.

Boudinot donated $10,000 to the ABS when an annual salary of $400 was considered respectable. What is often not known about Boudinot is that he wrote a lengthy response to Thomas Paine's *An Age of Reason* titled *The Age of Revelation* which was first written as a pamphlet to his daughter in 1795. In a letter to his daughter, Boudinot described his motives for his critique of Paine's attack on the Bible:

> I confess that I was much mortified to find the whole force of this vain man's genius and art pointed at the youth of America. . . . This awful consequence created some alarm in my mind lest at any future day, you, my beloved child, might take up this plausible address of infidelity; and for want of an answer at hand to his subtle insinuations might suffer even a doubt of the truth, as it is in Jesus, to penetrate your mind. . . . I therefore determined . . . to put my thoughts on the subject of this pamphlet on paper for your edification and information, when I shall be no more. I chose to confine myself to the leading and essential facts of the Gospel which are contradicted or attempted to be turned into ridicule by this writer. I have endeavored to detect his falsehoods and misrepresentations and to show his extreme ignorance of the Divine Scriptures which he makes the subject of his animadversions— not knowing that "they are the power of God unto salvation, to every one that believeth" [Rom. 1:16].[3]

While Paine' *Age of Reason* gets a great deal of press from skeptics, misinformed separationists, and atheists of every stripe, almost no one mentions Boudinot's book-length response. Paine is considered to be an American Founding Father, and yet, unlike Paine, Boudinot actually served in a civil capacity in the United States. Paine's only elective office was in France. Boudinot is a true American Founding Father. Paine had no role in the founding conventions of America and their documents.

Boudinot expressed the religious views of the majority of Americans at a critical point in America's history. Supreme Court Justice William Rehnquist wrote the following in his Dissent in the 1985 *Wallace v. Jaffree* decision that dealt with Church and State separation: "On the day after the House of Representatives voted to adopt the form of the First Amendment Religion Clauses which was ultimately proposed and ratified, Representative Elias Boudinot proposed a resolution asking President George Washington to issue a Thanksgiving Day Proclamation. Boudinot said he 'could not think of letting the session pass over without offering an opportunity to all the citizens of the United States of joining with one voice, in returning to Almighty God their sincere thanks for the many blessings he had poured down upon them.' Boudinot's resolution was carried in the affirmative on September 25, 1789"[4] with only two recorded objections. Constitutional scholar Robert L.

Cord remarks, "It is quite clear from the record that James Madison did not object to the resolution requesting the Thanksgiving Day Proclamation. It is also plain from the day's proceedings that [Roger] Sherman of Connecticut, who voted for the First Amendment and the Establishment Clause, apparently saw no conflict between his vote for the Amendment and his support for the Thanksgiving Day Proclamation. . . ."[5] It is this singular recommendation by Boudinot that sheds a bright light on the meaning of the First Amendment and the religious character of the constitutional participants. He argued by citing "further precedents from the practice of the late Congress" that had approved a series of thanksgiving-day proclamations. If the First Amendment was designed to exclude God from all areas of civil government, then why agree to call for a day of thanksgiving to thank God for allowing them to draft an Amendment that would forever exclude Him? Why did "they proceed to violate an important principle which, only a day earlier, they had voted to recommend to the States as a part of the constitutional amendment?"[6]

Boudinot waited some time before deciding to respond to Paine's *Age of Reason*. His measured rejoinder to Paine's work is contemplative and, contrary to Paine's treatise, a work of sound scholarship:

> For a considerable time past, I have ardently wished to see some more able hand, meet Mr. Paine more on his own ground, in a plain and simple manner—but after waiting several years, I have lost all hopes of being gratified; and therefore have been more easily persuaded to undergo, amidst a variety of other business, the labor of copying once more, what was designed for a particular and special purpose; and altering the address, by applying it more directly to the author of the *Age of Reason*, and through him to all his brethren in skepticism.
>
> I am averse to increasing the number of books, unless it be on important occasions, or for useful purposes; but an anxious desire that our country should be preserved from the dreadful evil of becoming enemies to the religion of the Gospel, which I have no doubt, but would be introductive of the dissolution of government and the bonds of civil society; my compliance with the wishes of a few select friends, to make this work public, has been more easily obtained.

Boudinot feared what we are experiencing today in America. "I confess," he wrote, "that I was much mortified to find, the whole force of this vain man's genius and art, pointed at the youth of America, and her unlearned citizens." Even though there are tens of thousands of churches and tens of millions of Christians, it seems that the skepticism of Paine has the upper hand. The prevalence of skepticism is more the inaction of Christians than the accomplishment of skeptics. Boudinot knew that he could no longer wait for someone else to respond. He understood that the duty was his, even if he did not consider himself worthy of the task. It's remarkable that *The Age of Revelation* was written by a layman who had a comprehensive knowledge of the Bible, classic philosophy, and history.

Like Paine, Thomas Jefferson, and John Adams, Boudinot saw flaws in the clergy of his day and was not shy about making his views public. In a letter to Edward Griffin in 1809, Boudinot wrote, "I have wished, among other improvements in Theological Studies, a professorship of Common Sense and Prudence was established in our Seminaries. I really have known as many ruinous Errors in practice, among our pious and zealous Ministers, for want of this celestial quality, that I am sure it is of more importance than is generally believed."[7] But unlike the skeptics of his and our day, the follies and foibles of *some* clergy were not enough for him to reject *all* clergy. Their misuse of the Bible was not the fault of the Bible anymore than the misuse of the Constitution by politicians is the fault of the Constitution.

It was Boudinot's opinion that if *The Age of Reason* had not been written by the popular author of *Common Sense*, the 1776 pamphlet that argued that America was justified in breaking away from the British monarchy, the book would not have been given much of a hearing. Boudinot shows that Paine did not uncover anything new under the sun. Modern-day atheists have only repackaged Paine for an audience that is not familiar with Elias Boudinot's *The Age of Revelation* which is a remarkable work of scholarship for that time. Boudinot quotes sources from nearly every field of knowledge. He seems to be acquainted with several languages, including Latin and Greek. He has a broad knowledge of the Bible and a keen sense of logical analysis. His work shows what an educated layman can do when spurred on by the need to answer a once-respected writer who abused his popularity to rail against a religious system that he either did not fully understand or had no wish to understand.

It will prove helpful at this point to learn something about the religious regression of Thomas Paine, from *Common Sense* in 1776 to *The Age of Reason* in 1794, that led Elias Boudinot to spend so much time in study to answer Christianity's most noted antagonist of his day.

Thomas Paine and *Common Sense*

Thomas Paine's *Common Sense* was constructed on "arguments from materials that were familiar to the average colonist, favoring allusions to popular history, nature, and scripture rather than Montesquieu, Tacitus, and Cicero."[8] There is no hint of deism in *Common Sense* or criticism of the Bible.

Alfred J. Ayer, a recent biographer of Paine, remarks that "the first argument that Paine brings against the institution of kingship is scriptural."[9] Paine declared that "government by kings was first introduced into the world by the Heathens, from which the children of Israel copied the custom. . . . As the exalting of one man so greatly above the rest cannot be justified on the equal rights of nature, so neither can it be defended on the authority of scripture; for the will of the Almighty, as declared by Gideon and the prophet Samuel, expressly disapproves of government by kings. All anti-monarchical parts of scripture have been smoothly glossed over in monarchical governments, but they undoubtedly merit the attention of countries which have their governments yet to form. 'Render unto Caesar the things which are Caesar's' is the scriptural doctrine of courts, yet it is no support of monarchical government, for the Jews at that time were without a king, and in a state of vassalage to the Romans."

Paine makes an often neglected point. Using Matthew 22:21 to support the claim that civil governments are not to be questioned or confronted by lesser magistrates or the people is misplaced and misunderstood. Israel was under the domination of Rome. We don't live under Caesar today, and the Americans didn't live under Caesar in the eighteenth century. Their dispute with the British monarchy and Parliament was over contractual issues. England had violated an agreement made by two sovereign powers and governments. Actually, in terms of the states, there had been multiple violations because there were 13 state governments.

Paine has an extended discussion of Judges 8:22-23 where he describes "the King of Heaven" to be Israel's "proper sovereign." He then spends several pages quoting, discussing, and making application of the importance of 1 Samuel 8 to the modern situation. He concludes this section of *Common Sense* with these words: "In short, monarchy and succession have laid (not this or that kingdom only) by the world in blood and ashes. 'Tis a form of government which the word of God bears testimony against, and blood will attend it." Yet, in his *Age of Reason*, Paine had no problem attacking the source of some of his best *Common Sense* arguments.

The Later Paine

It's the later Paine, the author of *The Age of Reason*, that secularists turn to in support of their claim that he was a deist and an ardent critic of Christianity and organized religion in general. While *Common Sense* was written in 1776, *The Age of Reason* was published around 1794, several years after the initial drafting (1787) and ratification (1791) of the Constitution. While Americans in general embraced *Common Sense* (surprisingly the French did not)—"fifty-six editions had been printed and 150,000 copies sold by the end of 1776"[10]—there was no public support for *The Age of Reason* by Thomas Jefferson, John Adams, Benjamin Rush, John Jay, and Benjamin Franklin:

> As for the supposition that the other Founders embraced "The Age of Reason" or its mindset: Jefferson advised Paine never to publish the book. Benjamin Franklin, Paine's patron and friend, gave his protégé the same advice. After reading a draft, Franklin noted: "He who spits against the wind spits in his own face. If men are wicked with religion, what would they be without it?"

> * * * * *

> John Adams, once a fan of Paines, having received his copy, called Paine a "blackguard"[11] who wrote out of the depths of "a malignant heart." And Washington, previously one of Paine's fiercest advocates, attacked Paine's principles in his Farewell Address (without referring to his name)[12] as unpatriotic and subversive.[13]

Paine's later views were so opposed by the public that he spent his last years in New York in relative obscurity. "Paine had expressed a wish to be buried in a Quaker cemetery, but the Society of Friends denied his request. In attendance at his graveside on his farm were his Quaker friend Wilbert Hicks, "Madame Bonneville, her son Benjamin, and two black men who wished to pay tribute to Paine for his efforts to put an end to slavery. It is probable that a few other persons were there but no one who officially represented either France or the United States."[14] Stokes and Pfeffer, writing in *Church and State in the United States*, state that "For a long time Paine, notwithstanding his great contributions to the Revolutionary cause, was held low in American public opinion."[15] Theodore Roosevelt's description of Thomas Paine "as a 'filthy little atheist' represented all too accurately the public estimate"[16] of him at the time. Although Paine was not an atheist—he believed in God and the immortality of the soul—the expression of his religious views in *The Age of Reason* put him outside the religious mainstream which was generally Christian. It's remarkable that so many of Paine's religious beliefs as expressed in his 1807 pamphlet *My Private Thoughts on a Future State* seem to have been drawn from the Bible. Michael Novak notes that "Paine hardly seems to be aware of how much of his new credo he owes, not to reason, but to the words of Jesus Christ. Neither the Greeks nor the Romans of the ancient world knew of 'the Creator,' nor of a divine justice and mercy, not of eternal life, nor that God called them to be His friends."[17]

The Thomas Paine of *Common Sense* and the Thomas Paine of *The Age of Reason* must be kept separate, both by time and philosophy. The later Paine cannot be superimposed on the earlier Paine. Without Paine's biblical arguments in *Common Sense*, the book would have been studied with great suspicion and might have sunk without a trace. Mark A. Noll, Professor of Christian Thought at Wheaton College, makes a similar argument:

> If Paine's *Age of Reason* (with its dismissive attitude toward the Old Testament) had been published before *Common Sense* (with its full deployment of Scripture in support of republican freedom), the quarrel with Britain may have taken a different course. It is also likely that the allegiance of traditional Christian believers to republican liberty might not have been so thoroughly cemented. And it is possible that the intimate relation between republican reasoning and trust in traditional Scripture, which became so important after the turn of the new century, would not have occurred as it did.[18]

The next time someone says that America was founded by deists, ask them to define deism and produce an official document from the founding era that explicitly uses deistic expressions. When Thomas Paine comes up in a discussion, ask if it's the early Paine or the later Paine. There is a big difference, as Elias Boudinot made clear more than 200 years ago in *The Age of Revelation*.

NOTES

1. Donald W. Whisenhunt, *Elias Boudinot: New Jersey's Revolutionary Experience*, ed. Larry R. Gerlach (Trenton, NJ: The New Jersey Historical Commission, 1975), 29

2. Forrest Church, *So Help Me God: The Founding Fathers and the First Great battle Over Church and State* (Orlando, FL: Harcourt, Inc., 2007), 401–403.

3.   Elias Boudinot, *The Age of Revelation, or the Age of Reason Shewn to be An Age of Infidelity* (Philadelphia: Asbury Dickins, 1801), xii–xiv.

4.   United States Supreme Court Justice Rehnquist's Dissent in *Wallace v. Jaffree* (472 U.S. 38, 105 S.Ct. 2479 [1985]): www.belcherfoundation.org/wallace_v_jaffree_dissent.htm.

5.   Robert L. Cord, *Separation of Church and State: Historical Fact and Current Fiction* (Grand Rapids, MI: Baker Book House, 1988), 28–29.

6.   Cord, *Separation of Church and State*, 29.

7.   Elias Boudinot to Edward Griffin, October 24, 1809. Boudinot Papers, Princeton University Library. Quoted in James H. Hutson, ed., *The Founders on Religion: A Book of Quotations* (Princeton, NJ: Princeton University Press, 2005), 66–67.

8.   Scott Liell, *46 Pages: Thomas Paine, Common Sense, and the Turning Point to American Independence* (Philadelphia Press, 2003), 20.

9.   A.J. Ayer, *Thomas Paine* (New York: Atheneum, 1988), 40. Ayer remarks that his appeal to the Old Testament is curious "in view of the want of respect he was later to show for the Old Testament" (40).

10.   Ayer, *Thomas Paine*, 35

11.   "The Christian religion is, above all the Religions that ever prevailed or existed in ancient or modern Times, the Religion of Wisdom, Virtue, Equity, and humanity, let the Blackguard [scoundrel] Paine say what he will; it is Resignation to God, it is Goodness itself to Man." (John Adams, *The Diary and Autobiography of John Adams*, ed. L.H. Butterfield [Cambridge, MA: The Belknap Press of Harvard University Press, 1962], 3:233–234).

12.   "Of all the dispositions and habits which lead to political prosperity, religion and morality are indispensable supports . . . And let us indulge with caution the supposition that morality can be maintained without religion . . . . Reason and experience both forbid us to expect that national morality can prevail to the exclusion of religious principle." (Excerpted from George Washington's 1796 "Farewell Address").

13.   Steve Farrell, "Paine's Christianity"—Part 1: www.newsmax.com/archives/articles/2003/9/4/212340.shtml

14.   Ayer, *Thomas Paine*, 180.

15.   Anson Phelps Stokes and Leo Pfeffer, *Church and State in the United States*, one-volume ed. (New York: Harper & Row, Publishers, 1964), 50

16.   Stokes and Pfeffer, *Church and State in the United States*, 50.

17.   Michael Novak, *On Two Wings: Humble Faith and Common Sense at the American Founding* (San Francisco: Encounter Books, 2002), 146.

18.   Mark A. Noll, *America's God: From Jonathan Edwards to Abraham Lincoln* (New York: Oxford University Press, 2002), 84.

Dedication

WHEN the warm and sincere affection, of a fond and anxious parent, is strongly manifested, by the interest he takes in the improvement and welfare of a beloved child; when it appears that, to promote her best interests, neither cares nor labour, even in an advanced and infirm age, will be spared; it may be hoped, that a corresponding temper of mind, may lead her to see the truth in a more clear and convincing light, especially when urged and inculcated by exertions of so tender a nature.

It was not from a doubt, of your principles being yet unsettled; or from an apprehension, that the extravagant and ludicrous ideas, of the vain and infidel author of a late publication, entitled, the AGE OF REASON, would, at present, in any respect, pervert your mind, that I have been led to spend so much of the precious remnant of time yet allotted me, in looking into his work, and endeavoring to show you its futility and weakness, in the following sheets: But, knowing the importance of your being able to give a ready answer for the hope that is in you, and seeing the melancholy prevalence of a spirit of infidelity, founded on a "pretended philosophy, and a vain deceit, after the tradition of men, after the rudiments of the world, and not after Christ," I thought myself, with regard to you, in the situation of the apostle Jude, with regard to the church of his day, that "I should give all diligence to write unto you of the common salvation, and exhort you, that you should earnestly contend for the faith which was once delivered to the saints; for there are certain men, who were before of old ordained to this condemnation; ungodly men, turning the grace of our God into lasciviousness, and denying the only Lord God, and our Lord Jesus Christ: wherefore, I ought not to be negligent, to put you in remembrance of these things, though you know them, and are established in the present truth."[1] "Yea, I think it meet, as long as I am in this tabernacle, to stir you up, by putting you in remem-

---

1. Jude, 4-5.

brance of these things; knowing, that shortly, I must put off this my tabernacle, I will endeavor, that you may be able, after my decease, to have these
things always in remembrance, for we have not followed cunningly devised
fables, when we made known unto you, the power and coming of our Lord
Jesus;"[2] "that the trial of your faith, being much more precious than gold
that perishes, though it be tried with fire, might be found unto praise and
honor, and glory, at the appearing of Jesus Christ, whom having not seen,
you love; in whom, though now you see him not, yet believing, you rejoice
with joy unspeakable and full of glory, receiving the end of your faith, even
the salvation of your soul."[3]

The whole tribe of unbelievers, object to the system of the gospel; that,
although there are mysteries in it, above the comprehension of human reason, yet it requireth, and that indispensably, the firm and unwavering faith
of its professors; it being one of its fundamental principles, that without
faith, you cannot please God

This certain fact, and not only reasonable in itself, but consistent with
the nature of the subject. No man believes, that credit is given to the veracity of another who reports a fact, by firmly believing it, on perfect demonstration, or of the fullest evidence. If a person of the most infamous character for falsehood and deceit, should assert, that the three sides of an
equilateral triangle, were equal to each other, every man who heard and
understood him, would immediately give the most hearty assent to the
truth of it, without putting the least confidence in the character or veracity
of the assertor. If one should inform you, that the sun was shining, and at
the same time should point to the meridian sun, appearing in his full splendor within your view, you could not but believe the fact, the truth would
force your assent; though without putting the least confidence in the in-
former. But if such a person were to tell you, of a fact that had come to his
knowledge, of which you could have no other evidence, and you were to give
full credit to it, then you would do honor to the veracity, and revere the
character of the informant. So it is with revealed religion, God, in his infinite wisdom, has given us sufficient evidence, that the revelation of the gospel is from him. This is the subject of rational inquiry, and of conviction,
from the conclusive nature of the evidence: but when that fact is established,
you are bound, as a rational creature, to show your full confidence in his
unchangeable veracity, and infinite wisdom, by firmly believing the great

---

2. Second Peter 1:12–16.
3. First Peter 1:7–9.

truths so revealed; although he has wisely kept from your knowledge, some things which may be mysterious in their nature. In this, his design, amongst others, may be, that thereby the pride of the human heart might be subdued; the human will brought to submit to the will of God; the character of Jehovah magnified and honored; and his unstained veracity perfectly confided in, and trusted to, while at the same time, the amiable humility of the Christian character, is promoted in the firm believer of his word.

These objectors find it difficult to submit to the faith of the gospel, because many things are above their reason; while they continually exercise the same principle in temporal things, which are subject, in one respect or another, to the like predication, in almost every action of their lives. In travelling, by sea and land—in eating and drinking—in plowing and sowing; do they all, with one accord, exercise this virtue in its full extent: no mysteries—no want of understanding principles or consequences, are opposed as sufficient to prevent their unfeigned faith in their fellow men: but in revealed religion, nothing is to be believed, even on the veracity of God himself, if they cannot fully comprehend and understand, every principle and mode of the truth, proffered as an object of their faith. They will trust themselves, their families, and their property, to a frail ship, and launch into the boisterous ocean, without a thought of examining the captain as to his theoretic or practical knowledge in navigation; or inquiring into the abilities of the seamen, with regard to the management of a ship in a storm. They exercise, without hesitation, an unfeigned faith in the general character of the one; and trust wholly to the owner and master, for the abilities of the others.

If they travel by land, they will mount the horse, recommended by its owner; or enter a public carriage provided for passengers, without doubting of their safety in the one case, or examining the Workmanship and construction of either carriage or harness, in the other. They trust to the care of the master and driver, and implicitly commit themselves to their knowledge and good conduct.

Men sit down to their usual meals, without ever inquiring, whether the meat they are to eat, is not part of a beast that died a natural death, or by some dangerous disease; neither is the cook ever called upon, as to the wholesomeness of the various additions made use of in dressing the food— all is prevented, by a firm faith in the butcher who sells the meat, and the host who employs the cook.

Does any person refuse to swallow his victuals, before he fully understands the method of digestion, or the manner in which the food will turn to his nourishment?

No man refuses to plough or sow, because he cannot comprehend, how the grain he casts into the earth, can take root, shoot up, and produce a much larger quantity than that which he sows—however inexplicable all this is to his finite nature, he exercises a lively vigorous faith in the consequences of his labors, and, without hesitation, acts accordingly. Will any man refuse to listen to the voice of his friend, because, with the utmost stretch of all his powers, he cannot comprehend how the motion of the air, can convey different articulate sounds to his ears; or how any sounds, however formed, can produce ideas in his soul, corresponding to the will of the mover. In short, innumerable important facts, the causes of which, with their modes of operation, we cannot comprehend, being perfectly mysterious and unaccountable, are yet firmly believed; and, in the course of life, acted upon by us. We hear the blowing of the wind, and feel its power; but we know not what produces it—why it is now mild and refreshing, and now violent and destructive—"We know not whence it comes, or whither it goeth"—we daily see and put the utmost confidence in the good effects of the loadstone, both as it regards our persons and property, by sea and land; and yet no one will pretend to understand, whence this peculiar virtue is derived, by which these effects are produced: our faith is firm and immovable, and no one objects its mysterious nature.

Nobody doubts of the motion of the heart, the circulation of the blood, or the action of the stomach and bowels; in all which the man exercises no act of his will whatever, neither can anyone define or comprehend the original cause or power by which these are accomplished: yet everyone believes the facts, notwithstanding their mysterious nature is far above his reason; and they risk their lives on the issue.

All then that revealed religion asks of men, is, that they would act in like manner, with regard to her requisitions—instead of rejecting all belief, till they fully understand every mystery of revealed religion, (and which is as applicable to natural religion) let their first inquiry be, is this the word of God, or not? If they find rational evidence, to prove that it is so, (which will most certainly be the case with every ingenuous mind) let them treat her great principles and doctrines, as they do the revelation of God in the natural world, and they will assuredly find additional and conclusive evidence arising from experience, and their faith will soon become to them the substance of the things hoped for, from the promises of the Gospel, and the evidence of the things there revealed as unseen. In submitting to the great mysteries of the Gospel, we believe, because God has said it—here then we rely on the divine veracity alone, and show our confidence in, and pay due honor to, his character and attributes; which is the life and soul of a true faith. But how does the unbeliever better himself, by the denial of revelation, and flying to his religion of nature? Is there not as strong faith required here, as in revealed religion? How does he know, that there is a God, who regards the affairs of men, or concerns himself with their well being? He tells you that he firmly believes that there is an eternal almighty first cause, and that this is fully proved by all the works of creation and Providence, around him. But why does he believe it? Certainly, by a strong faith in the declarations and assertions of those on whose sleeve he pins his faith, and on arguments drawn principally from that revelation he affects to despise. To judge aright in this matter, let us inquire into the opinions and belief of the wise and the learned, previous to the coming of Christ, and who had no aid from the knowledge communicated by the Savior, to a guilty world; though drawing much assistance, (unknowingly) from tradition, founded on revelation, to Adam, Enoch, Seth, and Noah. Hearken then to the language of Cicero, that oracle of antiquity, whose religious knowledge was superior to any of his contemporaries, in his treatise, written expressly on the nature of the Gods; "As many things in philosophy are not sufficiently clear, so the question concerning the nature of the Gods, which is in itself the most interesting and necessary for the regulation of religion, is attended with peculiar difficulty. Among those who supposed that there are Gods, their opinions are so various, that it is difficult to enumerate them. Much has been advanced concerning the form of the Gods; the place of their habitation, and their employment; and on these subjects there has been much disputation among the philosophers. But the principal difference among them, and a subject on which everything depends, is, whether the Gods undertake to do nothing in the government of the world; or whether everything were originally constituted, and is still directed by them, and will be so forever. Till this be decided, men must be in much error about things of the greatest importance.—For there are, and have been philosophers, who have maintained, that the Gods take no care of human affairs; and if this doctrine be true, what foundation can there be for piety and religion. This will be due to them, if we be noticed by them, and if in return they render any services to men; but if the Gods neither can, nor will do anything for us, and give no attention to our conduct, why should we render them any kind of worship, or pray to them ? Then will piety be mere hypocrisy, and all religion be at an end; and this will be attended with the greatest confusion in the business of life. Nay, I do not know, but that with the loss of religion, the foundation of all confidence of men in society, and even of justice, the most important of the virtues, would be taken away. But there are other philosophers, and those of the first distinction, who think that the world is governed by the mind and will of the Gods; that by them everything in the course of nature is provided for the use of man; and they express themselves in such a manner, as if they thought the Gods themselves were made for the use of man. Against these, Carneades has advanced so much, as to excite persons of any curiosity, to investigate the truth. For there is no subject, about which not only the unlearned, but even the learned, differ so much; and their opinions are so various and discordant, that only one of them can be true, though all may be erroneous." So confusedly and absurdly did Cicero write, with all the boasted light of nature, and human wisdom, without revelation.

If the Son of God has appeared in this our world, and has proved his mission by miracles and prophecies; in a word, by doing works, that no other man ever did, and that in proof of doctrines the most pure, moral, religious and benevolent; honorable to God, and beneficial to man; do they not demand, at least, as much respect, as men pay every day to their fellow creatures, whom they know to be fallible and imperfect; sometimes immoral, dissolute, and profane. In fine, is there any propriety in these objections to the firm faith of the gospel; while men so universally exercise a greater degree of faith, towards each other every day, in the common business of life? Let reason and conscience judge.

When I first took up this treatise, I considered it as one of those vicious and absurd publications, filled with ignorant declamation and ridiculous representations of simple facts, the reading of which, with attention, would be an undue waste of time; but afterwards, finding it often the subject of conversation, in all ranks of society; and knowing the author to be generally plausible in his language, and very artful in turning the clearest truths into ridicule, I determined to read it, with an honest design of impartially examining into its real merits.

I confess, that I was much mortified to find, the whole force of this vain man's genius and art, pointed at the youth of America, and her unlearned citizens, (for I have no doubt, but that it was originally intended for them) in hopes of raising a skeptical temper and disposition in their minds, well knowing that this was the best inlet to infidelity, and the most effectual way of serving its cause, thereby sapping the foundation of our holy religion in their minds.

To Christians, who are well instructed in the Gospel of the Son of God, such expedients rather add confirmation to their faith. They were fore-warned near two thousand years ago, of these things, by their great Lord and Master; "that when the time should come, they might remember, that he had told them of them." They indeed rest in this strong confidence, "that when the Lord Jesus shall be revealed from heaven, with his mighty angels in flaming fire, he will take vengeance on them, who know not God, and who obey not the Gospel of our Lord Jesus Christ; who shall be punished with everlasting destruction from the presence of the Lord, and from the glory of his power, when he shall come to be glorified in his saints, and to be admired in all them who believe in that day."

This awful consequence, created some alarm in my mind, lest at any future day, you, my beloved child, might take up this plausible address of infidelity; and, for want of an answer at hand to his subtle insinuations, might suffer even a doubt of the truth, as it is in Jesus, to penetrate into your mind.

You might then, perhaps, be alone, or without a friend near you, whom you might be willing to consult without delay; and my mind could not, with patience, endure the idea of your doubting, on such important points, though it were but for a moment.

I therefore determined, as God should give me health and leisure, were it only by improving a few moments at a time, to put my thoughts on the subject of this pamphlet, on paper, for your edification and information, when I shall be no more.

I chose to confine myself to the leading and essential facts of the Gospel, which are contradicted, or attempted to be turned into ridicule, by this writer. I have endeavored to detect his falsehoods and misrepresentations, and to show his extreme ignorance of the divine scriptures, which he makes the subject of his animadversions —not knowing that "they are the power of God unto salvation, to everyone that believeth."[4]

It is by their divine instructions, that, in the language of the elegant Hunter, the true Christian learns "what is the commanding object in the eye of eternal Providence, the salvation of a lost world, by Jesus Christ. Do you adopt the same object? Cleave unto it; keep it continually in view; all things else are vain and worthless; for they are passing quickly away. Our

---

4. Romans 1:16.

interest in, and hold of the world, is diminishing every hour. Our consequence, as candidates for immortal bliss, as heirs of glory, is rising in proportion. When we cease from importance as the citizens of this world, our
real importance begins to be felt and understood. I recommend no sullen
distance from your fellow-creatures, nor peevish discontent. Live in the
world. Associate with mankind. Enjoy the portion which God allotteth to
you. But use the world, so as not to abuse it. While you are cumbered about
many things, never forget, that one thing is needful, and choose that good
part, which shall not be taken from you."[5]

The experience of forty years, and upwards, has confirmed the conclusions I have drawn from the doctrines of the Gospel; and be assured, my
dear child, that this author's whole work, is made up of old objections, answered, and that conclusively, a thousand times over, by the advocates for
our holy religion. Some of them he has endeavored to clothe with new language, and put into a more ridiculous form; but many of them he has collected almost word for word, from the writings of the deists of the last and
present century.

May that God, who delighteth in the meek and humble temper, which
trembleth at his word, lead you to the cross of Christ; and there, by his holy
spirit, direct you into all truth. May he instruct you in his holy word, which
is able to make you wise unto salvation. Let that word abide in you richly—
become your daily companion, under every circumstance of life; "the man
of your council, a lamp to your paths, and a light to your feet."

For near half a century, have I anxiously and critically studied that invaluable treasure; and I still scarcely ever take it up, that I do not find something new—that I do not receive some valuable addition to my stock of
knowledge; or perceive some instructive fact, never observed before. In
short, were you to ask me to recommend the most valuable book in the
world, I should fix on the Bible as the most instructive, both to the wise and
ignorant. Were you to ask me for one, affording the most rational and pleasing entertainment to the inquiring mind, I should repeat, it is the Bible: and
should you renew the inquiry, for the best philosophy, or the most interesting history, I should still urge you to look into your Bible. I would make it,
in short, the Alpha and Omega of knowledge; and be assured, that it is for
want of understanding the scriptures, both of the Old and New Testament,
that so little value is set upon them by the world at large. The time, however,

---

5. Hunt, *Sacred Biog.* 2d vol. 24

is not far off, when they will command a very different reception, among the sons of men.

One thing I beg you would attend to, as a guard against the designs of infidels, to wit, that the Gospel revelation is a complete system of salvation, suited to our fallen nature, and should be taken altogether. Be cautious, then, how you ever hearken to objections leveled against detached principles, separated from the system, which are too often made use of, with success, by those who wish to weaken the force of revelation upon the mind of its professors, and by slow, if not imperceptible advances, to sap the foundation of their hope. It is not unusual to hear the punishment of sin, stated as incompatible with the perfections and attributes of Almighty God: that he cannot delight in the sufferings of the creatures that he has made, as he has no passions to gratify, and he delighteth not in cruelty—but the gospel reveals the great Jehovah, as the governor of all ranks of being in the universe. That it is necessary to keep all intelligences in the love of order, and obedience to his righteous laws. That the breach of them necessarily induces a separation from him, who is the fountain and source of all happiness and enjoyment; and, of course, necessarily induces misery in the extreme. This becomes a warning to all intelligences, to avoid the evil of sin; and therefore it is for the good of the whole, and founded in benevolence to beings in general, that the obstinate and unbelieving sinner is punished. But if the advocates for infidelity, can once weaken your faith, by the disbelief of future punishment, he finds you then ready for a new attack, by the denial of some other detached principle, till thus by degrees, your faith is undermined and destroyed, before you are aware of it.

For you I have written. To you I commit this labor of my old age, hoping that, as it is designed for your own private instruction, you will receive it, as in the fear of the Lord, without a criticizing eye, or opposing heart; and that you will be persuaded by it, to search the Scriptures, "knowing that they contain the words of eternal life," thereby you will gratify the most fervent desire of

An Affectionate Parent.
Rosehill

Preface

THE ushering into the world, an investigation of the nature of the following answer to the *AGE OF REASON*, at this late period, after so many conclusive answers have been given to it, and particularly that of the learned, pious, and excellent bishop of Landaff, certainly requires some apology.

The substance of the following sheets, were written after the first appearance of the *AGE OF REASON*, in this country. The original design was merely to guard a beloved child and intimate friend, against any skeptical doubts that might have been produced, by the many consequences that daily took place, when that awful book was first handed about in this city.

It was, at first, designed to be confined within the limits of a few sheets.

But after, having occasion to review the subject, it opened itself in such a manner, that before I was aware of it, the bulk increased to a manuscript of a considerable size.

When, in my opinion, it had answered the original design, I desisted from any farther pursuit of the subject, till a short time since, when, being credibly informed, that thousands of copies of the *AGE OF REASON*, had been sold at public auction, in this city, at a cent and an half each, whereby children, servants, and the lowest people, had been tempted to purchase, from the novelty of buying a book at so low a rate; my attention was excited, to find out what fund could afford so heavy an expense, for so unworthy an object.

I was soon convinced, that a principle of the illuminati in Europe, had been adopted by some unknown persons in this country, viz.—that of fixing on the rising generation, and the lower orders of the people, as the chief objects of an attack, for spreading the principles of infidelity; finding, from long experience, that the arts of deception must ever fail, where sound learning and pure science prevail.

This became the subject of much conversation among men of sober principles, with whom I was intimate; during which, two or three learned friends became acquainted with my attempt to answer that dangerous pamphlet. They assured me of their opinion, that although it was a repetition of reasoning, arguments, and facts, that had been published over and over again; yet, under present circumstances, it might be of real service to the young and unlearned, as the subject was placed in a light more adapted to their capacities and memories, than in those publications that had preceded me; and many facts enumerated, that were not easily attainable by them; that, at all events, it would be casting in my mite, towards opposing the flood of infidelity that was deluging our land; and coming from a layman, engaged in avocations foreign from the study of divinity, it might encourage others, under like circumstances, to devote their leisure hours to investigate so important a subject, as the religion on which their hopes of happiness hereafter, must depend.

It must be acknowledged, that however pleased I have been with Bishop Watson's very learned, able, and judicious *"APOLOGY FOR THE BIBLE,"* I do not think it altogether calculated for young people, and the lower ranks of the community; and it is really to be wished, that the title had been better adapted to the work.

Several other valuable answers have appeared, each containing many important arguments on the subject; and as many of them as have come to my hands, have been perused, and though much pleased and edified with most of them, I have not been entirely satisfied with them, as applicable to the youth of our country, and those whose opportunities have not been so advantageous, as to guard them against the sophistry of art, cunning, and an inbred hatred of everything sacred and holy. The boldness of impiety is often mistaken for knowledge, founded on an independent spirit, and thereby saps the necessary defense of simple innocence and unsuspecting modesty.

For a considerable time past, I have ardently wished to see some more able hand, meet Mr. Paine more on his own ground, in a plain and simple manner—but after waiting several years, I have lost all hopes of being gratified; and therefore have been more easily persuaded to undergo, amidst a variety of other business, the labor of copying once more, what was designed for a particular and special purpose; and altering the address, by applying it more directly to the author of the Age of Reason, and through him to all his brethren in skepticism.

I am averse to increasing the number of books, unless it be on important occasions, or for useful purposes; but an anxious desire that our country should be preserved from the dreadful evil of becoming enemies to the religion of the Gospel, which I have no doubt, but would be introductive of the dissolution of government and the bonds of civil society; my compliance with the wishes of a few select friends, to make this work public, has been more easily obtained.

However, I am not sanguine of great success, knowing my own insufficiency for the task; neither do I expect to carry much conviction to the minds of those, who have been long engaged in the vices of infidelity; what I principally look for, is, to persuade the rising generation, and those who are but beginning to doubt or waver, to make the divine Scriptures their serious and attentive study; and seek to understand the principles of the Gospel, before they pretend to judge of them, or to renounce them as untrue, or of but trifling importance. Thus they would do in any other science, and they cannot reasonably adopt a different practice in religion.

Few know to what lengths, conscious ignorance of a subject that every man ought to know, will lead a person to go, in order to cover the knowledge of it from the world.

If this attempt shall become the means of directing one solitary individual from the path of error, into that of truth, I shall consider myself richly paid for all my trouble, in altering and preparing the following sheets for the press.

Most willingly do I commit them, to the overruling direction of Sovereign Wisdom, who has heretofore made use of clay and spittle, to open the eyes of the blind; and do most devoutly pray, that in his own way, and by his own means, and in his own time, he will accomplish the promised kingdom of his beloved son.

1

Age of Revelation

"Oh that my head were waters, and mine eyes,
"Were fountains flowing, like the liquid skies;
"Then would I give the mighty flood release,
"And weep a deluge for the human race."
PAINE

"**H**EAR O heavens! and give ear O earth! for the Lord hath spoken: I have nourished and brought up children, and they have rebelled against me," was the pathetic and affecting language of the elegant and truly evangelical prophet, Isaiah, when addressing an highly favored, though obstinate and sinful nation—"a people loaded with iniquity—a seed of evil doers—children who were corrupted."

And can there be a more pertinent address, in any other form of words, put into the English language, which would better suit an introduction to a review of a late work, made famous, from no other cause, but having been written by the author of *Common Sense*, and which is absurdly entitled "The Age of Reason."

There is no intrinsic merit in this work, which might entitle it to an answer; and it would undoubtedly have been consigned to perpetual oblivion, with a thousand other profane and impious performances, had it not been from a conviction, that many young and uninformed people, wholly unacquainted with the genuine principles of our holy religion, and the subtle and dishonest practices of her apostate adversaries, had with avidity engaged in reading it. From the reputation the author had gamed, by his former political writings, in this country; writings, which, from local circumstances, and the state of men's minds at the moment of an important revolution, gave

1

celebrity to their author, the production before us has met with a more general approbation, than could otherwise have been expected.[1]

It is in this manner, that these inefficient fragments of the writings of the last century, repeated by the late king of Prussia, Voltaire, and others, now new vamped up, with the aid of ridicule, under the title of "The Age of Reason," and this addition, " By the Author of Common Sense," though so often fully answered by learned men, are again introduced into the world, as new matter, in hopes of deceiving the ignorant and unwary, by the influence of a name.

It is no new thing, for the enemies of truth and godliness, thus to descend to the meatiest arts, in order to accomplish the horrid purpose of ruining the of men.

As to the serious and devout Christian, who has the transforming power of the religion of Jesus Christ, and has experienced the internal and convincing evidence of the truth of the Divine Scriptures, the treatise referred to, will rather have a tendency to increase his faith, and inflame his fervent zeal in his master's cause, while he beholds this vain attempt, to ridicule and set at nought, the great objects of his hope and joy, by one who plainly discovers a total ignorance of every principle of true Christianity, as revealed in the Scriptures.

The vanity and confidence often produced by an appearance of superior knowledge and laborious investigation, will sometimes lead even wise men, undesignedly, into a supercilious and dogmatical mode of argumentation, on subjects, which they persuade themselves they fully comprehend: hence some apology may be made for their errors; and even the faulty manner of managing the argument may be forgiven. But, as to the performance before us, the author has proved himself to be totally ignorant of the subject he has undertaken to elucidate, not only as to the intrinsic merit of the question, but also the ideas and terms, which its advocates have been known always

---

1. "The general opinion (speaking of the influence that entitled *Common Sense*, had among certain classes of the people), and the unanimous testimony of all the known writers upon American affairs, leave scarce room for a doubt of the fact, though for the honor of the Americans, I would most willingly call it in question.—Thomas Paine's *Common Sense*, is a pamphlet just at contemptible almost throughout, just as remote from sound human, sense, as all the others, by which, in later times, he has made himself a name,"—Friedrich von Gentz (1764–1832), *The Origin and Principles of the American Revolution, Compared with the Origin and Principles of the French Revolution*, 56. The great effect which this pamphlet had on the revolution, (and it was certainly great) arose from its being written at the moment when the public mind was in a great alarm, and totally at a loss how to determine.

to hold up and use, as expressive of their sense and meaning of it. He has undertaken to explain, what he does not appear to have endeavored, by proper investigation and consideration, to understand; and at the same time he has reviled and abused a subject of serious and solemn importance, in the estimation of many of the most learned and best men, that ever lived.

This shows not only a wicked and perverse temper of mind, but a degree of forward and indecorous pertinacity, that ought not to be countenanced by any lover of mankind.

Argumentative investigation is one thing; but ignorant declamation and ridicule is another.

The miraculous facts of revelation, one might suppose, would have led every serious mind to believe, that human wisdom could not have devised the plan of the Gospel; and that the prudent and cautious mind, however darkened by the doubts and objections of men of the world, would at least have waited with some degree of patience, till the understanding should be farther opened, by the fulfillment, or failure, of the facts foretold, as taking place before, and preparatory to, the second coming of Christ. That awful and important period is approaching. The express declarations of Omniscience, as contended by the friends of prophecy, are fast fulfilling. In the mean time, as has been observed by an able writer, "let critics and learned men of all kinds, have full liberty to examine the sacred books, and let us be sparing in our censures of each other—let us judge nothing (rashly) before the time, until the Lord come, and then shall every man have praise of God. Sobriety of mind, humility and piety, are requisite in the pursuit of knowledge of every kind, and much more in that which is sacred."[2] But this rational principle, ought not to lead us to countenance any person in abusing sacred things, and misrepresenting important facts, whereby the ignorant may be deceived, and the searchers after truth be led out of the way. However, it may justify critical examination and free inquiry, it cannot support the vicious mind in reviling serious things, ridiculing as visionary, facts and principles established by the experience of ages, or palming on us dogmatical assertions for serious truths.

To enter into a minute and candid disquisition of any and every subject, which interests the welfare of our fellow men, as rational and accountable creatures, and that with boldness and decency, is the part of a noble mind; but to treat those things as jests and fables of children, which, in the con-

---

2. David Hartley, *Observations on Man, His Frame, His Duty, and His Expectations* (London: Thomas Tegg and Son, [1748] 1834), 374

templation of his opponents, are considered as involving infinite and eternal consequences, is inexcusable, and will admit of no palliation.

If the most important communication should be made to an unlettered Englishman, in the Greek language, it would not be thought harsh to say, that he did not understand it, though he had been in the habit: of hearing Greek spoken ever so long; and an attempt by him to explain the communication, without having endeavored to learn the language, would be thought little short of idiotism. Why then should a man be countenanced by the public attention, in his animad versions on any subject of which it does not appear, that he has ever entertained one just idea; not even of the language of its authors ? How comes it to pass, that in every other science, except that of religion, it is necessary to become a learner, before it is expected to be understood. Principles, axioms, and definitions, must be settled and established, before men will form conclusions, or adopt decided sentiments on important subjects of civil or moral obligation: but, as to revealed religion, every vain sophist and pretender, not only undertakes to give an opinion on its all interesting doctrines, bat even dogmatically to deny and contemn its essential, well attested facts and historical occurrences, which have stood the test of the severest and most critical examination. At the same time, these pretenders to knowledge, have never given themselves the trouble of inquiring into the A. B. C of religion, the alphabet of the Divine Scriptures.

What is there in the nature of revealed religion, when compared with other sciences, and the present degraded state of human nature, that a man should comprehend all its great and important truths, without labor and investigation, whilst most subjects, even of human knowledge, are not to be obtained but by industrious application, with all the aids of learning and experiment?

It is my present design then, to make a few observations on the work before us, in a manner that may serve as a trial of its merits by the rules of *common sense*, and to this the author ought not to have any reasonable objection, as all his pretensions to celebrity are founded on the assumption of that title.[3]

In doing this, I shall confine myself to a few essential facts of the Gospel, on which all the rest depend, and which are denied and ridiculed in this pamphlet. I shall examine the arguments attempted therein, (if any of them can deserve so respectable a name) independent of the artful language in

---

3. Referring to a well known publication of his, previous to the dedication of our independence, entitled, *Common Sense*.

which they are dressed; and endeavor to expose the falsehoods made use of to give a sanction to impious and delusive sophistry.

The object being to convey rational and honest information, on a subject all-important to the everlasting interests of my fellow-men, and not personal fame or reputation—to guard the young and uninformed from the dangerous vortex of infidelity, I shall feel myself at perfect liberty, in the prosecution of this design, to draw knowledge from every source—to borrow from any treasury, that I shall consider more productive than my own; and where I find superior abilities and greater extent of information than I can pretend to, I shall not only use the ideas of such authors, but their language, if thereby the great end of my undertaking may be promoted; I mean a conviction of the truth, in the minds of those, into whose hands it may fall.

2

The Author of the *Age of Reason*'s Introduction to His Work; Shewn to Be Without Proof or Argument

THE author of the *Age of Reason*, in all the pride and obstinacy of infidelity, introduces his objections to the Christian system, by an exhibition of his own creed, both affirmatively and negatively, as if his established character for sobriety, integrity, and exemplary moral conduct, entitled him to the respect and veneration of his fellow-citizens, and the world at large. In an authoritative manner, he declares, that he does not believe in the creed of the Jewish church, the Roman church, the Greek church, nor of any church he knows of. From this declaration, or rather from this his disbelief, it would seem, as though he intended, we should infer, that the benevolent author of our being, hath left mankind in total ignorance of the nature of the worship he requires from them; and that all the worship that has prevailed in the world since the creation, till the present time, has been founded in error and deception. But the concluding part of this his extraordinary creed, is as, if not more extraordinary; "that his own mind is his own church."[1]

Among all nations, the idea of a church, imports a society or body of rational beings united together for the purpose of worshiping God, agreeably to some established rule or system, agreed upon by them as most acceptable to the Deity. What then are we to understand by this profound casuist's assertion, that "his own mind is his own church?"—A man so well

---

1. One of the principles of the illuminati in France, at the head of which among others, was Charles Maurice de Talleyrand-Périgord, bishop of Autun, was "That every man was his own God—his own lawgiver—and amenable only to himself."—*Vide Smith's letter to the editor of Dr. Robertson on the Illuminati*

versed in the language necessary to communicate distinct ideas of his subject, must be an able interpreter of religious doctrines.

Another position of his introduction is as void of principle, as that above mentioned. He asserts "that infidelity does not consist in believing or disbelieving; but in professing to believe, what he does not believe." What jargon is this, to substitute hypocrisy for infidelity! Thus a man really and professedly denying the being of a God, and the obligations of revealed religion, is not guilty of infidelity: but if a man professes to disbelieve a system, for special purposes of his own, though really and truly in his conscience, he does fully believe the truth of such system, he is an unbeliever in that system, an infidel and does not believe it.

I know of no way of accounting for this absurdity, but by supposing that our author has a secret wish, hereafter to be reckoned among the believers in the Christian system, though he now openly denies every word of it. From this creed of our author, some proper expectations may be formed of the residue of this curious performance.

His observation on revealed religion, in this part of his work, is also false in fact, viz. "That every religion has established itself by pretending to some special mission from God, communicated to certain individuals, as Moses, Christ and Mahomet, *as if the way to God was not open to every man alike.*"

This conclusion, unfounded in truth, seems particularly designed to prepare the way, as an excuse for his ignorance of the Christian system, and to countenance his animadversions on religion, without being at the trouble of investigating its nature and tendency. But facts are asserted in this whole work, with an uncommon defect of modesty, under the apparent expectation that the world will take them as established upon the bare assertion of the author.

It is true that Moses, Christ and Mahomet, all claimed the authority of a divine mission: but is it supposable that our author has ever read with attention the respective histories of these celebrated characters, and yet, that he could allow himself to make the above observation to the Christian world with a view of placing them all on a footing. Does it follow that, because wicked men will be guilty of counterfeiting the most valuable paper, that therefore the original and the counterfeit are to be considered as equally genuine? Or does not rather the existence of the counterfeit, prove the reality of the original? Did not Moses and Christ show their divine mission, not only by the nature and effects of their doctrines and precepts, with unblemished purity of life and manners; but also by doing, *in the presence of all the people*, works, that no other men ever did; and by appealing to them as the visible manifestations of Heaven, in confirmation of their claim, in which the multitudes could not be deceived? But Mahomet aimed to establish his pretensions to divine authority, by the power of the sword and the terrors of his government; while he carefully avoided any attempts at miracles in the presence of his followers, and all pretences to foretell things to come. His acknowledging the divine mission of Moses and Christ confirms their authority as far as his influence will go, while their doctrines entirely destroy all his pretensions to the like authority. His doctrines and precepts, are calculated to gratify the prejudices of every party, and to confirm them in the established principles of a fanciful religion, to the Jews he was a disciple of Moses,—to Christians, he was a believer in the prophetic character of Jesus Christ, while he indulged the heathen inhabitant of Arabia in sensual ideas, that were most captivating and pleasing to the human heart. Instead of doctrines and precepts inculcating the entire renovation of our natures—the becoming a new creature and overcoming the world:—Instead of a felicity consisting of pure and spiritual pleasures, "did he not establish a system of carnal indulgences, ever grateful to the natural man, founded in the fascinating allurements of its promised rewards?—In their agreeable to the propensities of corrupt nature in general, and to those of the inhabitants of warm climates in particular,—in the artful accommodation of its doctrines and its rites to the preconceived opinions, the favorite passions, and the deep rooted prejudices of those to whom it was addressed."[2]

Mahomet's pretensions to inspiration and the submission of the people to his authority, in the degree in which they are found, as has been observed by Mr. Hartley, may be accounted for, from the then circumstances of things, without having recourse to real inspiration, and particularly if we admit (as Mahomet did) the revelations related and intimated by Moses, with his own divine legation. It will appear that Mahomet copied much of his scheme from them, to make it palatable to those he meant to attach to his interests, which is a strong argument in favor of the Mosaic and Christian systems. There is no other instance (than that of the Mosaic code) of a body of laws being produced at once, and remaining without addition afterwards;—but those of Mahomet and other impostors have generally been compiled by degrees, according to the exigencies of the states,— the prevalence of particular factions; or the authority who governed the people at his own will.

---

2. White

Mahomet made his laws, not to curb, but humor the genius of the people; they were therefore altered and repealed from the same causes. Whereas the body politic of the Israelites took upon itself a complete form at once, conformable not only to its then present necessities in a wilderness, but to all its future circumstances, when settled in a regular government, surrounded by neighboring nations, in the land of Canaan; and has preserved the same form, in a great measure to the present time, and that under the highest external disadvantages, which is an instance without a parallel.

The doctrines, and whole system of the Gospel, breathe also a quite different spirit, from those changes and accommodations to human passions, which have been always calculated to answer the end of merely temporal governments: its language has ever been, "if any man shall add unto these things, God shall add unto him the plagues that are written in this book; and if any man shall take away from the words of this book, God shall take away his part out of the book of life, and out of the holy city, and from the things which are written in this book."[3]

Moses appealed to the miracles done in Egypt, before Pharaoh, his court, the wise men, and the whole congregation of the children of Israel—to their passage through the Red Sea—to the pillar of fire by night, and the cloud by day, attending them, not once or twice, but through their whole journeyings in the wilderness—to the thunders and lightnings, and the voice of God speaking from the mount—to forty years experience of miracles and prophecies—while Christ raises the dead—heals the sick—feeds the hungry—makes the lame to walk, and the blind to see—commands the winds and the waves, and they obey him—foretells the events that shall happen to his church for 2000 years to come, in proof and confirmation of his having come from God, and possessing divine authority. And now, where is the comparison between the supposed prophet of Mecca, and the Son of God; or with what propriety ought they to be named together? "The men of Nineveh shall rise up in the judgment with this generation, and shall condemn it; for they repented at the preaching of Jonah; and behold a greater than Jonah is here."[4] The difference between these characters is so great, that the facts need not be further applied.

The conclusion of our author's observation, "that the way to God, is open to every man alike," is equally unfounded, on his own principles and representation. Such are his vanity and confidence, that he does not even pretend

---

3. Revelation 22:8, 19.
4. Luke 11:32.

to cover his presumption, by an attempt to produce proof of his position, either from facts or argument; or to show from whence he gets his information, or to assign reasons for his assertions; but he proceeds at once, to build his system of objections upon them, as undisputed data; and concludes his readers must receive conviction, on the first blush of the argument. The fact asserted is, " that the way to God, is open to every man alike." This assertion has been heretofore often made by infidels, and as often answered: it is contradicted by every man's daily experience, as well as by a thousand fatal and melancholy examples.

If mankind were found in a state of perfect rectitude and innocence, free from all the dreadful consequences of sin and iniquity, such an assertion might be made with more propriety. But, not to mention the fatal apostasy of man from the original purity of his nature, which, although proved by all his actions, yet I well know is denied by infidels in general, and by some who call themselves Christians;[5] I appeal to every man's observation, as convictive, that our author's position, on his own principles, is false in fact. He himself allows, in page 35 of his pamphlet, "that there is a revelation, the word of God, in the creation we behold." And again, in page 36, "It is only in the creation, that all our ideas and conceptions of a word of God, can unite."

Every man must and will acknowledge, the various and differing powers of the human mind, in different persons, from the idiot, to the philosopher,

---

5. The radical corruption of human nature, is one of those truths, which their very plainness renders it the less easy to support by formal proofs. If a person be unmoved by the decisive arguments which press upon him every moment, at every turn, you can scarcely know in what manner to address him on the subject.—Let any one look diligently into their own minds, and they will be convinced, that the continual indisposition to righteousness, and proneness to transgression, which they will discover there, can be ascribed to no other cause. Let them behold what passes in the world around them, and they will be satisfied, that the prevailing wickedness of mankind, can be traced to no other source. They will perceive, that in this, as in every other instance, reason and experience unite in bearing testimony to the truth of the word of God. (Thomas Gisborne, *Familiar Survey of the Christian Religion, and of History* [Dublin, Ireland: William Porter, 1800], 14).

The late discoveries in the Eastern World, greatly add to the testimony relative to this subject. Mr. [Thomas] Maurice says, "From the whole of the preceding statement, it must be evident to every reader, that the Brahmins are no strangers to the doctrine esteemed absurd *in some Christian countries*, but admitted by the Brahmins from time immemorial, *that of original sin*. It is their invariable belief, *that man is a fallen creature*.—The doctrine is universally prevalent in Asia, and originally gave birth to the persuasion, that by severe sufferings, and a long series of probationary discipline, the soul might be restored to its primitive purity.—They had even sacrifices denominated those of regeneration, and those sacrifices *were always profusely stained with blood*." (Thomas Maurice, *Indian Antiquities*, 7 vols. [London: H.L. Galabin, 1793-1800], 5:956-957).

most famous for his wisdom and application. And can any man of reflection, be ignorant, that the way to God, in our author's sense of it, is not alike open to him, who never raised his thoughts to the great Author of universal nature, or contemplated his power, wisdom, and goodness, in his works of creation and providence? and to the studious, contemplative philosopher, who, pursuing the plastic hand of nature through all the streams of pure benevolence and love, hath been led, with astonishment and surprise, to the inexhaustible ocean there, in holy rapture, to love and to adore?

Can it be possible, that any man in his senses, should suppose this way to God, is alike open to the wretch, who, destroying all the powers of nature in debauchery and wickedness, never mentions the name or attributes of the great, self-existing First Cause of all things, but to deny his being, or to blaspheme his sacred and venerable name; and to the devout and obedient soul, who, sensible of his own natural weakness and insufficiency, is continually casting himself at the feet of Divine Mercy, and humbly supplicating for grace to illumine his darkened understanding, and wisdom to direct his researches into the things of God?—Is this way open alike to the man who is blind and deaf, and so incapable of improving the revelation of our Author, in the works of creation; and to him, who, enjoying every assistance, both physical, moral, and artificial, sees deeply into the mysteries of nature? Are the enlightened, philosophic Newton, or Rittenhouse, and the wandering savage of the Mississippi, on equal terms, with regard to this way to God? Or the poor laborer, confined during his whole life, to some mechanical business, for the bare support of his nature; and the rich, affluent citizen, who can devote both time and fortune to the investigation of nature, and "nature's God, seen through all his works?" These observations, not only teach the falsity of the position, in our author's sense, but fully prove the certainty of some great and essential change wrought in the nature and state of man, since he was originally formed by his merciful Creator; and show, in glowing colors, the ignorance of our author in the first principle necessary for his investigating the truths of the Christian religion: I mean his own nature, as well as the sublime doctrines of salvation by a Redeemer, founded upon it.

The way to God, even under the express and positive revelation of his will, manifested in the life, character, and doctrines of Jesus Christ, requires study, application, instruction, divine grace, and continual improvement, before it can be properly sought out, even with the aid of the sacred Scriptures. Do the advocates of the Christian system, at this day expect to know the great truths of their holy religion, by immediate inspiration, while they acquire the knowledge of every art and science, relative to human things, by laborious investigation? Even in the natural world, God, who created man, hath made him a dependent creature, so that it is necessary for his support, from day to day, that he should be fed, clothed and covered from the inclemency of the weather; but does any man pretend to disbelieve the goodness and mercy of God towards him, because he cannot exist, without care, labor, and active attention to his various wants? Must he not plough, and sow, and reap, and defend himself from his known enemies, or perish ? Is this ever thought a solid argument against the superintendant Providence of God, or his abundant goodness to the children of men?

In the religion of the Gospel, the Spirit of God has been promised by Jesus Christ, to lead his people into all truth; but it is the diligent, the active, the persevering and sincere inquirer, who is encouraged to depend upon this heavenly gift; and therefore the apostle exhorts his fellow Christians "to work out their own salvation with fear and trembling, for it is God," saith he, "who worketh in you, both to will and to do, of his good pleasure,"

Nothing short of consummate vanity, or the grossest ignorance, therefore, could lead to the unfounded conclusion, "that the way to God," in our author's sense, "is open to every man alike."

The author of the Age of Reason, having thus introduced himself to the attention of his readers, and, as he supposed, paved the way to a skeptical temper of mind, proceeds to his objections to the leading facts of revealed religion.

3

The Virgin Mary

*"When I am told," says our author, "that a woman, called the Virgin
Mary, said, or gave out, that she was with—child, without any cohabi-
tation with a man; and that her betrothed husband, Joseph, said that
an Angel told him so, I have a right to believe them or not; such a circumstance required a much stronger evidence, than their bare word for
it; but we have not even this; for neither Joseph nor Mary wrote any such
matter themselves. It is only reported by others, that they said so. It is
hearsay upon hearsay."*

THIS gross misrepresentation, however plausibly clothed in artful language, is unworthy of a man, who pretends to integrity of character,
and to write for the edification of mankind. He surely has never taken the
pains to read, with attention, the narration which he thus attempts to contradict; and thereby he is deceiving the young and unlearned reader, in matters of serious importance to his best interests.

The sacred writings of the Jews, many hundred years before Joseph or
Mary were born, predicted, in positive terms, the extraordinary event, that
a virgin, of the tribe of Judah, should conceive and bear a son, and that in
the town of Bethlehem, in Judea. It was not only thus early promulgated, but
became a principle firmly believed and relied upon by the whole people of
the Jews, for many generations; and was the great object to which most of
their inspired prophets directed their public labors. "The ancient Jewish
doctors expected their Messiah to be born of a virgin; therefore it was, that
Simon Magus, who set himself up for the Messiah, pretended that his
mother Rachel, bore him without the loss of her virginity."[1]

---

1. Huet. Questions Almat. lib. ii. ch. xv.

Previous to this mysterious phenomenon, the time foretold by the prophets for its completion, expired; and many other circumstances that were to attend it, actually came to pass. The expectation of the Jews, as a people, and the learned men of the neighboring nations, who were acquainted with their Scriptures, was raised to the highest pitch, by the fulfillment of the previous events foretold, as the signs of the approaching glory.

Daniel had very early, and while he was a resident in Babylon, by his prophetic declaration, foretold the coming of the Messiah among the Jews, at the end of seventy weeks, or four hundred and ninety years, which must have been well known to all the nations of the east—add to this, that the Jews were then scattered over all Asia, Africa, and Europe. Tacitus, the Roman historian, who lived in the first century, says, "Many of the Jews were persuaded, from the contents of their sacred writings, that the eastern country would prevail, and that from Judea would come those, who were to have the sovereignty of the whole world."[2] Suetonius, another famous historian of the same century, says, "An ancient and uniform opinion had prevailed *all over* the east, that it was destined for the people of Judea, about this time, to rule over the world."[3] Josephus, the Jewish historian, mentions the same thing; and further says, "That what principally excited the Jewish people, *the wise men* as well as others, to the war with the Romans, was the expectation of a great deliverer to arise among them, who should obtain the empire of the world," He also says, "That when Alexander the Great was at Jerusalem, the prophecies of Daniel were pointed out to him, by Jaddus, the high priest."[4] Dr. Sykes says, "It is evident that this opinion was fixed and settled; was generally received among the Jews, that some one of their nation was to get universal dominion. It is testified on all hands, by heathens and by Jews, as well as Christians, and consequently cannot be denied."

The miraculous event is made known to the subject of this divine grace by an angel from Heaven. She is not found among the nobles of her country, or the princes of her tribe.—She is an obscure virgin of the tribe of Judah, dwelling in the despised city of Nazareth. Her betrothed husband receives equal proof of the awful truth.—They make it known to their friends.—It is confirmed to them by her cousin Elizabeth, who had previous notice from the same heavenly messenger, of the mercy of God to her nation. They are necessarily, tho' undesignedly, brought to the village of Bethlehem by the

---

2. Lib. v. cap. xiii. fol. 502.

3. De Vita, Vesp: ch. iv.

4. Josephus, vol.

public authority of the government, that no part of the ancient prediction should be unfulfilled.

At the birth of this wondrous child, certain simple and unsuspecting shepherds, engaged in their lawful and innocent occupations, but wholly ignorant of any extraordinary occurrence, are surprised with a visit from a heavenly choir, and informed, in the most sublime language and harmonious strains, of the love of God to man.

The shepherds, with astonishment, visit the stable and the manger by direction of the messengers of Heaven, and find the more than royal babe, agreeably to their information.—They publicly announce the glad tidings, and publish abroad the fulfillment of ancient prophecy.

The wise men from a distant and eastern country, under the influence of tradition, added to a divine revelation, and the supernatural appearance and direction of a new star in the Heavens, attend the new born babe with magnificent presents, and hail him king of the Jews.[5]

Chacldius the Platonist, a pagan historian who wrote, soon after the coming of Christ, his Commentary on Timaeus, says, "There is another more holy and more venerable history, which relates the appearance of a new star, not to foretell diseases and death, but the descent of a venerable God, who was to preserve mankind, and to show favor to the affairs of mortals; which star the wise men of Chaldaea observing as they travelled in the night, and being very well skilled in viewing the heavenly bodies, they are said to have sought after the new birth of this God; and having found that majesty in a child, they paid him worship, and made such vows as were agreeable to so great a God."

Baalam, on the arrival of the Israelites from Egypt into the wilderness, had prophesied of the coming Messiah, by declaring, that "a star should come out of Jacob, and a sceptre rise out of Israel;" and no doubt but the knowledge of this prophecy was preserved in the east, and, with other historical facts,

---

5. De Vita, Vesp: ch. iv. Abul-Pharagius, an Arab writer mentioned in the Historla Dynastarium, page 54, tells us, that "Zoroaster, the head of the Persian magians, (or clergy) foretold to his magians the coming of Christ, and that at the time of his birth there should appear a wonderful star, which should shine by day as well as by night, and therefore left it in command with them, that when that star should appear, they should follow the directions of it, and go to the place where he should be born, and there offer gifts and pay their adoration unto him: And that it was by this command that the three wise men came out of the east—that is, out of Persia, to worship Christ in Bethlehem." Dean Prideaux says, this author, though an Arab, professed the Christian religion, and supposes it as most likely, that he took this idea from them, though he assigns no reasons for his belief.

handed down by tradition. The people of the east had also the advantage of the knowledge and piety of Melchizedeck, Abraham, Lot, Isaac, Jacob and Job, and his friends; the worship and example of the Hebrews in Egypt—the account of all the miracles performed by Moses—their supernatural deliverance from that house of bondage—the remarkable destruction of the Egyptians in the sea—the miraculous support, in the wilderness, of three millions of souls for forty years, with their unexampled success, against all the united force of the kings of Canaan, with their numerous hosts, according to the express predictions of Moses—the final settlement of the Hebrews in the promised land—the celebrity of David, Solomon, and the kings of Judah and Israel—the conduct and prophecies of Daniel, Isaiah, Jeremiah, and other prophets—with all the various decrees of the kings of Babylon, acknowledging the God of Israel, to be the God of all the earth, as did many of the neighboring nations from time to time. All these extraordinary means of knowledge, and the occurrences consequent thereon, must have turned the attention of the wise men of every nation, to the history and religion of a people thus favoured of God; and hereby it is reasonable to suppose they became acquainted with the leading facts of revelation.[6]

Strabo, another heathen historian, in his 16th book, mentions Moses and the ancient Jews with commendation. He says, "That many, in honor to the divine majesty, went out of Egypt with Moses, rejecting the worship of the Egyptians and other nations, inasmuch as Moses had instructed them that God was not to be worshipped by any image, and that he would reveal himself only to the pure and virtuous." He observes, "That Moses had great success in the establishment of his government, and the reception of his laws, among the neighboring nations; and that his successors, for some ages pursued the same methods, being just, and truly religious."

Varro, the most learned Roman historian, though a heathen, much approved of the Jewish worship, as being free from that idolatry, which he could not but dislike, in the heathen religion.

Abraham, Isaac, Jacob and Joseph, were mentioned of old in Philo Biblyus, out of Sanchoncathan, who wrote about 200 years after Moses—in Berosus, a priest of Belus, who lived about 300 years before Christ—Hecataeus—Nicolaus Damascenus—Artipanus—Eupolemus—Demetrius—Theorphicverses—and in Justin, out of Trogus Pompacius; all of whom relate the history of Moses, and his principal acts.[7]

---

6. St. Augustine, *Civitas Dei*, lib. iv. ch. xxxi.
7. Hugo Grotius, *De veritate religionis Christianae*.

This fact is also confirmed by the language of Rahab, the harlot of the city of Jericho, to the spies. "And she said unto the men, I know that the Lord hath given you the land, and that your terror has fallen upon us, and that all the inhabitants of the land faint because of you: for *we have heard how the Lord dried up the water* of the Red Sea for you, when ye came out of Egypt; and what ye did to the two kings of the Amorites, that were over the other side of Jordan, Sihon and Og, whom ye utterly destroyed, for the Lord your God, he is God in Heaven above, and on earth beneath."[8] The learned bishop Tillotson says, "The gentiles had, from the prophecies of the Sybils, an expectation of a great king, that was to appear in the world." So Virgil says, "that the time of Augustus was the utmost date of that prophecy, *ultima cumaei venit jam carminis Aetas*."

These wise men then, under all these advantages, might, on the appearance of this star, about the time of the completion of Daniel's four hundred and ninety years, have been fully convinced of the truth of the prediction, and the certainty of his being born, who should literally become the king of all the earth. They therefore did not enter Judea in a secret manner, or make a mystery of their mission. Their application is not to the parties concerned, or friends engaged to make out the truth of the fact; but as ambassadors from a foreign prince, they with confidence apply to Herod, the king of the country, and under a conviction of the certainty of their mission, with an air of authority demand to know, *"Where is he that is born king of the Jews? for we have seen his star in. the east, and are come to worship him."* This was unwelcome and alarming news, to the cruel, jealous, and tyrannical Herod. He did not rejoice in the glorious confirmation of all their hopes, founded on ancient prophecy, and endeavor to countenance the idea, and the general expectation of the people, but "he was troubled, and all Jerusalem with him." The people had often experienced the dreadful effects of revolts, and therefore, without considering the difference between these times and events, trembled at the extraordinary tidings. The chief priests and Scribes, are all solemnly convened by the king's order, that he might know from them, with precision, the place pointed out by the inspired penmen of their sacred writings, where Christ, or their expected Messiah, should be born, They do not hesitate about, or deny the facts, but unanimously answer, "In Bethlehem of Judea." The wise men no sooner receive the answer, than they repair to that place, and lo! the star, which they had seen in the east, again

---

8. Joshua 2:9-11.

appears to them, and directs to the most unlikely place in the world, in human apprehension, (a stable and a manger) to look for a royal infant, the expectation of a great nation, and the hope of the world.

As soon as this extraordinary child is brought into the temple, (most likely with many others, without distinction) Simeon the priest, an order of men among the Jews, not famous for countenancing the humble Jesus, and Anna, a prophetess, under the influence of a prophetic spirit, single out the blessed child, and unite their testimony in confirmation of this supernatural event.

But it will be asked, how are these things known, but by bare " *hearsay upon hearsay?"*

I answer, these are facts related by the chosen disciples of this same child, who was thus born king of the Jews. They accompanied him, during his ministry, and received their knowledge from his own information, as well as that of Joseph and Mary, and by the inspiration of the Holy Spirit. These are facts related by them, not in a secret history, or in a corner; not for their private or personal advantage in this life, but at the risk of their reputation, peace, comfort, and even of their lives. Arnobius, as early as the third century, says, "that it is extremely improbable that men should be so absurd and infatuated, as to agree together to pretend that they had seen things, which they had not seen; especially if we consider, that they were so far from making any advantage of such an imposture, that they exposed themselves to the hatred of the world in general."—Not hundreds of years after the events, but during the life of their master, and immediately on his death—in the life time of Mary, if not of Joseph too; and most likely of the shepherds and other witnesses of these extraordinary circumstances, which they relate—of numbers who must have been privy to the visit of the wise men, priests, scribes, and pharisees—to the cruel slaughter of the innocent children by the relentless Herod—many an inconsolable mother, and weeping father, must have been living witnesses of these important facts, when first published by the disciples of the crucified Jesus, to an astonished world. On no other natural principle, can you account for the amazing success, that attended the preaching of a poor illiterate fisherman, when three thousand men were brought over to the faith, at one sermon. It is most likely, that not only these, but thousands more, did then testify to their truth, otherwise the apostles must have been detected in the most shameful imposition on mankind, if they had been false. But so far from this, neither scribes, nor pharisees, with other learned Jews, who always discovered so much inveteracy to the Christian faith, ever pretended to controvert, in that day, the great leading facts of the Gospel history.

These opposers of the Christian church, had the most urgent reasons for using every means in their power, to expose the falsehood or forgery of the apostles, if such had been the case. The apostles condemned both scribe and pharisee for their unbelief, hypocrisy and formality—the whole body of the Jews, for their darling partiality to their own nation, and ceremonial law; and threatened the most dreadful punishment in a future state, upon all. Dr. Priestley very properly observes, that "We believe the facts recorded in the New Testament, not on the evidence of four persons, but on that of thousands, who were well acquainted with the facts, and by whom it cannot be denied, the contents of these books were credited. The books called the Gospels, *were not the cause, but the effects of the belief of Christianity in the first ages*: and these were received by the primitive Christians, because they knew beforehand, that the contents of them were true; consequently the leading facts of Christianity will always remain deserving credit, whatever may be found to be the truth concerning the authenticity of particular books. The circumstances of the Christian church, which received these books and transmitted them to us, were such, as there cannot be a doubt with respect to the competency of their evidence; because they were published in the life time of thousands and myriads, who were as competent witnesses of the *facts, as the writers themselves*; and there cannot be any question of their veracity, unless we suppose they all combined to tell and to propagate a falsehood, to their own prejudice, and merely to impose on all posterity—which would be a greater miracle, as being more contrary to what we know of human nature, than any thing recorded in these books."[9]

But what can our author say to the confirmation of all these great events, by the after life and conduct of Christ himself, who is acknowledged to be "a virtuous and amiable man and a preacher of the most excellent morality."[10] He acknowledged his mother on the cross, and declared his supernatural birth and high original, publicly and openly, before friends and enemies.

Let any candid man, with a mind open to conviction on rational evidence, take up the account of this transaction, as related by the apostle, and confirmed by all the attendant and concurring circumstances contained in the sacred Writings, and let him say, if he could then presume to assert,

---

9. Joseph Priestly, *Letters to a Young Man.*
10. Thomas Paine, *The Age of Reason.*

without a shadow of truth, that the birth of Jesus Christ of the Virgin Mary, as related by the evangelists, is mere *hearsay*, or rather *hearsay upon hearsay*. Did not the writers of the Gospels testify, by their whole conduct, that they were men of integrity, impartiality and virtue ? Did they not teach and inculcate the most pure and strict morality ever taught to man, and that on pain of the utmost displeasure of Almighty God? Christ's disciples, says the learned [John] Jortin, were examples of fervent zeal for the welfare of mankind—of an inoffensive behavior—of disinterestedness and self-denial—of indefatigable industry—of the most extensive charity—of patience, courage and constancy—and of a regular practice of all they taught. The first Christians resembled their teachers in their good qualities, and it was no small advantage to them, in their apologies for themselves and their religion, to be able to appeal boldly to their innocence and integrity.—That we may have a right sense of this, we should consider what it was to be a Christian in that day, lest we be deceived by the vulgar use of the word, and by the notion which we at present entertain about it. To be a Christian at that time, was to be an example of well-tried virtue—of true wisdom and consummate fortitude; for he surely deserves the name of a great and good man, who serves God, and is a friend to mankind; and receives the most ungrateful returns from the world; and endures them with a calm and composed mind; who dares to look scorn, infamy and death in the face. Whoever stands forth unmoved, and patiently bears to be derided as a fool and an idiot—to be pointed out as a madman and an enthusiast; to be reviled as an atheist, and an enemy to all righteousness; to be punished as a robber and a murderer— He who can pass through these trials, is a conqueror indeed; and what the world calls courage, scarce deserves that name when compared to this behavior.[11]

Some of these disciples who afterwards wrote the Gospels, were personally acquainted with Jesus Christ, attended him during his life, and were actually concerned in many of the events they relate. They were intimately acquainted with Joseph and Mary; and one of them took Mary to his own house after the crucifixion, at the request of his dying Lord, and she dwelt with him for fifteen years. The brothers and sisters of Jesus Christ after the flesh, were among his disciples, and several of them sealed their faith with their blood. If these circumstances did not constitute the Apostles the most proper historians to record the life, actions and doc-

---

11. John Jortin, *Discourses Concerning the Truth of the Christian Religion* (London: 1746) , 113.

trines of their master, and do not operate as a strong confirmation of the facts they relate, I know not what human testimony, can amount to proof: neither can I see, what reason there can be, for giving credit to the most approved histories either of nations or individuals.

Our author, with all his infidelity, will allow in page 8, "that no one will deny or dispute the power of the Almighty, to give such a revelation, if he pleases,"He acknowledges that there was such a man as Jesus Christ; and that he was a virtuous and amiable man. "That the morality he preached and practised was of the most benevolent kind."These are concessions, more than sufficient to overthrow our author's whole system of objections, and his infidelity founded thereon.

That Jesus Christ lived in the reign of Tiberius Caesar and suffered death under the Roman governor Pontius Pilate, is acknowledged—that he appointed during his life a set of men, who had been with him, during his ministry, to publish and propagate throughout the world, to Jew and Gentile, the doctrines he had taught—the miracles he had performed; and the predictions he had declared, as consequences of his death and resurrection, is scarcely doubted; he plainly and explicitly foretold to them, the success they should meet with in executing their commission, and the state of the Jewish and Christian churches till his second coming in glory, which he assured them should take place—these are all facts too notorious at this day to require proof.

That this same Jesus Christ did also, during his life, promise to his followers, that after his death and resurrection, he would send his holy spirit into the hearts of his disciples and followers; whereby they would be enabled to remember whatever he had told them while with them in the flesh ; and by whom they should receive the further knowledge of those things, which they 'were not then prepared to bear, is also recorded by these same apostles. Now the event has happened, as it was foretold, in full confirmation of the truth. That this promise was fulfilled in the presence of thousands of witnesses of all nations, providentially assembled at Jerusalem at the feast of Pentecost, for the purpose of public worship, is not only recorded by them as historians, but the after success of the preached Gospel, in all the neighboring nations, and the miraculous powers and knowledge of so many different languages, remaining in the apostles, and many of the first converts to Christianity for more than one hundred years, were evident demonstrations of the truth of the event. By this means churches were founded in the most famous cities then in the world, and men of all ranks, stations and characters, were brought by the force of these facts, to acknowledge the faith as it was in Jesus. So public and notorious was the descent of the spirit on the Apostles, that three thousand souls were added to the church in one day. This happened immediately after the event took place; and many of them must have had a previous knowledge of the facts published by the Apostles; and their belief, at that time, is a strong confirmation of the veracity of those facts. The descent of the spirit, must have been early contradicted, if it had not been founded in truth, as so many witnesses were appealed to; but even the high priest himself, was forced to acknowledge, "that unless they did something, all men would believe on him."

It ought not to be omitted here, that the whole plan of the Gospel, as delivered by these historians, is far superior to the natural abilities, of men so ignorant and unlettered, as were the planners and preachers of it—at the same time, they boldly declare, that every real professor shall experience in himself such powerful effects from a conformity to its doctrines and precepts, as that they should become uncontrovertible evidence to him, that God is their author. This has been verified in the lives and conduct of thousands, and thousands in every age of the church.

These historians have given us the account of the birth of their Lord and master, not only as they received it from Joseph and Mary, but as they had it from him in his life time, as well as from the influence and direction of the holy spirit, with which they were so openly and publicly filled, in presence of so many witnesses. Besides it is acknowledged, that the morality they inculcate, is of the most pure and benevolent kind: and that to mislead their adherents and followers, by publishing untruths to ruin and deceive them, would have been contrary to every principle of morality and benevolence.

If you look through their whole history, every part of it bears the mark of truth and credibility. They urge in all their teachings, the strictest attention to truth, and threaten the severest displeasure of Almighty God against falsehood, dissimulation and hypocrisy.

While they declare in plain but sublime language, the dignity and glory of their master's real character, they do not attempt to cover his actual state of humility, in not even having a place to lay his head. And though they claim for themselves the rank of ambassadors of the Son of God, and the representatives of a King and Sovereign, they fail not to record their own shameful misconduct, and the many mistakes and failures they had been guilty of, during their misapprehension of his true character; having been deceived with the rest of their nation, in looking to their Messiah as a temporal Prince and Saviour.

Add to this, that most of the great leading facts they relate, are confirmed by profane historians of good character, though known enemies to the Christian name; and then let it be asked, who can point out even equal human authority for any ancient history, with which the world is acquainted.

The universal expectation of the Messiah, or some divine person, about this time, is a fact generally acknowledged, Nebuchadnezzar, in his time, speaks of one of the persons who appeared in the fiery furnace, being like unto the Son of God; and Haggai[12] the prophet, expressly says, that *he*, i. e. the Messiah, was to be the desire of all nations. If so, mankind must have had tradition from the ancient patriarchs of the character of the expected Saviour. Suetonius refers to this expectation in his life of Vespasian, as has been already mentioned. Virgil's Pollio is an unanswerable argument in favor of the same event. The sacred books of the Jews foretold it, with the time and many circumstances preparatory to and attending it; and they were well known to the then learned world, and for a long time before, as has been shewn. The conduct of the wise men prove it.

There were three celebrated universities of the Jews in the provinces of Babylon, viz. Narbardia—Pompeditha and Soria, besides several other places famous for learning.[13] The Jews relate that the ten tribes were carried away not only into Media and Persia, but into the Northern countries, beyond the Bosphorus. Ortelius finds them in Tartary. II In Egypt the Jews had a temple, like that of Jerusalem, built by Onias and continued for the space of 343 years, till the reduction of Jerusalem by Titus. The Jews at that time, says the Talmud, were double the number in Egypt, of those who left it under Moses, that is, six millions.[14]

The reign of Augustus and the government of Pilate are established facts. Dion in his life of Octavius Caesar, mentions the murder of the Babes of Bethlehem; and Macrobius, another historian of early date and a heathen, says that "Herod the king ordered to be slain in Syria, (by which the Romans often meant Judea) some children that were under two years old. Among

---

12. Haggai 2:7.
13. Buxtorf, Tib. Cats. 6. Lightfoot's *Harmony, N. T.* 335, *Reasons of Christianity* 85. Hiaer in Zech. x. *Reasons of Christianity*, 85.
14. Josephus *Antiquities of the Jews.*

whom he included his own son, which made Augustus pleasantly say, it was better to be Herod's hog, than his son."[15]

The appearance of a wonderful star at the time of Christ's nativity is mentioned by Pliny[16] in his natural history, under the name of a bright comet.[17]

Celsus, Julian and Porphyry, all mortal enemies to the religion of Jesus, acknowledge the miracles and doctrines of Christ, at the same time that they ascribe them to the power of magic. It is a great complaint of Porphyry (a famous heathen Philosopher of the third century who wrote against the Christian religion) that our blessed Lord had the power of curing the possessed with devils and destroying their dominion, wherever he came. He makes it no wonder, that their cities should be overrun with sickness, since Esculapius and the rest of the gods, ever since the admission of the Christian religion, have withdrawn their converse with men. For since Jesus began to be worshipped no man hath received any public help or benefit by the gods.[18]

Tacitus and Lucian both mention the crucifixion under Pontius Pilate. Hear the first in his own words, when speaking of the Christians, "They had this denomination from *Christus*, who, in the reign of Tiberius, was put to death as a criminal, by the procurator Pontius Pilate. This pernicious superstition, though checked for a while, broke out again and spread not only *over Judea*, but reached this city (meaning Rome) also."

---

15. Macrob. Saturnal. Lib. 2. c. 4. folio, 279, cited by Cave, 1 vol. Introduction 2.

16. Lib. 2. c. 25.

17. Huetius says, *Scribit Plinius, exortum fuisse aliquando comaetam, candidum, argente crine ita fulgentem, ut vix contueri possit quisquam, specieque humana Dei effigiem in se ostendentem.* Quest, alnet. lib. 2. ch. 16.

The same author in his demonstration, proposition 3d, says, "that at new star or body of light seen by the wise men, is acknowledged by Julian, though he ascribes it to natural causes." And it is set off with great eloquence by Chalcidius, in his comment upon Plato's Timaeus. Haram. Annot. in Matthew 2:2.

18. Euseb. ch. 1. 179. 1 Cave, Lives Introduction 10. Thallus a Greek historian in his 3d Book, speaks of the darkness at our Saviour's death, which he calls an eclipse.

Phlegon who was the Emperor Adrian's freed man, in his 13th Book of Chronicles, acknowledges that our Lord was a Prophet; and in his history relates several events which he had foretold. Phlegon composed a history digested by Olympiads as far as the year of Christ 140.—In this he takes notice, that in the 4th year of the CCIId [202nd] Olympiad which determines about the middle of the 33d year of our common aera, there happened the greatest eclipse of the sun, that had ever been seen, insomuch that the stars were visible at noon day: and that afterwards there was a great earthquake in Bithynia. This is quoted by Eusebius, Hyeronimus in his Chronicon and origen against Celsus. Stack. I. N.T. 148.

The Christian authors for the first six centuries constantly appealed to the testimony of Phlegon, Thallus and the Roman records without hesitation. Whiston Test, of Phlegon, vindicated—Calmets disputation sur lestenebres.

The darkness at that time is taken notice of by Dion, Thallus, Phlegon and Suetonius, but by Tertullian in a particular manner, when he appeals in his apology to the Roman Archives, then in existence, for the particular account of it, given by Pontius Pilate to Tiberius Caesar; and the rending of the veil of the temple is mentioned by Josephus.

Thus, when actuated by a firm and lively faith in the truth and certainty of the Gospel, the Christian beholds the actions of even the enemies of the cross, (in the words of a worthy Dignitary of the church of England) "insensibly ministering to those sublime intentions of Providence; and ignorantly concurring to advance the triumphs of the cross; his thoughts are relieved and enlarged amidst the amplitude of such conceptions: inferior considerations pass away and no affection remains to the overwhelmed and enraptured mind, but that of holy joy and gratitude, in return for such exuberant goodness, which hath thus amply provided for the present and future happiness of his creature man."[19]

As a confirmation of the history thus written by the apostles, may here be added, the amazing progress made by the religion of Jesus Christ, on the preaching of a few illiterate fishermen, in opposition to the religion of Jew and Gentile, and to the entire subversion of both, as then practised, as is ably observed by an eminent writer at the beginning of the second century, during the lives of many of the eye witnesses to some of those important facts. "The Christian religion," says he, "is spread through the greatest part of Europe, Asia, and Africa. It extends from the British islands, to the farthest India; and is established not only in cities and populous places, but in towns and country villages, as Pliny testifies.

The metropolitan cities are all under bishops of the greatest eminence and piety. Rome, Alexandria, Antioch,and Jerusalem, are governed by apostolical men—Publiusis at Athens—Polycarp at Smyrna—Onesimus at Ephesus—and Papias at Hierapolis." And Tertullian addressing himself to the Roman governors, in behalf of the Christians, assures them, "that although they were of no long standing, yet that they had filled all places of their dominions; their cities, islands, castles, corporations, councils, armies, tribes, companies; the palace, senate, and courts of judicature; that if they had a mind to revenge themselves, they need not betake themselves to secret and skulking arts; their numbers were great enough to appear in open arms, having a party, not in this or that province, but in all

19. Hurd. 3d Sermon, 70-71.

quarters of the world; nay that, naked as they were, they could be suffi-ciently revenged upon them; for should they but all agree to retire out of the Roman empire, the world would stand amazed at that solitude and desolation, that would ensue upon it; and they (the Romans) would have more enemies than friends or citizens left among them."[20]

Among these converts, a great proportion were Jews, not only in Jerusa-lem, but in every town and village in Judea, as well as in the cities of the Gentiles. Even the persecuting Saul, who thought he did God service by his great zeal in bringing the best Christians to judgment and to death, is made himself to cry put, "Who art thou Lord? what wouldst thou have to do?" and afterwards to seal with his blood the truth of that Gospel which he had so furiously persecuted.

Permit me now to address myself to every reasonable man, and ask, *if facts thus related, attended with so strong corroborating circumstances*, by men of unblemished characters, with such advantages, and whose general statement is thus supported, can with justice be charged with wanting even "the authority of the persons from whom the facts came, and with being mere *hearsay*, if not *hearsay upon hearsay*, and which no one is bound to believe." Am I at liberty to believe or disbelieve, that there is such a city as London, or such a republic as France, because I have not seen them; but draw my knowledge from the testimony of others? Am I not bound to give credit to facts related to me, on rational evidence, though human and falli-ble?—Is there a sensible man in the United States, who doubts whether Thomas Paine wrote the pamphlet, called the Age of Reason, where every page is characteristic of the man, and unites to confirm the testimony of others, that he is the author; although perhaps there may not be a man in America who saw him write it—and if any one should have seen him write it, or should have heard him acknowledge it, yet, on the principles of the author of the Age of Reason, I am not bound to believe it, unless I had seen him write it, or heard him acknowledge it, myself.

Am I to believe this world existed from all eternity, and will continue to eternity, because I was not present at its creation? Nor can I have personal demonstration of its end, although I enjoy the concurrent testimony of rea-son and revelation, to convince me both of its beginning and end.

It is a very strange doctrine that I am not to believe a fact, though it comes from God himself, and is authenticated in the fullest manner by the

---

20. Apol. ch. xxxvii. fol. 30. I

person to whom it is first communicated, because it was not also made to me in person. If one is bound to believe human testimony, relative to human transactions, when given by men of veracity, having the means of knowledge, is the weight of the evidence lessened? or is the obligation to believe, weakened, when the testimony relates to the acts and declarations of God himself, which in his infinite wisdom and condescension, he has thought proper to make known to any of his servants, for the general benefit of mankind? If it should please God to make a special revelation of his will to an individual, with regard to any rule of conduct which he chose should influence those who wished to serve and obey him, and that individual is authorized to communicate it to me, attended with full and convincing evidence of its truth and certainty, am I nevertheless at liberty to disbelieve and reject such revelation with impunity? What would have been said of the primitive church in Jerusalem, if, after knowing from others, the command of their Lord and master while in the flesh, "that on seeing the approach of the Roman armies, they should leave the city and fly for their lives," if they had reasoned with our author, and refused to believe, because they had no knowledge of the injunction, but from the testimony of others? But, blessed be God! they believed, and were preserved from the exemplary fate of that unhappy city.

In human knowledge, it is generally thought that the mind necessarily assents to a fact fully proved by such testimony as the nature of the case will admit. Now it is directly opposed to the whole nature of man, and every principle of responsibility in him for his moral conduct, to suppose an immediate personal revelation from God, to every individual of the human race, before he is bound to believe.—This would render it necessary for God, either to affect the mind of man so irresistibly by the influence of his spirit, as to destroy all free agency in him, and thereby do violence to his nature; or else, being thus convinced by the knowledge of the facts revealed, and knowing the will of his master, he might have gone on in disobedience, having his natural heart still unsubdued and impenitent, and increased his condemnation more and more, by acting contrary to so much light and knowledge. St. Paul testifies this perverse bias of human nature, and opposition of the heart of man to the conviction of his understanding, when he says, though "they knew God, yet they did not glorify him as God."

Could our author have, by an immediate revelation from Heaven, better evidence of the facts revealed in the Scriptures, than he has of the being and attributes of that God, in whom he lives and moves, and has his existence?

And yet, if we were to examine into the effects of this knowledge on his daily practice, we should have reason to fear, that an express and individual revelation to him, without a thorough change of heart and mind, would meet with much the same reception as the Scriptures. If he can act against the conviction of a fact, so clearly revealed to every rational and reflecting mind, as the eternal power and godhead of the one great and glorious Jehovah, with the consequent duties and obligations; it is not irrational or unjust, to suppose a similar conduct, in opposition to the most personal revelation of God to his own mind. This is the idea suggested by St. Paul, that great judge of human nature, hinted at before:—"For what can be known of God," says he, "was manifested to the Gentiles by God himself, who enlightened them. His invisible perfections are clearly seen by the visible creation; yea, his eternal power and godhead, by the things that are made; wherefore they are inexcusable, because having known God, they did not glorify him, nor were they thankful, but became vain in their imaginations, and their foolish hearts were darkened; and *fancying themselves wise*, they became so stupid, as to change the glory of the incorruptible God into an image made like to corruptible man."[21] I have not followed the common translation, but one that better agrees with the spirit of the original.

It is time now to draw this conclusion from what has been said—that the facts, relating to the miraculous conception and birth of Christ of the Virgin Mary, are established by evidence and proof far superior to her word, and are of that nature, which one would imagine must command the assent of every honest, ingenuous mind, till the truth and rectitude of the characters of Christ himself, and the sacred historians, can be impeached, and their veracity doubted. And although we have not the writings of Joseph and Mary for vouchers, we have the authenticated testimony of those, who had it from them, with the additional evidence of miracles, prophecy, and the experience of thousands and thousands of the subjects of this divine grace, from the first promulgation of the Gospel, to this day.

---

21. Romans 1:19-22.

4

The Divine Mission of Jesus Christ

The Age of Reason, not content with ridiculing the miraculous conception of the Saviour of the worlds calls in question his divine mission also, by asserting, "that it is not difficult to account for the credit that was given to the story of Jesus Christ being the Son of God. He was born at a time when the heathen mythology had prepared the people for the belief of such a story—almost all the extraordinary men, who lived under the heathen mythology, were reputed to be the sons of some of their Gods. The story, therefore, had nothing in it either new, wonderful or obscene: it was conformable to the opinions that then prevailed among the Gentiles, or mythologists, and it was those people only, that believed it. The Jews, who had kept strictly to the belief of one God, and no more, and who had always rejected the heathen mythology, never credited the story."

THIS is something worse than bare misrepresentation.—It must be admitted to arise, either from a total want of knowledge of the subject, or a wilful perversion of the truth.

The assertion is, that "the heathen mythology had prepared the minds of the people, about the time of the birth of Jesus Christ, for the belief of such a story, as that of his being the Son of God; and that the Gentiles only believed it, but the Jews had never credited the story."

Our author seems to have collected together a few technical expressions, belonging to particular subjects, and with which he seems much pleased, in hopes, that by repeating them over and over, he might persuade himself, and perhaps his readers too, that he was acquainted with the doctrines to which they were attached. This appears to be the case with regard to the heathen mythology; but from his application of them to the subject before him, he appears to know as little of the Pagan principles of worship, as he does of the Christian system.

To every person, versed in the history of the nations of the world, at the time of the publication of the Gospel of Jesus Christ, nothing can be more evident, than the contrariety of its doctrines and precepts to the mythology of the Gentiles. So far, indeed, were their minds from being prepared, by their religious principles and practices, to admit the doctrines of the Son of God, that perhaps no two things in nature could be more opposite, or better calculated to destroy each other.

The religion of the gentiles, was the then religion of all the nations of the earth, the Jewish nation excepted, which was execrated by them all, as barbarous and savage, on account of the exclusive nature of its worship; not admitting communion with any other religion, known or practised in the world, but reprobating them all, as the doctrine of devils. Jesus Christ was professedly a Jew, and therefore was despised by the Gentiles; during his whole life he addressed himself only to the Jews; after his death, his apostles confined their preaching, for many years, to the same people, till taught to do otherwise by divine revelation. They did not consider the Gentiles as subjects of the grace of the Gospel, if we except the distant hope held out to them by Christ, in his parables and prophetic declarations, grounded on the rejection of his Gospel by the Jews, and which were not understood by his apostles till after his resurrection.

The whole genius of the Pagan religion, consisted in the occasional worship of a multitude of Gods, of their own making, for the attainment of mere temporal good, or the indulgence of their passions, without having an idea of the spiritual nature of the great self * existent First Cause of all things; or the least expectation of the resurrection of the dead. Their hints of an immortality after death, were very obscure and imperfect. Cicero, in his Tusculan Questions, says, "Show me first if you can, and it be not too troublesome, that souls remain after death; and if you cannot prove this, for it is difficult, declare how there is no evil in death?" Again—"I know not what mighty things they have got by it, who teach, that when the time of death comes, they shall entirely perish; which if it should be, (for I do not see any thing to the contrary) what ground of joy or glorying does it afford?" Hence, an admission of any new God, or different mode of worship, was easily assented to by them; so that it did not derogate from the established principles of intercommunity of divine homage to their various deities, agreeably to their national institutions.

The Christian system, grounded on the religion of the Jews, so odious to the whole world of Gentiles, opened a new scene to mankind. Jesus Christ commenced his prophetic office, by preaching repentance and forgiveness of sins, through his name alone, in opposition to all the Gods of the nations; declaring their worship to be that of demons and devils—that no salvation could be procured by any of them to their votaries, and that there was but one only living and true God—that life and immortality was now brought to light by his Gospel, in which, for the first time, was clearly revealed the resurrection of the body—that every man, *every where*, was now command-ed to repent and believe his Gospel, as by no other name under Heaven, but that of his own, could eternal life be obtained—that,whoever believed on him, should be saved; but all who refused, and would not believe, should be damned—that no man could come to God, but by him—that he was, em-phatically the resurrection and the life—that there could be no communion in the worship of the heathen deities, even their most supreme, no not so much as to eat or drink with them at their festivals and solemnities, their being no possible connection between the cup of the Lord, and of devils.

The heathen world was now in an awful state of darkness and vice. It will therefore throw some light on the necessity mankind were in at this time, of great reformation, to attend to the nature and practice of the heathen mythol-ogy. A respectable author, has given an epitome of it in the following words— "The chief oracles among the heathens, appointed human sacrifices; that of Delphi, of Dodona, and of Jupiter Saotes. It was the custom of all the Greeks, to sacrifice a man, before they went out to war. It was a custom among the Phoenicians and Canaanites, for their kings, in the times of great calamity, to sacrifice one of their sons, they loved best; and it was common both with them, the Moabites, and Ammonites, to sacrifice their children. Herodotus says, "That in the expedition of Xerxes into Greece, arriving in the country of the Edonians, in Persia, the magi took nine of the sons and daughters of the inhabitants, and buried them alive—and that when Amestris, wife of Xerxes, had happily attained to mature age with confirmed health, she ordered four-teen children of the noblest families of Persia, to be buried alive, in grateful sacrifice to the subterraneous deity."[1] The Egyptians, the Athenians and Lacedemonians, and generally all the Grecians, Romans and Carthagenians—

---

1. Lib. vii. p. 477.

the Germans, Gauls and Britons—and indeed almost all the heathen nations throughout the world, offered human sacrifices upon their altars; and this, not on certain emergencies, and in imminent dangers only, but constantly, and in some places, every day; but on extraordinary accidents, multitudes were sacrificed at once to their bloody deities.

Diodorus Siculus and others, relate, that in Africa, two hundred children, of the principal nobility, were sacrificed to Saturn at one time; and Aristomenee sacrificed three hundred men together to Jupiter Ithometes, one of whom was Theopompus, king of the Lacedemonians.

Plutarch, in his Tract on Superstition, says, "Had it not been much better for the so much famed Gauls and Scythians, that they had neither thought nor imagined, nor heard any thing of their Gods, than to have believed them such as would be pleased with the blood of human sacrifices, and who accounted such for the most complete and meritorious of expiations. How much better had it been for the Carthagenians, if they had had either Critias, or a Diagoras, for their first law-giver, that so they might have believed neither God nor Spirits, than to make such offerings to Saturn, as they made. But they *knowingly and willingly* devoted their own children; and they who had none of their own, bought of some poor people, and then sacrificed them, like lambs or pigeons; the poor mothers standing by, without either a sigh or a tear—or if by chance she fetched a sigh, or let fall a tear, she lost the price of her child, and it was nevertheless sacrificed. All the places round the image, were in the mean time filled with the noise of hautboys and tabors, to drown the poor infants' crying."

Let those who are instrumental, with so much industry, to destroy our holy religion, and bring us back to this awful state of things, seriously reflect on the just deserts of so aggravated a crime, and fear the tremendous punishment that awaits their absurd conduct.

Livy makes mention of human sacrifices at Rome—Dion Cassius relates that two men were sacrificed in the Campus Martius, under Julius Caesar. He says it was a custom, begun under Augustus, for men to be devoted to death for the safety of the emperor.

Suetonius mentions, that some writers affirmed, that Augustus offered a great number of enemies, who had surrendered themselves, to be slain on the ides of March, in devotion to the manes of Julius Caesar. We are informed by Pliny, that in the year of the city 658, a decree of the senate passed, that no man should be sacrificed, and that, till then, such sacrifices were public. This prohibition seemed to concern only the common and frequent use of them;

for besides what has been already observed, Plutarch says, "They continued in his time; and it was not till about the time of Constantine's reign, that a final stop was put to so strange and abominable a practice; for though it was forbidden by Adrian, and very much abated in his reign, yet Antinous was made a sacrifice by Adrian himself." Tatian declares, "That the human sacrifices offered to Jupiter at Rome, and to Diana, not far from thence, were the chief cause of his leaving the heathen religion, and turning Christian."

Pliny acquaints us, that they were practised in the age in which he lived; and Minutius Felix, that they were used when he wrote. Porphyry mentions them as notoriously practised at Rome, in his time; and Lactantius speaks of them, as not laid aside in his.[2]

Did not this degenerate and cruel state of things loudly call for a speedy and effectual remedy? The Jews, as a people, had lost every sense of the spirituality of their divine religion, and had settled down into mere form and hypocrisy. Their example no longer edified and instructed the neighboring nations, to forsake their vain idols and turn to the living God, Among the heathens, their diabolical sacrifices, with other as impure practices, made up so great a part of their worship, and were become so habitual and fashionable, that arguments and reasonings drawn from the nature of God, and the proof of his perfections in the works of creation and Providence, had lost all their convictive force and energy. In this gloom of more than midnight darkness, the sun of righteousness arose on a benighted world, with meridian splendor.

When Jesus Christ began his ministry, he courted neither Jew nor Gentile—declaring the Jewish economy at an end, and fully completed in him; and showing, that all the other nations " had changed the glory of the incorruptible God, into images made like corruptible man, and to birds and four footed beasts, and creeping things; wherefore God hath given them up to uncleanness, through the lusts of their own hearts, to dishonor their own bodies between themselves—being filled with all unrighteousness, fornication, wickedness, covetousness, maliciousness; full of envy, murder, debate, deceit, malignity, whisperers, backbiters, haters of God, despiteful, proud, boasters, inventors of evil things, disobedient to parents, without understanding, covenant-breakers, without natural affection, implacable, unmerciful."

---

2. *Reasons of Christianity*, 362.

Does this black catalogue contain a picture, likely to attract the friendship of those, who were said to be the originals? Had it a tendency to prepare the minds of the Gentiles to believe the author to be a Son of God?

The author of the Age of Reason must have well known, if he had given himself time to reflect, that there was a wide difference, in the estimation of the Gentiles, between their ideas of deifying a man, who had pretended to have been begotten by some imaginary God, and who would claim divine honors jointly with a thousand other Gods of the like origin, and the claim of Jesus Christ to an exclusive worship—He not only severely, and with sovereign power, reproved their abominable practices, as a moral teacher, but he declared himself in an exclusive sense, (though apparently the son of Joseph and Mary, and confessedly incarnate and the son of man) the only begotten Son of God, begotten before all worlds, even from eternity—the Creator of all things—one with the Father, the sole object of all true worship in Heaven and earth—who was, and is, and is to come— the first and the last—the beginning and the end—and besides whom there was no God.

Is there any thing in all the mythology of the ancients, that tended to prepare the minds of the people, for such a story as this? Or is not every word and every idea totally repugnant to all the notions ever formed by the wisest among the Gentile nations of the earth, on the subject of religious worship?

Add to all this, that Jesus Christ not only thus declared himself to be the Son of God with power, in Ms preaching, and proved the claim by doing the works that no man before him ever did; but that the crime for which he was crucified, was, that "being a man, he had made himself equal with God;" and this imputed crime he confessed at the bars, both of the high priest of the Jews, and of the Roman governor. Yet Jesus Christ is acknowledged by this author, "to have been a virtuous and amiable man; and the excellent morality he preached and practised, to have been of the most benevolent kind, and not exceeded by any who had gone before, or succeeded him."

How a man, pluming himself on the title *Common Sense*, can reconcile Jesus Christ having been a preacher of such excellent morality, with his own principles detailed in this extraordinary treatise, I leave others to determine.

Is it possible that this writer could have seriously believed, "that Jesus Christ, or the Messiah of the Jews, being the Son of God, was a doctrine of no higher a date, than the birth of Christ; and that therefore it was a wretched story, formed for the critical moment, when the peoples minds were prepared for the belief of it, by the peculiar complexion of the heathen mythology ?"

Nothing could have convinced a reader of this fact, but the author's apparent want of knowledge, in both the Jewish and Christian histories, when he asserts, "That the Jews who had kept strictly to the belief of one God and no more, and who had always rejected the heathen mythology, never credited the story."["]

It is almost incredible, that any man, however absurd his conduct might have been in some other respects, should have attempted so' important a subject, without reading the sacred writings of the Jews, with the opinions of their chief authors. To these I appeal for a conclusive answer.

Their prophetical books expressly foretold, (besides the declaration to Adam, that the seed of the woman should bruise the serpent's head) many hundred years before the event, that in the fullness of time, God would send his prophet (so termed by way of eminence) to whom the people should hearken, and that in the seed of Abraham, all the nations of the earth should be blessed. The prophecies relating to the promised Messiah, were delivered at different times, and under very differing circumstances. To Adam and Eve he was promised, in general, as a man, the seed of the woman. It is somewhat remarkable, that we never read of the seed of the woman but in the instance of the promised Saviour: We hear of the seed of Abraham, Isaac and Jacob—of Aaron and of David, but never of the seed of any woman, but that of the Virgin Mary, the mother of our Lord according to the flesh. To Abraham he is promised as his seed, or the seed of his posterity. Thus (in the words of the sacred Biographer[3]) "He who was promised to Adam, immediately on the fall, under the obscure description of the seed of the woman, who should bruise the head of the serpent, was now announced to the world as the seed of Abraham, in whom all the families of the earth should be blessed. And hence—forward, we have prediction upon prediction—ordinance upon ordinance—promise upon promise—event upon event, leading to, rising above, improving, enlarging upon each other, like the gradual light of the ascending sun, from the early dawn to the perfect day: we perceive types, shadows, ceremonies, sacrifices disappearing little by little: patriarchs, priests, prophets, lawgivers and kings, retiring one after another, and giving place to the Lord our Judge, our Lawgiver, our King to save us, as the twinkling fires of the night hide their diminished heads; and as the vapors disperse before the glorious orb of day."

---

3. Vol. ii. 17.

To Jacob, the Messiah is promised as one descending from the tribe of Judah. To David, that he should be of his family, and of the fruit of his body. That he was to be a great King forever and ever—the anointed of the Lord—his only begotten Son, who should have the heathen for his inheritance, and the uttermost parts of the earth for his possession.—Yet he was to be forsaken of his God; to be despised and laughed to scorn; his garments were to be parted among his persecutors, and they were to cast lots for his vesture. He was to be betrayed by his own familiar friend, who eat of his bread. To Isaiah it was foretold, that the spirit of the Lord should be upon him, that his birth should be miraculous, and his mother a virgin:—that he should be a man of sorrows and acquainted with grief; and that the chastisement, by which our peace is to be effected, should be laid upon him, his death being for the redemption of mankind; yet the government should be upon his shoulders, and his name should be called, Wonderful Counsellor—the Mighty God—the Father of the Everlasting Ages—the Prince of Peace.

To Micah, he was to be born in Bethlehem. To Daniel was made known the precise time of his suffering. To Haggai, Zechariah, and Malachi, that all these events should be accomplished before the destruction of the second Temple. The not breaking a bone of the paschal Lamb—the fending the garment and casting lots for his vesture—the offering gall and vinegar—the looking on him whom they have pierced—the prophecies relating to the humiliation and death of the Messiah, and the spirituality of his office, all tend to elucidate and show the established doctrines of the Jews with regard to their expected Messiah.

Agreeably to this view of the prophetical declarations relating to our Saviour's incarnation, the general prediction was 2000 years, before the promise made to Abraham. From that, to the pointing out the particular tribe from which he was to descend, was 280 years. From thence to the designation of the family in which he was to be born, was 600 years. It was above 300 years from thence to the prophecy of his miraculous nativity: and from thence to his public appearance as a preacher of righteousness, was 350 years.

This is a very concise view of the expectations of the Jews, relative to Messiah their King's coming in the flesh. They believed that he should be the Son of God, yet, emphatically speaking, the Son of Man—exalted and debased—master and servant—priest and victim—king and subject—clothed with mortality, yet the conqueror of death—rich and poor—glorious in holiness, yet a man acquainted with grief. He was the Father of the everlasting ages, yet involved in our infirmities, and reduced to a state of extreme humiliation. All these seeming contradictions were to be reconciled in the person of their expected Messiah; and they centered, as in a point, in the man Christ Jesus, the only begotten Son of God.

The Jews as a people, then professed firmly to believe, that their king Messiah, though the Word and eternal Son of God, was to be born of a Virgin—of the tribe of Judah—of the family of David—in the village of Bethlehem: that he was to continue for ever and ever, and his name as long as the sun and moon should endure: that he was to be both son and Lord of David: that he should die an ignominious death and rise again: that he should have a fore-runner in the power and spirit of Elias. That, as a proof of his mission, he should heal the broken hearted, preach deliverance to captives, raise the dead, and preach the Gospel to the poor. That he should perfect and fulfil the law—be a stone of stumbling and rock of offence to many; and that the Gentiles should submit to his government. In full proof of these facts, the whole book of Psalms, with the prophets Isaiah, Jeremiah, Ezekiel, Daniel, Zechariah, Haggai, and Malachi bear witness.

Yet, notwithstanding this explicit declaration of the person and character of this glorious personage, the Talmud of the Jews informs us, "That, when the Messiah shall appear, he shall be acknowledged only by a small number of the Jews (in comparison with the whole people), and shall be rejected by the bulk of the nation: that the Messiah shall be a rock of offence to the two houses of Israel, and an occasion of falling to the inhabitants of Jerusalem: that the Jews shall then be overwhelmed with evils."[4]

When Christ appeared and began his ministry, he did not go to the Gentiles, but confined himself exclusively "to the lost sheep of the house of Israel," to the Jews alone, as the immediate object of his mission. From these he first chose twelve disciples, who remained with him, the constant witnesses of his life and doctrines, to the end. After some time, his followers greatly increasing, he chose seventy disciples more, and sent them to the various cities of Judea, still confining his mission to the Jews. At one time he had attendant, on his personal ministry, four thousand, and at another five thousand followers, besides women and children; these were all Jews. His popularity became so very conspicuous among the Jews, and his friends and followers so greatly increased, that, in the Sanhedrim, the chief priest declared, *that all men* were running after him; and among his warm friends

---

4. Bab. Talm. Tract. Sanhedrim C. Halies in Galatin, lib. ix. ch. ii.—Jean Baptiste Bullet, *The History of the Establishment of Christianity*, ix.

and disciples, we find Nicodemus, a ruler of the Jews; Joseph of Arimathea, a counsellor; and Matthew and Zacheus, noted Jewish publicans, or tax-gatherers, officers under the Roman government; these were all Jews; and to these, with the whole city of Jerusalem, and the country round about, did he publish the glad tidings of salvation, declaring himself to be the Son of God, and the appointed Messiah, and they believed on his name: and after his death, even the persecuting Saul, a pharisee of the strictest sect, was added to the number. But never, in any one instance during his life, did he address himself to the Gentiles.

His being the Son of God, was so remarkably and emphatically the burden of his doctrines while on earth, that his inveterate enemies confined their charge against him, when arraigned on the trial for his life, to this important fact; and, as they were employed and bribed to make this accusation, by the chief priest and pharisees, it is pretty conclusive evidence of their opinion of the true character of the expected Messiah.

The testimony given against him on his trial, before the Jewish Sanhedrin, was, that he should have said, "If they should destroy the temple, he would rebuild it in three days," as a proof of his Almighty power, otherwise there could not have been any pretence of blasphemy in the charge; but even in this, the witnesses could not agree so as to make their testimony amount to legal proof; and the innocent Jesus remaining silent, nothing could be obtained from his confessions—on which the chief priest, in order to aid the defective testimony, adjured him, by the living God, to answer, if it was true, "That he was the Christ or Messiah, or not?" This was putting the accused to his oath, after the manner of the Jews, or examining him on interrogatories. Silence was now no longer allowable. Without hesitation, therefore, he fully confessed it; and as a further acknowledgment of his divine mission, added, "Hereafter you shall see the Heavens opened, and the son of man standing at the right hand of God." Hereupon the chief priest, considering this as an unequivocal declaration of his claim to the character of the Messiah, rent his clothes, and passed sentence of condemnation against him, *not as guilty of falsehood, deceit, or imposition upon the people, but of blasphemy*; and therefore pronounced him worthy of death; and afterwards, to put the idea they formed of the true character of their expected king *Messiah* out of question, he refused his assent to Jesus being released by Pilate, because he had made himself the Son of God; that is, by claiming the character of their Messiah.

The like consequence was drawn by the people at large from his preaching long before, when he charged them with attempting to stone him for his good works—they denied the fact, but said, that it was "*for his being only a man, yet making himself equal with God.*"

After his resurrection, and the descent of the Holy Spirit on the day of Pentecost, the apostles began to preach in his name; and, at one of their first sermons, converted three thousand souls; and soon after, we are informed, that the number of the brethren were about five thousand; and, a little afterwards, that "a great company of the priests were obedient to the faith." Here then were numerous converts, who must have been as well acquainted with the general statement of facts relative to the life and actions of the Saviour, as the apostles themselves; and, by their conversion, under the dangers to which they exposed themselves by their adherence to the cause of a persecuted end crucified master, they became as good and sufficient witnesses of the facts on which the Christian doctrines are founded, as if they had been of his family in his life time. These were all Jews; and they were at Jerusalem, the seat of all the great occurrences of his life and death, where a church was immediately established, and from whence their doctrines spread throughout all Judea, so as to raise a persecution against the whole profession. Hereby these followers of the despised Nazarene, were scattered throughout the country, and finally forced among the Gentiles, whom they were taught of God, by a revelation of his will, to admit also to fellowship; the Jews as a nation having rejected the Messiah their king; and not till then did they turn to the Gentiles.

Thus it is plain to demonstration, that, before the crucifixion of Christ, and for a considerable time after the resurrection, so far from the Jews "never crediting the story, and the Gentiles being the only people that believed," it was the direct reverse. The Jews were the only people who did believe the Gospel, it never having yet been preached or offered to any other nation.

Indeed, whoever is the least acquainted with ecclesiastical history, and the history of the Jewish nation, must be surprised at the boldness of this adventurous author, in asserting, "that the story of Jesus Christ being the Son of God, was introduced under cover of the heathen mythology, and that the Gentiles only received it;" when it is so apparent, both from sacred and profane history, that the church of Christ consisted of thousands of Jews, before a single Gentile convert was known to the church. And when it did first happen, a special revelation from Heaven became necessary, to reconcile the minds of the apostles to it. And, after the calling of the Gentiles, about fourteen years from the crucifixion, we are told, that on the preaching of Paul, "A great multitude of both Jews and Greeks believed." About thirty years after the death of our Lord, the doctrines of the Gospel had spread throughout Judea, Gallilee and Samaria; so that, on Paul's arrival at Jerusalem, the apostles inform him, that many thousands, (literally myriads or tens of thousands) were in Jerusalem, who believed.

Thus is the wisdom and foreknowledge of the glorious Redeemer manifest, in his having ordered an exclusive application to the Jews, till, as a nation, they should reject him, not only in fulfilment of ancient prophecy, but in full contradiction to the spirit of infidelity, which he foresaw would arise in these latter days, charging him with introducing the doctrine of his divinity under cover of the heathen mythology.

The devils themselves will rise in judgment against this pretended philosopher; for although he knows not Jesus, nor who he is, and will not believe in his being the Son of God; those unhappy spirits, even in the days of his flesh, could cry out in the bitter anguish of despair, "*We* know thee, who thou art, Jesus thou Son of God; art thou come to torment us before the time?"

5

The Christian Theory Misrepresented

In the like spirit of misrepresentation, and utter aversion to the pure system of the Gospel, does this writer assert, "That the theory of the Christian church, sprung out of the tail of the heathen mythology. A direct incorporation took place in the first instance, by making the reputed founder, celestially begotten. The trinity of Gods that then followed, was no other than a reduction of the former plurality, which was twenty or thirty thousand. The statue of Mary, succeeded the statue of Diana of Ephesus, &c. &c. The Christian theory is little else, than the idolatry of the ancient mythologists, accommodated to the purposes of power and revenue, and it yet remains to reason and philosophy to abolish the amphibious fraud."

IT is an old observation, take any thing for granted, and any thing will follow. Should not every reader expect, after these round assertions, that some proof of this extraordinary position would have been adduced; especially as the whole system of the Gospel is declared by its advocates, to be a direct attack on every principle and species of idolatry, and wholly designed to establish the worship of one only living and true God through Jesus Christ whom he hath sent. But this writer appears to have supposed, that the knowledge of the Gospel might be gained by intuition; and of course is wholly unacquainted with the nature of its doctrines, and seems to suppose his readers equally ignorant, or he would have seen the necessity of some kind of proof or argument to support his *bold and unsupported charges* against the Christian church as founded in the Gospel of the Son of God.

Whatever plausible pretexts he might have had, from a cursory view of the unchristian practices of the church, when degenerated and apostatized under darkness and declension, as foretold by the author of our holy religion and his apostles, that it would be under the reign of Antichrist; yet surely he must have been beside himself to assert, "that the *Christian Theory* is little else than the idolatry of the ancient mythologists, accommodated to particular purposes."

If ever a system of pure doctrine, or holy practice, founded on the belief and worship of one God, has been inculcated and urged on the consciences of men, surely it is to be found in the Christian Theory.—Hear our author himself; "Jesus Christ was a virtuous and amiable man; the morality that he *preached and practised*, was of the most benevolent kind."

The Decalogue, which is the epitome of all its precepts, begins by the express commandment, "that thou shalt not have more Gods than one."—And the New Testament opens with a rebuke that may well be applied here, "get behind me Satan, for it is written thou shalt worship the Lord thy God, and him only shalt thou serve."

When the great author of our holy religion addresses himself to God the Father, he says, "I thank thee O Father, Lord of Heaven and Earth, because thou hast hid these things from the wise and prudent, and hast revealed them to babes and sucklings, for so it seemed good in thy sight" [Matt. 11:25; Luke 10:21]; and the substance of many of his instructions were, "that no man can serve two masters—ye cannot serve God and mammon" [Matt. 6:24].

"The law and the prophets were until John; since that time the kingdom of God is preached, and every man presseth into it" [John 6:16]. For God so loved the world, that he gave his only begotten Son, that whosoever believeth on him should not perish but have everlasting life. {John 3:16]. God is a spirit and they who worship him must worship him in spirit and in truth" [John 4:24]. And his disciples after his resurrection, who established all the primitive churches, and taught them both their theory and practice, set out by declaring, "that the God of Abraham, Isaac and Jacob, the God of their Fathers had glorified his Son Jesus Christ." And when the people of Lystra, who were both heathen and idolaters, but much more excusable than the author of the *Age of Reason*, had mistaken the apostles for their gods in the likeness of men; and would have offered sacrifice to them; instead of justifying the conclusion or assertions of our pretender to reason, "they rent their clothes, and ran in among the people, saying why do ye these things? we preach unto you, that ye should turn from these vanities unto the living God, who made heaven and earth, the sea and all things that are therein" [Acts 14:15].

When the Gentile converts, in the beginning of their church, were trammelled with the false reasonings of some weaker brethren, who would have obliged them to be circumcised according to the law of Moses; they made application to the church under the apostles at Jerusalem, for their instructions on this head. In their answer, the apostles appear to aim at summing up their duty according to the Christian theory in as few words as possible. These were, "that they should abstain *from pollutions of idols*, from fornication and from blood" [Acts 15:20].

When Paul, the great apostle of the Gentiles, was preaching at Athens, he assures his hearers, "that, as they worshipped the unknown God; therefore, whom they ignorantly worshipped, *Him* he declared unto them; that is, God who made the world, and all things that are therein, seeing that He is Lord of heaven and earth, and dwelleth not in temples made with hands" [Acts 17:23–24]

The doctrine of the gospel, which Jesus Christ and his apostles taught throughout the world was the worship of one only true God, in spirit and in truth, through Jesus Christ his beloved Son, and all their instructions, relative to practical religion, do indeed breathe a spirit of the purest morality ever taught to man. In addition to the incomparable sermon on the mount, and the whole strain of our Lord's teachings, hear the apostle Paul in his address to the Romans, "I beseech you brethren, by the mercy of God, that ye give up your bodies a living sacrifice, holy, acceptable unto God, which is your reasonable service.—Let your love be without dissimulation; abhor that which is evil; cleave to that which is good; be kindly affectioned one to another with brotherly love, in honor preferring one another; not slothful in business; fervent in spirit, serving the Lord; rejoicing in hope, patient in tribulation, continuing instant in prayer; distributing to the necessity of saints, given to hospitality; bless them who persecute you; bless, and curse not. Rejoice with them who rejoice, and weep with them who weep. Be of the same mind one towards another; mind not high things, but condescend to men of low estate; be not wise in your own conceit; recompense no man evil for evil; provide things honest in the sight of all men; if it be possible, as much as lieth in you, live peaceably with all men; avenge not yourselves, but give place unto wrath. If thine enemy hunger, feed him; if he thirst, give him drink; be not overcome of evil, but overcome evil with good" [Rom. 12:1-21]. And again, the same apostle, when addressing the Thessalonians—"For this is the will of God, even your sanctification, that ye should abstain from fornication [1 Thess. 4:3];

that no man should defraud his brother in any thing, but encourage and promote brotherly love; that they should study to be quiet, and do their own business, and work with their own hands, walking honestly to them that are without, that they should have lack of nothing; that they should be sober, and at peace among themselves" [1 Thess. 4:6]. [The apostle Paul] exhorts them "to warn the unruly; comfort the feeble minded; support the weak; be patient to all men; rejoice for evermore; pray without ceasing; in every thing give thanks; prove all things; hold fast that which is good [1 Thess. 5:14–21], and abstain from all appearance of evil" [1 Thess. 5:14]. And when he speaks of the fruits and effects of these doctrines, as he does to the Galatians, "They are, love, joy, peace, long suffering, gentleness, goodness, faith, meekness, temperance" [Gal. 5:22].

This was the sum of the essential doctrines of the church for the first three hundred years of the Christian era, connected with an unremitted attention to them in all their theory and practice. The assertion, therefore, "That the Christian theory is little else than the idolatry of the ancient mythologists," may, without the just charge of uncharitableness, be termed a perversion of the truth, when made by a man, who had the means of knowledge in his power, but who has neglected to make use of them.

What could the *Age of Reason* mean by *theory*? Surely that of the Christian church is only to be found in the New Testament. It would be even too absurd for our author, who seems, however, capable of almost any attempt, to charge the Gospel, or the Christian church, with the errors and abominable practices, of many of its mistaken, or disingenuous professors, when manifestly opposed by every precept and instruction of its system. As well might he say, that the theory of the Christian church, was that of the Gnostics, Manicheans, or Nicolaitans, because they once professed to belong to that church.

The Gospel is the only test of all the theory and allowed practices of the Christian church; and whenever that is swerved from in either, its emphatic language is, "Remember therefore from whence thou art fallen, and repent, and do thy first works, or else I will come quickly, and remove thy candlestick out of its place, except thou repent" [Rev. 2:5].

The writer of the *Age of Reason*, may think it harsh to be charged with falsehood in every page of his work; but it would ill become an advocate for the Gospel, not to declare it boldly, and would be doing great injustice to the cause of truth, when the everlasting interests of his fellow men are at stake; and the guilty person has no one but himself to blame for this severity, having presumed to enter on a subject with which he had not taken pains to make himself acquainted; no, not with its *alphabet.*

Had he thought proper to have used reasoning and argument, founded on proof, to enforce his observations, he might have expected a suitable reply; but when he contents himself with advancing the most palpable falsehoods and misrepresentations as facts, from which to draw the most important conclusions, and these so enveloped in sophistry, and tainted with ludicrous insinuations, as seem only calculated to impose on the young and unwary mind in matters of infinite importance, he has no right to expect any thing farther, than a positive denial of the gross misrepresentation of facts he has imposed on the public.

The language of Justin Martyr, in the first ages of the church, to Crescens the philosopher, who had ungenerously, as wickedly, traduced the then Christians as atheistical and irreligious, is very applicable to our author. He says, "That Crescens talked about things which he did not understand—feigning things of his own head, only to comply with the humour of his seduced disciples and followers—that, in reproaching the doctrines of Christ, when he did not understand them, he discovered a most wicked and malignant temper, and showed himself far worse than the most simple and unlearned, who are not wont rashly to bear witness and determine on things not sufficiently known to them; or if he did understand their greatness and excellency, then he showed himself much more base and disingenuous, in charging upon them what he knew to be false, and concealing his inward sentiments and convictions, for fear test he should be suspected of being a Christian."[1]

Neither can our author complain with justice, that our Scriptures, the authority of which he denies, are made the test of truth on this occasion, as it is the theory established therein, which he charges with idolatry and falsehood. There can be, therefore, no other criterion or evidence of the truth or falsehood of the assertion, but from those Scriptures, let them be true or false. They must afford the exclusive testimony of what is contained in them, and to which alone we can appeal; and they contradict the charge in every page.

Our author indeed seems to plume himself on his imaginary idolatry of the Christian church, "in substituting a trinity of Gods, as a reduction of the twenty or thirty thousand of the heathen mythology." Could he have shown a single instance of a Christian church acknowledging a trinity of Gods in

1. William Cave, *Primitive Christianity*, vol. 1. fol. 7.

their worship, it would *then* have been necessary for him to have shown, that this was countenanced by the Gospel of Jesus Christ. But, while that teaches the mysterious doctrine of the Father, Son, and Holy Spirit, it never fails to inculcate as a truth, essential to his religion, that these three are but one inconceivable Jehovah.

Can our author be so ignorant as to suppose, that the doctrine of the Trinity is peculiar to, and the in-Tendon of, the Gospel? Had he read the Jewish Scriptures, or the heathen mythology in its first principles, with care; or attended to the known doctrines and principles of the Jews as a religious people, and the primitive religion of many of the heathen nations, he would have known, that a trinity in unity, was a doctrine taught many hundreds of years before the birth of Christ, and indeed from the beginning of the world.

As to the doctrine of the Trinity, it is not my design to enter into a dispute of so important a nature. It will suffice to show, as well his ignorance as his malice, in the charge, *"That the theory of the Christian church sprang out of the tail of the heathen mythology—and that the trinity of Gods that then followed, was no other than a reduction of the former plurality, which was twenty or thirty thousand."*

This may be done by barely evincing it, whether true or false, to have been the doctrine of the earliest heathen mythology, derived by tradition from the first patriarchs; and also that of the Jews, before the coming of Christ.

If the Christian religion is true, and was really a revelation from God, by Jesus Christ, then it must always have been essentially the same, from the beginning of the world.

God having formed man out of the dust of the earth, and breathed into him a rational soul, it was impossible on his first starting into existence, that he should, by his natural powers, ever have attained to the true knowledge of his Maker, or become acquainted with his will, otherwise than by an express revelation from Heaven; for as Tertullian justly observes, "What is infinite, can only be known of itself." God, as a wise and good Creator, could not have left his creature under this incapacity of rendering him the homage due to his name. All the attributes of the Divine Majesty required that this should be done; and there can be no doubt, but that the beneficent Creator did instruct Adam in that knowledge of his will, which was necessary to his well-being, by the revelation of the divine nature and attributes, and the mode of worship he required of him.

It clearly appears from the Mosaic history that the Messiah, who was to come, the second person in he Christian Trinity, was early made known to

Adam, by God himself, *as the seed of the woman*. The Spirit of God, the third person in the same trinity, is expressly said to have moved upon the face of the waters, at the creation; and the language made use of on that great occasion, is there said to be, *"Let us make man in our image"*—from which short account we may safely conclude, that Adam was not left without divine instruction.

Hence also, in the Mosaic account of the creation before the fall, we find God frequently and personally communing with Adam, whose mind, in that pure and sinless state, was better calculated to receive the communication of spiritual and divine knowledge, and to bear a constant contemplation of the perfect attributes of the Divinity, than any of his fallen race. And after the fall, we are told of Cain and Abel, worshiping the God of Heaven; one in an acceptable manner, by offering his devotions through victims slain on the altar, before man fed on the flesh of beasts; thus pre-figuring *him* who was to come, as the great propitiatory sacrifice. The other, in a very unacceptable manner, by refusing obedience to the revealed will of his Maker, and preferring the bloodless productions of the earth, raised by his own labor, as at least equal in the sight of God. The issue was answerable to the tempers and conduct of the men, and one sinful act begat another; impiety in principle, soon producing extreme cruelty in action; a brother was found shedding a brother's blood.

Adam then, being instructed in the will of his Creator, in a much higher and more spiritual manner than any of his descendants, must have taught his children, and his children's children, for many generations, with anxious solicitude, the words and expectations of eternal life.

If we proceed a step farther, we shall find Enoch walking with God—the children of Seth distinguished from the children of Cain, by the appellation of the sons of God.

Noah receives an express revelation from God, relating to the flood, when he complains that his *Spirit* should not always strive with men.

As a good man, Noah must have carefully instructed his children in the principles and knowledge of the true worship of their Maker; and at the dispersion of Babel, this knowledge must have been carried by every separate party to the several nations of the earth, which were founded by them, especially in the line of Shem.[2]

---

2. Sanchoniathan calls Shem, by the name of Magus, as the prince of the order of the Magi, or wise men, who were the first, and patriarchal priests after the flood.

Hence if we examine into the first principles every religion in the world, before they were debased and profaned by the ignorance, arts or designs of those men who were intrusted with the public instruction, we shall discover evident traits of the trad religion as revealed to Adam, Enoch, Seth, and Noah.

Their posterity did certainly receive by tradition and hieroglyphics, (the only modes of perpetuating facts and events known to the world before the invention of letters) many of the essential truths of revelation.[3] Abraham is agreed by all parties, both sacred and profane, to have been a holy man, and taught the worship of the one and only living and true God. He lived early enough to converse with Shem, the son of Noah, who lived in Methuselah's day. Abraham's children, with their posterity, preserved this knowledge and worship, and instructed all the neighboring nations in it, both by precept and example, till the coming of the Saviour.[4]

Abraham was so remarkable for his purity and zeal in the service of God, and for his faith and confidence in his promises, that he refused not, at the divine command, to sacrifice his only son, who thus was held up as a striking figure of him who was to bruise the serpent's head. As a reward

---

3. Mr. [Robert] Henry, in his *History of Great Britain* [1800] speaking of the ancient Druids, says, "The first and purest principles of their religion, at least descended to them, together with their language, and many other things, from Gomer, the eldest son of Japhet, from whom the Gauls, Britons, and all the other Celtic nations, derived their origin. For it is not to be imagined that this renowned parent of so many nations, who was only the grandson of Noah, could be unacquainted with the knowledge of the true God, and of the most essential principles of religion; or that he neglected to communicate this knowledge to his immediate descendants, and they to their posterity, from age to age. But unhappily, the method by which this religious knowledge was handed down from Gomer to his numerous posterity in succeeding ages, was not well calculated to preserve it pure and uucorrupted. This was by tradition, which however limpid it may be near its fountain head, is, like other streams, very apt to swell and become turbid in its progress." Vol. i. fol. 92.

4. "The name of Abraham hath, for many ages past, been had in great veneration all over the east, and among all sects, so that every one of them have thought it would give reputation to them, could they entitle themselves to him. For not only the Jews, the Magians, and the Mahometans, but the Sabians and the East-Indians, all challenge him to themselves, as the great patriarch and founder of their several sects, every one pretending their religion is the same that Abraham professed. The veneration for Abraham in those parts, proceeded from the great fame of his piety, which was (it is supposed) there spread among them, by the Israelites in their dispersion all over the east, first on the Assyrian, and after the Babylonish captivity." (Humphrey Prideaux, *The Old and New Testament Connected in the History of the Jews and Neighbouring Nations,* 2 vols. (London : Printed for R. Knaplock and J. Tonson, 1716-1718), 1:225.

for Abraham's piety, God revealed to him, that all the earth should be blessed in his seed; or in other words, that the promised Messiah, known by the epithet, *the seed of the woman*, should spring from his loins.

Thus we have very strong evidence from the history of Moses, that the religion of Adam, Enoch, Seth, Noah, Shem, Abraham, and his children Isaac and Jacob, led them to look to the Messiah that was to come, the promised seed of the woman, pre-figured in all their sacrifices and oblations of blood shed upon their altars.

This is the only rational account of the prevalence of so strange a mode of worshipping the beneficent Creator of the Heavens and the earth, unaccountable in any other view than as it was designed to show forth the great sacrifice of the Messiah, in offering himself up for the sins of his people.

Now with what propriety could these eminent servants of God have uniformly continued in this mode of worship, as evidencing their faith and hope in him that was thus to come; or have any confidence in his sufficiency for their redemption, unless they had been instructed by a divine revelation in this mysterious doctrine, which, from all their conduct, it appears they were.

Abraham retained the knowledge and worship of the true God, amidst all the idolatry of his country, and at last separated himself and family from the contagion of their example, by removing into a distant land, not before inhabited.

In the process of time, Joseph, his great grandson, by the special providence of God, became governor and lord of all Egypt; and from the purity and holiness of his character, must have made use of his grandeur, power, and influence, to spread the truth throughout that populous country; and this must have had great weight, not only from his example, but from the truth of his predictions, and the distress that afterwards came upon that people from the severity of a seven years famine.

These doctrines must have greatly prevailed, by the addition of Jacob and his family to the inhabitants of Egypt. Hence, upon a careful examination into antiquity, we shall find, that Egypt afterwards became the divinity school of all the surrounding nations, and especially the Greeks. Into their religions, however different from each other in detail, the great principles of revelation must originally have been ingrafted, though afterwards greatly darkened and debased by the inventions of philosophers and the superstition of priests, to make them acceptable to the mass of the common people, who were extremely ignorant and perverse.

If this reasoning be just, history and the works of the ancients must throw some light on this subject; and considering the tempers of the author of the Age of Reason and his disciples, it may be prudent, in the first place, to trace the necessary facts from heathen antiquity, as they may have more influence than any thing from a purer source, and as at the same time they will greatly corroborate the Mosaic history.

We are informed by the earliest Egyptian histories, that about the time of Abraham, the Egyptians had their first king, who was called Zoroaster Misfaim, by some Misra, and by others Osiris. He is said to have reigned about two thousand years before the Christian era.

Afterwards came the famous Hermes-trismegis, Tus, or Taut, or Thoth, by whom the first Egyptian pyramids were raised. Many authors have supposed this Hermes to have been Moses, but the late Mr. Bryant (as we are informed by an elegant, learned and able writer) very satisfactorily contends, "that he was no other than the patriarch Joseph. He is persuaded that the Osarsiph of the Egyptians, one of the names by which *Hermes* was called, if Manetho, their earliest historian may be credited, is nothing else but a mistake in arrangement, for *Sar-Oseph*, or Lord Joseph of the bible. And if another name by which Hermes was known, as some ancient authors have asserted, was *Siphoas*, Mr. Bryant thinks it a similar confusion of the letters; for what saith he, is *Siphoas*, but Aosiph misplaced, which is the Egyptian name of Joseph." But, however the truth may be, the argument is strong, that the Egyptians derived several important branches of divine revelation from the patriarchs, as will now appear from the character of Hermes.

Diodorus Siculus bestows the highest encomiums on Hermes-trismegistus as the founder of all the Egyptian learning, and it is said that he received his name from his teaching the explicit doctrine of the Trinity.[5]

The Chronicum Alexandrinum, quoted by Kircher, relates, that there lived among the Egyptians, the first of the family of Charm Sesostris, that is a branch of Osiris, a man venerable for his wisdom and admirable learning, who held that there were three principal powers, virtues, or forms in

---

5. The Caduceus of Hermes, is adorned with the old Egyptian symbol of Deity, the globe, wings, and serpent; and is described by the ancients as producing *three leaves* together, a sacred trefoil, intimating the three-fold distinction in the Deity, for which he was so strenuous an advocate. Thus Homer, in the Hymn to Mercury, calls it the golden *three leafed wand.*—Ind. Ant. 811.

God—that the name of the ineffable Creator, implied one Deity, for which reason, this wise man was called Hermes-tris-megistus.[6]

Suidas, another profane historian, in his historical Greek Lexicon, says, "that Hermes-trismegistus the wise Egyptian, flourished before Pharaoh (supposed to be the oppressor of the Israelites) and that he was so named, because he asserted, that there was a Trinity, and that in the Trinity there was but one Deity.

We are told by Tertullian and Lactantius, that Tris-megistus and the Sybils had obtained a tradition, that God created all things by his Co-omnipotent Son: and the Christian Greeks emphatically call Christ *the Logos*, meaning both speech and reason, because he is the voice and wisdom of God, Lactantius particularly observes, that the philosophers had some idea of this grand truth; and that Zeno, the father of the porch, calls the creator of the world *Logos*, which he also terms *Fate* and *God* and the *Mind of Jove*.

In short, all the very ancient accounts of the Egyptians confirm this fact; that they were acquainted with the doctrine of a trinity in the divine Being.

So in the first chapter of Hermes Paemander, he represents God as saying, "I am *Light* and I am *Mind*, even thy God—older than moist or fruitful nature, which he created from darkness; and the Son of God is that glorious *Word*, which came forth from the *Mind*. The *Word* of God, sees and hears whatever is in thee: but the *Mind* is God the Father. These however do not differ between themselves or in essence; and the union of both is the union of life." He further treats of the *Word*, which he uniformly calls, *the Son of God*, as co-essential and co-eternal with the Father, and as the creator of all things—and he speaks of the *Divine Spirit*, as the nourisher and imparter of life; and the supporter and ruler of all other spirits. He addresses the three persons together, and concludes his address with this remarkable expression, which gives the reason of it, "*O Lord thou art one God.*"

The learned Mornaeus observes, that Hermes-trismegistus uses the same words, in explaining the trinity, as were afterwards used by the apostle John.

If we examine the most ancient heathen historian Sanchoniathan, who flourished near thirteen hundred years before Christ, we shall find

---

6. Kircher also informs us, that the Egyptians actually made use of the equilateral triangle, as a symbol to describe the *Deity in his threefold capacity*. in Oedip. Egypt. vol. 2. page 24.

him confirming this truth, that the neighboring nations, had the same principles of religion.

In his Phoenician history, in explaining the hieroglyphics of their worship, he says, "Jove is a winged sphere, out of which a serpent is brought forth. The circle implies the divine nature, without beginning or end. The Serpent shows his *Word* which animates and fructifies the world; and the wings refer to *the Spirit of God*, which vivifies the world by his motion." This fact is confirmed by Dr. Stukely, a British author, who wrote about seventy years ago.

In that part of his work stiled *Aubury*, he says, "we learn repeatedly from Sanchoniathan, Porphyry, and other ancient authors quoted by Eusebius in the Praeparatio Evangelica, that the first sages of the world had just and true notions of the nature of the Deity, conformable to those of the Christians; that in their hieroglyphic way of writing, they designated the Deity and his mysterious nature by the sacred figure of the circle, serpent and wings. Of these the circle meant the fountain of all Being; for this being the most perfect and comprehensive of all geometrical figures, they designed it for the symbol of the First and Supreme Being; whose resemblance we cannot find; whose centre is every where, and whose circumference is no where. The serpent symbolized the Son, or first divine emanation from the Supreme. This they called by the name of *Ptha*, which is derived from the Hebrew, meaning *the Word*. The wings symbolized that divine person or emanation from the former, commonly called Anima Mundi; but the Egyptians called him *Knepth*, which in Hebrew signifies winged." He further says, "This symbol of the snake and circle, which is the picture on the temple at Abury, we see on innumerable Egyptian monuments—always it holds the uppermost, the first and chief place; which shows its high dignity."

He can by no means admit this to be an Egyptian invention. "The Egyptians took this, and hieroglyphic writing, in general, from the common ancestors of mankind. This is sufficiently proved from the universality of the thing, reaching from China in the East to Britain in the West, and into America too."[7]

Aristotle in his first Book, *De Caelo et Mundo*, ch. 2d. s. 2d numb. 10, says, "That he, together with others, offered a threefold sacrifice to the gods, in acknowledgment of the threefold perfection discovered in them." And again speaking of the number three, "therefore we make use of this number,

---

7. Stukely's Abury, page 56.

in celebrating the sacrifices of the gods: nature itself seeming to have pointed it out, as the most perfect of all."

That the later philosophers received the first principles of their mythology from the Egyptians, is proved from Iamblichus another heathen author, who was a Syrian, and a disciple of Porphyry the great enemy of Christianity, and Preceptor to Julian the apostate. In his book of the Egyptian mysteries he says, "if you would propose any difficulty in philosophy (which then principally meant religion) we will decide the matter by those ancient columns of Hermes, upon which Plato, and before him Pythagoras, formed the principles of their philosophy." And Justin Martyr, who was not only a zealous Christian, but a learned philosopher of near the apostolic age, deeply skilled in the mythology of heathen antiquity, asserts that the doctrine of the Trinity was known to Plato and the other philosophers.[8]

Procleus, an heathen philosopher, asserts of the Trinity as contained in ike Chaldaic Oracles, that it was at first a theology of Divine revelation, or a Divine cabala (tradition); to wit, among the Hebrews first and from them afterwards communicated to the Egyptians and other nations.[9]

Plotinus, another heathen philosopher, asserts, "that the doctrine of a Trinity was an ancient opinion before Plato's time, and delivered down by the Pythagoreans to the Platonists—and Josephus, in his tract against Apion, says, that Pythagoras was well acquainted with the Jewish rites and introduced many of them into his philosophy.[10]

Chalcidius, the disciple of Plato, distinguished the divine nature into the Father—the Son and Creator of the world—the Spirit which enlivens. The first arranging—the second commanding—and the third actuating all things.[11]

Thus stands the testimony from antiquity, which is here adduced, not to show the correctness of their knowledge of the divine nature, but that they received the general doctrine from the Egyptians; who received it from the Hebrews, who originally recieved it from Abraham, who received it from Shem, who received it from Noah, or rather perhaps Methuselah, who received it from Adam, who must have received it by divine revelation from God himself. Let us now look into more modern histories, and see if we cannot find these facts confirmed by their authority also.

---

8. 2d. Apol. 73.
9. Cudworth, Intel. Syst. lib. 1. ch. 4.
10. Lib. 1.
11. Cudworth, Lib. 1. ch. 1. page 22.

Persia being the country from which the Magi or wise men, who visited our Saviour at his birth, are supposed to have come, and in which Daniel, with others of the Hebrew prophets, had been resident,[12] we will look into their history, as published by the learned Dr. Hyde, Hebrew and Arabic professor in the University of Oxford, in his *Historia religionis veterum Persarum, eorumque Magorum*. Here we find that there still exists in that ancient Country, a sect of the Persians, who strictly adhere to their original principles in the midst of established Mahometism, and live separately from the rest of the inhabitants, as much as possible, in order to preserve their purity. They worship one only God, of whom they seem to entertain very just notions, although some mix with them, too great a reverence for the stars and planets, bordering on Sabaism. It seems that they received the principles of their religion from Shem and Elam, who were their great ancestors. That in process of time, having degenerated into Sabaism, Abraham recovered them from their errors, and restored the worship of the true God. They greatly boast of Abraham, and call their religion, the religion of Abraham. We know that Abraham conquered Cherdelaomer, king of Persia. It is probable, therefore, that he, with his allies, embraced the religion of the conqueror, which was common in former clays, and that their example was followed by his people.

Dr. Hyde found it very difficult to obtain a correct knowledge of the present principles of their religion, as their great prophet Zoroaster, (of which name there are many in different nations) had expressly prohibited the instruction of strangers in their language or religion. Dr. Hyde, however, interested a friend who lived in Persia, to gain information on this head from their priests, if possible, and particularly as to the worship they pay to *Mithra* (whom they term the *Triplasian*, or three-fold *Mythras*.)[13] He was answered, that the Persian priests positively denied, that they paid any divine worship to the Sun, Moon, or Stars—That they only turned to them when they prayed, because they resembled fire, which they consider as an

---

12. From the time of the Babylonish captivity we find the Jews dispersed through all the provinces of the Persian monarchy, and that in great numbers; and many people of the land becoming Jews: and after their return they were scattered through Africa, Asia and many Cities and Islands of Europe. Josephus tells us, that wherever they dwelt they made many proselytes—See Esther 3:8:13; 9:2. Jos, Antiq. lib. 14. ch. 12. Thomas Stackhouse, vol. i. N. T. 196

13. Dionysius, the Pseudo-areopagite, says, "The Persian Magi to this very day celebrate a festival solemnity, in honor of the Triplasian, or three-fold Mythras. Cudw. Intel. Syst. ch. iv. page 288.

emblem of the Deity, but that they do not worship them. They regard the Sun as the image of God; and some suppose it to be the place of his more immediate residence; others, that it was the seat of the blessed; but they insist that they worship God alone. They are acquainted with the history of the creation—Adam and Eve—the deluge—Moses and Solomon.

They style Moses "the ruddy shepherd, who holds a staff or rod." In short, Dr. Hyde clearly shows, that they have continually believed in one God, almighty and eternal, possessed of all those perfections which Christians ascribe to him. They believe in an universal resurrection, both of the good and bad, and a last judgment, in which every one will receive according to his works. They believe that they offend God every day; but they protest that they repent of all their sins, both of mind and body, in thought, word and action. They do not fast, alleging, that true fasting consists in an abstinence from all sin. Some fix the state of happiness in the sun; but others suppose that, after the resurrection, the blessed will live on this earth, which shall be renewed after a general conflagration. Dr. Hyde, with other learned writers, believes that the birth of Christ was made known to the Persians, they having persevered in the worship of the one true God.[14] Daniel and other prophets had

---

14. Arnobius, who wrote in the third century, says, that the name of Christ reigns among the Indians, the Persians, the Serae (or the Chinese) and all the islands and provinces, which are visited by the rising or setting sun; yea, and in Rome itself, the empress of all. Lib. ii. fol. 23.

Since the late discoveries in the East-Indies, which Mr. Maurice, whose invaluable work I am reading while this is printing, has so advantageously set before the public view, it appears that even the Cross has been had in great reverence from time immemorial, among the nations of the east, though they have not preserved the original design of it. He says, "Even the form of the Cross, as allusive to the four elements, was no unusual symbol in the Pagan world," and indeed Tavernier describes two of the principal pagodas of India, *Benares* and *Matbura*, as erected in the form of *vast crosses*, of which each wing is equal in extent. Let not the piety of the Catholic Christian be offended at this assertion, that the Cross was one of the most usual symbols among the hieroglyphics of Egypt and India. Equally honored in the Gentile and the Christian world, this emblem of universal nature—of that world, to whose four quarters its diverging radii pointed, decorated the hands of most of the sculptured images in the former country: and in the latter, stamped its form upon the most majestic of the shrines of their deities. It repeatedly occurs on the pamphilian and other obelisks; and the antiquarians, Kircher and Montfaucon, have both honored it with particular notice.

The Cruxansata of Hermes, is represented by the former as a most sublime hieroglyphic, as a most mysterious and powerful amulet, endowed with an astonishing virtue, and as exhibiting one of the most complete mathematical figures, "*babentem longitudinem atque latitudinem, et quar-tuar angulos rectos,* i. e., possessing at once both length and breadth, and having four right angles," at once allusive to the four cardinal points of the world, and typical of the four elements." And again, after stating a number of symbolical representa-

been in their country, and might have left the knowledge of the expected Messiah. The prophecies of the Old Testament was not unknown to them; and Zoroaster, who assumed the title of their great prophet, and lived in the time of Darius Hystaspes, though a Persian by birth, yet, from the poverty of his father, is said to have become a servant to Esdrass, the great Hebrew prophet, from whom he got many principles of the Jewish religion, and particularly the plan of reforming the religion of his country. The Persians have also a very ancient book still extant among them, older than Zoroaster, entitled, The Eternal Wisdom, which shows their original worship to have been that of the true God. And a Chaldean or Persian oracle, quoted from Damascius, by Patritius, shows that they believed a Trinity in the godhead. It is in these words—"In the whole world shineth forth a Triad, or Trinity, which is a perfect monad or unity."[15]

A volume might be filled with proofs of this kind, but I shall conclude the testimony on this head, with but one instance more, and proceed to the Chinese, whose mythology, though very old, has been known but a short time to the inhabitants of Europe.

Dr. Parsons, in his Remains of Japhet, has given a curious explanation of a Siberian medal, in the cabinet of the late empress of all the Russias, found in an old ruined chapel, near the river Kemptschyk, contained in a memoir of Col. Grant. "The design of this medal, exhibits the idea, which the *lamas*, or high priests of the country called Tibet, have beyond all memorial, entertained among themselves, concerning the *godhead*. On one side of this extraordinary medal is a representation of the Deity, with three heads and one body, evidently designed to convey the notion of a Trinity in unity. On the reverse is an inscription in the Magogian language, and translated by the colonel into Latin, thus: *"Alma imago sancta Dei in Tribus imaginibus hisce; colligite sanctam Voluntatem Dei ex illis; diligite eum"*—that is, "The pure holy image of the Deity is under these three forms; gather ye the holy will of God from them; and love him." They hereby acknowledge one Divinity, which consists of three persons, equal among themselves; each of infinite

---

tions of the four elements, he adds, "All these figures thus emblematical of the elements, which are highly worthy a minute examination, bear the *hallowed Cross*, by which they were collectively and strikingly represented," Indian Antiquities, page 359, 360, 361.

If the Cross, thus inscribed on these ancient hieroglyphics, appropriated to the Gentile worship, should only be allowed to be descriptive of the four elements and four quarters of the world, what a noble idea does it give us of the universality of that salvation which was wrought out for guilty man by Christ Jesus expiring upon it.

15. Vol. ii. Philos. Princip. 123.

wisdom and power; all three of a beneficent nature; inseparable in one spirit; constituting but one Being, infinitely wise and powerful, the Creator and Ordainer of all things."[16]

It is a fact very remarkable, and not easily to be accounted for by infidels, that all the heathen writers, who have mentioned the subject, unanimously concur in imputing the creation of the world to the *word of the Deity*, which so closely corresponds with the language of the Scriptures, This is an argument of its original derivation from those who knew the truths of God by his own revelation. Hence the apostle, speaking of the heathen, says, "Because that which may be known of God, was manifested to them, (as in the margin of the Bible) *for God hath shewed it unto them*—when they knew God, they glorified him not as God."[17]

The Chinese are the most ancient people we know of unmixed with other nations. They have a sacred book called King, in which, if we may trust the translations from their language, "God is named Changti" or the Sovereign Emperor; and Tien, the supreme Heaven, the self-existent Unity, who is present every where, and who produced all things by his power. Tehuhi, in commenting upon these expressions, says, "The Supreme Unity is most simple and without composition—He lasts from all eternity without Interruption—He is ancient and new—He is the source of all motion and the root of all action."18 In the book Tonchu we read, "The source and root of all is one. This self-existent Unity produces necessarily a second; the first and second, by their union, produces a third; in fine, these three produce all." One of their

---

16. Ch. vii. page 184.

Mr. Maurice on this medal says, "From India, if we direct our eyes northward to the great empires of Tangut and Thibet, and over the vast Tartarian desarts to Siberia itself, we shall find the same sentiments (relating to the Trinity) predominate. In the former country, if the authors quoted in Parson's Remains of Japhet may be credited, medals, having the figure of the *Triune Deity* stamped upon them, are given to the people by the *Dalai-Lama*, who unites in his own person the hierarchal and regal character, to be suspended as a holy object around their necks, or conspicuously elevated in the chapels where they perform their devotion." With respect to the Tartars and Siberians, Van Strahleaburgh, after remarking how universal a veneration prevails through all Northern Tartary for the sacred number *three*, acquaints us, "That a race of Tartars, called Jakathi, who are idolators, and the most numerous people of all Siberia, adore, in fact, only one indivisible God, under three different denominations, *Artugon, Schugo-Tugon, Tangara*; the first of which Col. Grant translates, *Creator of all things*; the second, the *God of armies*; and the third he venders, *Amor ab utroque procedens*, the Spirit of Heavenly Love, proceeding from the two former." Ind. Antiq. page 775.

17. Romans 1:19-20.

18. Philos. Prin vol. ii. 40.

commentators, called Lopi, says, "That the Unity is triple, and this triplicity, one." Laostee, another commentator, in his fourteenth chapter, called Tsan-huen, or the Eulogium of Hidden Wisdom, says, "He that produced all, and is himself unproduced, is what we call Hi. He that gives light and knowledge to all things, and is himself invisible, is what we call Yi. He that is present every where, and animates all things, though we do not feel him, is called Ouei. Thou wilt in vain interrogate sense and imagination about these three, for they can make thee no answer—contemplate by the pure Spirit alone, and thou wilt comprehend that these three are but one." Li-yong, in commenting upon this passage of Laostee, says, Hi, Yi, Ouei, have no name, colour, nor figure. They are united in the same spiritual abyss, and by a borrowed name they are called Unity; this Unity, however, is not a bare Unity, but an Unity that is triple, and a triplicity that is one."[19]

If we pass to the East-Indies, there we find from the latest discoveries, by the learned Sir William Jones, that the Hindoos have always had a sacred tri-literal name, as only applicable to the Supreme Being, which must have been the consequence of traditions handed down from Noah. The name is O. U. M. [20]

---

19. Phil. Princip. vol. ii. 120.

20. Since this work has been prepared for the press, the author has accidentally met with the first volume of Mr. Maurice's *Indian Antiquities*, wherein to his great surprise, and greater pleasure, he finds Mr. Maurice ably supporting the same doctrines from the latest discoveries in the East-Indies, since Sir William Jones's observations above quoted. His words are—"A species of Trinity forms a constant and prominent feature in nearly all the systems of Oriental theology."

"This extensive and interesting subject engrosses a considerable portion of this work, and my anxiety to prepare the public mind to receive with indulgence, my efforts to elucidate so mysterious a point of theology, induces me to remind the candid reader, that visible traces of this doctrine are discovered, not only in the three principles of the Chaldaic theology; in the triplasian Mithra of Persia; in the triad Bhrahma, Veshna and Sceva of India, where it evidently was promalged in the GEETA fifteen hundred years before the birth of Plato; but in the Numen triplex of Japan; in the inscription upon the famous medal found in the deserts of Siberia, "to the Triune God," to be seen at this day in the invaluable cabinet of the empress at Petersburgh; in the *Tanga-Tanga*, or three in one, of the South-Americans; and finally, without mentioning the vestiges of it in Greece, in. the symbol of *the wing, the globe, and the serpent*, conspicuous on most of the ancient temples in Upper Egypt." And again in his 6th vol. p. 65, he observes, "That the Druids represented him (their Hermes or Taut or Theutates) and the peculiar allegorical delineation of the doctrines which he taught the Oriental world, in the figure of the orb, serpent and wings, which is engraved in not less conspicuous characters on the extensive plains of Abury, in Wiltshire, (Great Britain) than the Thebais of ancient Egypt."

These few instances, out of a thousand that might have been adduced, may suffice to shew our author's incorrectness, though it may not be amiss, for general information, to add, in confirmation, some quotations, as cited by the excellent and learned author of the *Horae Solitariae*.

Augustine Philastrus says, "That the doctrine of the Trinity was esteemed as ancient as the world., and reputed an heresy to think the contrary." Augustine positively declares, "That the substance of what is now called the Christian religion, was maintained by the ancient believers, and existed from the very beginning of human nature." God's people were Christians, even in the time of the Patriarchs, and so denominated by God himself, in Psalms, 5th chap. 5th ver. "Touch not my anointed," or Christians, (both words having one meaning) "and do my prophets no harm."And Philastrus, bishop of Brixen, says, "That the Trinity of Christianity was asserted from the foundation of the world."

Thus stands the testimony, taken very briefly from the principles of the heathen mythology handed down by tradition from Noah. We will now proceed to the Jewish tenets on this subject, as they are contained in their sacred books, and their best writers, before Christianity generally prevailed in the world. They had this doctrine, as has already appeared, regularly handed down to them, from the same source of Divine revelation. Their Scriptures are full of it; otherwise with what propriety could John the Baptist, our Lord himself, and his apostles after his resurrection, so freely use the terms *Father, Son, and Holy Spirit*, in their instructions of the people, without any previous introduction, explanation, or comment, to reconcile their hearers to so new and alarming a doctrine, if it had not been familiar to them in their own system of religion. The Jews were so jealous of their religious principles, that they did not suffer any one to use the ineffable name of Jehovah, but on the most solemn and awful occasions.

There are thirty different places in the book of Genesis—one hundred in the law, and five hundred throughout the Old Testament, where the words Elohim or Alehim, Eloheka and Adonai, (Gods, the Lord thy Gods) are made use of. All three of the Trinity are equally called Jehovah, the self-existent or the eternal Being, with the difference of a termination—as Jehovah-ab—Jehovah-el—Jehovah-ruach although our translators have not thought proper to make the necessary distinction. The sacred Scriptures of the Jews contain many other instances to our purpose on this subject. Abraham calls one of the three Beings, who came to him before the destruction of Sodom, "The Almighty God, the judge of all the earth." Jacob, in his journey to Canaan, at Mahanaim, called the place Peniel, because he had seen God face to face. Moses beheld the Lord in the burning bush. The whole process at Mount Sinai, shows that it was Jehovah-el, who met Moses there. "Then went up Moses and Aaron, Nadab and Abihu, and seventy of the elders of Israel—and they saw the God of Israel, and there was under his feet, as it were, a paved work of a sapphire stone, and as it were the body of Heaven in its clearness—also they saw God, and did eat and drink."

Now no reasonable man will assert, that the essential, infinite, unveiled essence of the Deity, was seen by these holy men of old, or that any created being ever conversed with the pure and spiritual nature of God, or beheld him face to face. But all these glorious displays of Jehovah-el, in his communication with his ancient people, were that of the *Word* or Logos, in his glorified body, before his incarnation; for Christ himself expressly prays, "That he may be glorified with the glory which he had before the world was;"[21] and the apostles declare, that "They beheld his glory as that of the only begotten of the Father, full of grace and truth.[22] In Psalm 2, David says, "That the kings of the earth set themselves, and the rulers take counsel together against the Lord and his Christ, or anointed. The Lord hath said unto me, thou art my son, this day have I begotten thee. Kiss the Son, lest he be angry—blessed are all they that put their trust in him." Again, "The Lord said *unto my Lord*, sit thou at my right hand, until I make thine enemies thy footstool"[23] This is translated in the Targum, "The Lord said unto his word." So in Proverbs 30:4. "What is God's name, and what is his son's name, if thou canst tell." To the like purpose is Isaiah 11:1-2—"And there shall come forth a rod out of the stem of Jesse, and a branch shall grow out of his roots, and the *Spirit of the Lord* shall rest upon him, the *Spirit of Wisdom* and Understanding." And again, "Thus saith Jehovah the *Redeemer*, the Lord of hosts; I am the first and I am the last, and beside *me* there is no God;" and in 48:16-17, "And now the *Lord God, and his Spirit*, hath sent me." And in 44:24, " Thus saith the Lord thy Redeemer, the holy one of Israel, I am the Lord thy God." Isaiah, lv. 5. "Thy Makers are thy Husbands, the Lord of Hosts is his name." And in chap. lix. 19, "When the enemy shall come in like a flood, the *Spirit of the Lord* shall lift up a standard against him." In 59:1, "The Spirit of the Lord God is upon me." In the Second Esdras 13:32, "And then shall my Son be revealed, whom thou sawest go up as a man." Also

---

21. John 17:5.
22. John 1:14.
23. Psalm 110:1.

13:37, "And *this*, *my Son*, shall rebuke the wicked inventions of the nations." Wisdom 9:1, "O *God of my fathers*, and *Lord of mercy*, who hath made all things by thy *Word*" So, in Ecclesiasticus 24:3, 9, speaking of *Wisdom*, "I am come out of the mouth of the Most High; he created me from the beginning, before the world was." Again, 51:10, "I called upon the Lord, the father of my Lord." Wisdom of Solomon 18:15, "Thine *Almighty Word* leaped down from Heaven, out of thy royal throne." In chap. 7:25-26, speaking of Wisdom, "For she is the breath of the power of God, and a pure influence flowing from the glory of the Almighty—for she is the brightness of the everlasting light, the unspotted mirror of the power of God, and the image of his goodness; and being *but one*, she can do all things." Judith, 16:14. "Thou didst send forth *thy Spirit*, and it created them."

And to those who may not be inclined to credit the assertion that this doctrine was known in Palestine, a learned author already quoted, begs leave to propose the following Symbol, by which the ancient Jews were accustomed to designate the ineffable name Jehovah, in manuscripts of the most venerable antiquity, for their serious reflection. This symbol is a characteristical representation of a *Trinity in unity*. The former represented by three Jods, denoting the three hypostasis or persons in the Divine essence; the Jod being the known character of that Jehovah, of whose name, in Hebrew, it constitutes the first sacred letter. The latter is shadowed out by the circle that surrounds them, as well as by the point *Kametz*, T, subjoined to the three Jods, which denotes the essential unity, common to the three hypostases. This symbol is to be found in the writings of the younger Buxtorf, one of the profoundest critics in Hebrew literature, that ever flourished out of the Jewish church, and it is likewise preserved in that curious repository of Oriental antiquities, the Oedipus Egyptiacus of Athanasius Kircher. The first asserts, that in the ancient Chaldee paraphrases, kept sacred from the vulgar by the Jewish doctors, the name Jehovah is thus designated. And the second declares, that he himself has seen that name thus invariably characterized in all the ancient Hebrew manuscripts of the Old Testament in the Vatican."

But the Jewish writers themselves confirm this idea, when they are considering this very subject. Philo, one of their most learned men, (as Dr. Allix asserts) acknowledges a generation in God from eternity. He says, in many different places, "That God begets the Word in himself—that this *Word is Wisdom*, and that this Wisdom is the eternal Son of God. That God is called the God of Gods, not with relation to created intelligences, whether human, angelical; or seraphical, but in relation to his two consubstantial powers, which are not simple attributes, but eternal, uncreated, infinite principles of action, represented by the two wings of the cherubim that covered the Tabernacle." He further says, in his *Treatise de Somniis*, " That the Supreme Ens (i, ii v) whom he terms Logos or the Word, sometimes put on the appearance of an angel to mankind, but that his divine nature remained ever unchangeable. Philo expressly calls the *Logos* Θεος [*theos*], *God*, and in one place uses the remarkable expression Δευτερο Θεος [*deutero theos*], the second God."[24]

The Targum of Jonathan affirms it was the Logos who spake to Moses, the same who spake and the world was made. This Targum was written 30 years before the Christian aera.

The Chaldee Paraphrasts and Targumists, speak in the same manner—they ascribe to the Word, the creation of the world, the pardon of sin, and the mediating between God the Father and the creatures. The Cabalistical Jews, of a still later date, and who have recorded all the traditions of the patriarchs, &c. hold the same doctrine. "They fix the number of three persons in the Divine essence—they speak of the emanation of the two last from the first; and say that the third proceeds from the first, by the second. They call the first *Eusoph* and Kather; the second, *Memra* or Cbocbbma; the third *Binah.*

The learned Kircher gives many reasons to show, that the ancient Jews, and the later Cabalists, derived their knowledge of the Trinity, by a continued tradition from the first patriarchs, and he cites the Jetzirah, (a book which the Jews ascribe to Abraham himself, but which is said to have been written by a rabbi of the name of Abraham, a very ancient Cabalist) where the first person is described as *Kather* the crown, or profound intelligence —the second person, as Cbocbbma or Wisdom, or the intelligence illuminating—and the third person, as Binah, or the sanctifying intelligence; the builder of faith, and the author of it. The ancient Jewish prayer, called *Hosanna Rabba*, or the Great Hosanna, publicly sung on the last day of the feast of Tabernacles, proves this—"For thy sake, O our Creator, Hosanna—for thy sake, O our Redeemer, Hosanna—for thy sake, O our Seeker, Hosanna." So the great benediction which was pronounced under the law, by Aaron and his sons—"Jehovah bless thee and keep thee—Jehovah make his face to shine upon thee, and be gracious unto thee—Jehovah lift up his countenance upon thee, and give thee peace." Similar to the Christian bap-

---

24. Philo. Judaei apud Euseb. 190.

tism—(The Father is here, the author of blessing and preservation—grace and illumination are from the Son, by whom we have the light of the knowledge of the glory of God, in the face of Jesus Christ—peace is the gift of the Spirit, whose name is the, Comforter.)[25]

The learned Mornaeus says, "That it was once the received doctrine, and the true cabala of the Jewish schools, that the famous words of the 42 letters, used as an expository name of the great trilateral name, or *Jehovah*, which was not allowed the Jews to pronounce, was explained to have been, the Father is God—the Son is God—the Holy Spirit is God—three in one, and one in three."

The Rabbi Ibba, who is said to have lived long before Christ, and who is quoted in the book Zoder, written by Simeon Ben Jochai before the Talmud, as the Jews confess, if not before the Christian era, in descanting upon Deuteronomy 6:4. "Hear, O Israel, the Lord our God is one Lord," urges, "That the first Jehovah is God the Father—the second is God the Son, for so he is called by the prophet, Immanuel; or God with us—the third word *Jehovah*, is God the Holy Ghost—and the fourth word *one*, is to show the unity of essence in this plurality of persons."[26] Many of the Cabalists used the same names of Father, Son, and Spirit, for the three hypostasis, (declaring at the same time, that the doctrine of the persons in the Trinity, by no means opposed that of the essence in unity.[27]

Gallatinus cites a comment of Rabbi Isaac Arama, upon the 110th Psalm, which is peculiarly explicit: "From the womb of the morning is the dew of thy birth." "We do not find," says he, "any man, although a prophet, whose birth is predicted before the birth of his father and mother, excepting the Messiah, our just one; and therefore," he says, "from the womb of the morning is the dew of thy birth;" that is, thy birth is foretold long before the womb of her that bear thee was created. To this agrees what is said in Psalm 72:17—"His name, *the begotten, or Son*, is before the Sun," which implies' that before the Sun was created, the name (or person) of our Messiah, subsisted and was established, and that he sat at the right hand of God.[28]

The Jews, before the advent of Christ, often explained themselves on this subject, though the modern Jews since have concealed as much as possible, the writings of their ancestors, or mutilated them lest they

---

25. Jones's Cath. Doct. of the Trinity, page 61, 3d edition.
26. Grot, de ver Rel. Christ. lib. v. chap. xxi.
27. Hor. Sol. S60.
28. Gal. de Arc. Cath. Verit. lib. iii. ch. 17.

should be brought in evidence against them. On this ground the learned Pocock defends Galatinus, who quoted many testimonies from the ancient Jews, which cannot now be obtained. And the famous Picus, earl of Mirandola, whose honor and integrity are not candidly to be doubted, professed to have read (about 300 years ago) some very ancient Jewish manuscripts, which he purchased of a Jew at a very high rate, and in which he found the mystery of the Trinity—the incarnation of the word—the divinity of the Messiah, and many articles of our faith.[29] There are many other proofs of this point, but the following shall suffice. Rabbi Simeon Ben Jochai, treating of the name *Aloheim*, says, "Come and see the mystery of this word. There are three degrees or affinities, and each degree is to be distinguished by itself; but the three are one, and united to each other in one, nor is one to be divided from another." The same Rabbi, and Jonathan, the Chaldee paraphrast, who both wrote many years before Christ, commenting on Isaiah 6:1 where the Lord (Adonai) is represented as sitting upon a throne, applies the passage to the Messiah; and the former of them has this remarkable exposition of the thrice holy, in the 3rd verse—"Holy, that is the Father—Holy, that is the Son—Holy, that is the Holy Spirit.[30]

For most of the latter authorities, as well as those of the ancients, I am indebted to the elegant, learned, and judicious author of Horse Solitariae, already mentioned; a work worthy the attention of every learned or pious man.

It is wholly beside my purpose, to proceed further in the important dispute relative to the Trinity. I am contented with knowing, that the Scriptures are the word of the ever-living God; and that therein he has revealed to me, that the Father, the Son, and the Holy Spirit, in whose name I was baptized, bear record in Heaven; and that these three are the one only infinite and eternal God, whom I am to worship, love and adore, in spirit and in truth. It is sufficient in the present dispute, to have shown, that this doctrine (whether true or false) was the doctrine of the Jewish church before the coming of the Saviour; not invented first by the Christian theory, but as old as the creation; I believe I may add, as eternity.

Had it been consistent with my plan, I should not have shrunk from a fuller inquiry into this great mystery, as far as the nature of the question would admit; which could be only to show, that however it may exceed, yet

29. Leusd. Phil. Heb. Diec. 26. Maimon. More Nov. ch. 62.
30. Ant. Univ. Hist. vol. iii. folio 11.

it is not contrary to human reason; for I think it would have puzzled my opponent to have controverted a common principle, however far above our comprehension in its consequences, *that infinite power, infinitely active, must produce an infinite effect.* But such discussion, as I have said, is beyond my purpose; and it well becomes me, a finite creature, whose character and practice should ever be expressive of deep humility, to believe every report of revelation, when attended with rational evidence of its divine authority; and believing, to adore in silence what I cannot fully comprehend. I shall conclude this digression in the words of a learned writer, whom I have often quoted. "Equally above the boldest flight of human genius to invent, as beyond the most exalted limit of human intellect fully to comprehend, is the profound mystery of the ever blessed trinity.—Through successive ages it has remained impregnable to all the shafts of the most impious ridicule, and unshaken by the bolder artillery of blasphemous invective.—It is even in vain that man essays to pierce the unfathomable arcana of the skies.—By his limited faculties, and superficial ken, the deep things of eternity are not to be scanned. Even among Christians the sacred trinity is more properly a subject of belief, than of investigation, and every attempt to penetrate further into it, than God in his holy word has revealed, is at best an injudicious, and often a dangerous effect of mistaken piety.—It is in vain that we make reason the umpire: that finite man, however, can form no adequate conception of this great truth, by no means implies impossibility or contradiction in the thing itself.—This circumstance arises from the limited nature of the human faculties. It is mere ignorance; but it is an ignorance which we can never overcome.—Let it ever be remembered, that Christianity by no means proposes to mankind a theological code, encumbered with no difficulties, involved in no perplexities.—Its great mysterious truths (like most other of the ways of God) are not to be solved by the light of nature, nor scanned by the boldest flights of human intellect.—Neither the trinity, nor the incarnation can be proved, nor were intended to be proved, by philosophical arguments.—The word of God is the sole basis of the proofs and solutions of these stupendous doctrines. They are wisely shielded from our view, the better to excite in us the ardor of faith, and exercise the virtues necessary to obtain the sublime rewards which it proposes to persevering piety.—The Almighty has been pleased to erect mounds and ramparts, as of old at Sinai, around the abode of majesty, to ward off the dangerous curiosity of man; he hath wrapped himself in clouds, that we might not be consumed by the full blaze of that glory which invests the eternal throne."[31] I would by no means be understood to disparage human reason, "for, if rightly exercised, it cannot be contrary to revelation; neither can revelation, rightly understood, be contrary to reason, though it must often exceed it; for they are both rays from the same father of lights, with whom there is no variableness, neither shadow of turning."[32]

I repeat it, therefore, that it is sufficient, in this investigation, to have shown the opinion of both Jews and heathens, before the coming of Jesus Christ, and of course that our author has been wholly unacquainted with his subject.

Perhaps he might be content to be taught the truth from so many heathen authorities. Yet, I confess, it is to be feared, that it is too late for him to hearken to the words of wisdom from any quarter whatever; because, in so doing, he must acknowledge either his ignorance or wickedness, in asserting with so much confidence, "That the theory of the Christian church sprung out of the tail of the heathen mythology, and that the Trinity of Gods that then followed, was no other than a reduction of the former plurality, which was twenty or thirty thousand.

If it "yet remains for reason and philosophy to abolish the amphibious fraud," it must be a very different reason and philosophy from that of the author of the Age of Reason. It must be that of truth and argument, neither of which have fallen to his lot. What have reason and philosophy done for near two thousand years, but confirm the glorious doctrine of the cross of Christ, and multiply the followers of the once despised Nazarene. A nation in our day has made the attempt to try, what our author calls, reason and philosophy, will do without religion; and let me ask what has been the issue? The Scriptures told it before it came to pass. "Adultery, fornication, uncleanness, lasciviousness, idolatry, hatred, variance, emulations, wrath, strife, seditions, heresies, envyings, murders, assassinations, and such like."[33] Indeed it seems that as a nation, having forsaken and cast off all dependence on, and acknowledgement of, a Divine Providence, he had left them to strong delusions, and to the accumulated miseries and distresses incident to anarchy, confusions, insurrections, assassinations, wars and pestilence, to convince an astonished world what would be their portion, if once they should be given up by God to believe a lie, and to cast off all the

31. Ind. Antiq.
32. Doyl's Serm.
33. Galatians 5:20.

fear and reverence of his sacred majesty. They seem to be set forth as full evidence to all mankind, of the truth of the prophetic declaration, that in the latter day "false teachers should come among them, who privily should bring in damnable heresies, even denying the Lord that bought them, and bring upon themselves swift destruction; and many should follow their pernicious ways, by reason of whom the way of truth should be evil spoken of—that they should despise government—be presumptuous, self willed; not afraid to speak evil of dignities—they are spots and blemishes, sporting themselves with their own deceivings—having eyes full of adultery, and that cannot cease from sin—beguiling unstable souls—having hearts exercised with covetous practices—cursed children—these are wells without water—clouds that are carried with a tempest, to whom the mist of darkness is reserved forever—for when they speak great swelling words of vanity, they allure through the lusts of the flesh, through much wantonness, those who were escaped from them; who live in error; who while they *promise them liberty*, they themselves are the servants of corruption."[34]

---

34. Second Peter 2:1-20.

6

Particular Notes on This Subject

WHILE this answer was striking off at the press, I have been favoured with the perusal of all the volumes of that learned, laborious, and expensive work, *The Indian Antiquities*, by Thomas Maurice; a work which has entered so fully into this subject, as to render nugatory all I have attempted in this part of my answer; and if I had seen it in time, I should have contented myself with either referring to it, or giving a few extracts from it. I attempted to add some notes from it in the margin, but found it would greatly embarrass the printer; and being very desirous of enriching this answer with many facts and useful observations contained in it, and well knowing that a majority of my readers were not likely to peruse so large a performance, I have concluded to annex to this head, a number of quotations together, leaving it to my reader to apply them to this important subject as he may think proper.

Being impressed with the truth of the following observation, found in the preface to this admirable performance, I shall begin with it. He says— "The present is by no means the period for suppressing any additional testimonies to the truth of one of the fundamental articles of that noble system, (our holy religion); and the author trusts that he has brought together such a body of evidence, as will decisively establish the following important facts—first, that in the *Sephiroth*, or three superior splendors of the ancient Hebrews, may be discovered the three hypostasis of the Christian Trinity— secondly, that this doctrine flourished through nearly all the empire of Asia, *a thousand years before Plato was born*—and thirdly, that the grand cavern-pagoda of Elephanta, the oldest and most magnificent temple in the world, is neither more nor less than a superb temple to a Triune God."

In this volume, the Oriental Triads of Deity, are extensively discussed, and referred to what I cannot but conceive to have been the true source of them all; to certain mutilated traditions of a nobler doctrine revealed to man, in a state of innocence. As we advance still farther in these Indian researches, we shall find many other important points of religious belief, surprisingly elucidated; and thus, the Mosaical records and Christianity, so far from being subverted by the pretended antiquity of the Brahmins, will derive a proud trophy from the corroborative testimony of their genuine annals, and the congenial sentiments of their primaeval creed.

When the reader is informed, that the creation of the world, according to the Hindu cosmogony, was affected by an incumbent Spirit, the emanation of Deity impregnating with life the primordial waters of Chaos; *that the fall of man from a state of primaeval purity and innocence in the Satya-Yug or perfect age*, forms the basis of the Indian metempsychosis, that the Indians believe *in a future state of rewards and punishments*; that the first history, of which they can boast, has for its subject, the destruction of the human race, for their multiplied enormities, *in a certain great deluge, from which only eight persons were saved in an Ark, fabricated by the immediate* command of Veeshnu: that in their principal Deity, *a plurality of Divine persons is discovered*, since that Deity is symbolically designated by an image with three heads affixed to one body; and that the second person in that Trinity is, in their mythology, invested with the office *of a Preserver and Mediator*, and in both these characters incarnate. Finally, to omit other interesting particulars, that the duration of the *Cali-Yug*, or age immediately succeeding the great deluge, according to their own calculations, does not but by a few centuries, exceed the period asserted by Christian chronologers, to have elapsed since the deluge of Noah; and *that the existing world is to be consumed by a general conflagration.*

When all these circumstances, to be accounted for by no immediate connection or intercourse whatsoever with the Hebrew nation, in any period of their empire, are calmly considered by an impartial and unprejudiced mind, the result, I am persuaded, must be an increased confidence in the great truths of revelation—though the timid Christian may at first be somewhat surprised, yet a little reflection will soon convince him of the truth of what I have asserted to be the genuine fact, that in the pure and primitive theology, derived from the venerable patriarchs, there were certain grand and mysterious truths, the objects of their fixed belief, which all the depravations brought into it by succeeding superstition, were never able entirely to efface from the human mind. These truths, together with many of the symbols of that pure theology, were propagated and diffused by them in their various peregrinations through the higher Asia, where they have immemorially flourished, affording a most sublime and honorable testimony of such a refined and patriarchal religion having actually existed in the earliest ages of the world.

Mr. Maurice asserts, that " Mattra," (the Methora of Pliny) "is situated about 18 miles from Agra, on the direct road to Delhi, and is particularly celebrated for having been the birth place of *Creeshna,* who is esteemed in India, not so much an incarnation of the Divine Veeshnu, as the Deity himself in a human form. The history of this personage is among the most curious of all that occur in Indian mythology.

The sanscreet narrative of his extraordinary feats, in some points approaches so near to the Scriptural account of our Saviour, as to have afforded real ground for Sir William Jones to suppose, that the Brahmins had, in the early ages of Christianity, seen or heard recited to them, some of the spurious Gospels, which in those ages so numerously abounded, and had ingrafted the wildest parts of them, upon the old fable of the Indian Apollo. The birth of this divine infant was predicted, and a reigning tyrant of India, by name *Cansa,* learning from the prediction, that he should be destroyed by this wonderful child, ordered all the male children born at that period, to be slain; but *Creeshna* was preserved by biting the breast, instead of sucking the poisoned nipple of the nurse commissioned to destroy him. From the fear of this tyrant, he was fostered in Mattra, by an honest herdsman, and passed his innocent hours in rural diversions at his foster father's farm. Repeated miracles, however, soon discovered his celestial origin. He preached to the Brahmins, the doctrines of meekness and benevolence. He even condescended to wash their feet, as a proof of his own meekness; and he raised the dead by descending, for that purpose, to the lowest regions. He acted, not always indeed, in the capacity of a prince or herald of peace, for he was a mighty warrior; but his amazing powers were principally exerted to save and to defend.

Even the great war of Mahabbarat, which he fomented, was a just war, undertaken against invaders and tyrants, whom he triumphantly overthrew, and then returned to his seat in the Heavenly region.[1]

---

1. Vol. iii. page 45.

One of the most prominent features in the Indian theology, is the doctrine of a Trinity, which it plainly inculcates; a subject by no means to be passed over in silence; but at the same time connected with the abstrusest speculations of ancient philosophy. It has been repeatedly observed, that the mythological personages, *Brahma, Veeshnu,* and *Seeva,* constitute the grand Hindu triad of Deity.—That, nearly all the Pagan nations of antiquity, in their various theological systems, acknowledged a kind of Trinity in the Divine Nature, has been the occasion of much needless alarm and unfounded apprehension, especially to those professors of Christianity, whose religious principles rest upon so slender a basis, that they waver with every wind of doctrine. The very circumstance which has given rise to these apprehensions, the universal prevalence of this doctrine in the Gentile kingdoms, is, in my opinion, so far from invalidating the Divine authenticity of it, that it appears to be an irrefragable argument in its favor. It ought to confirm the piety of the wavering Christian, and build up the tottering fabric of his faith.

The doctrine itself bears such striking internal marks of a Divine original, and is so very unlikely to have been the invention of mere human reason, that there is no way of accounting for the general adoption of so singular a belief by most ancient nations, than by supposing what I have, in pretty strong terms, intimated at the commencement of this chapter, to be the genuine fact, that the doctrine was neither the invention of Pythagoras, nor Plato, nor any other philosopher in the ancient world, but a *sublime mysterious truth,* one of those stupendous arcana of the invisible world, which through the condescending goodness of Divine Providence, was revealed to the ancient patriarchs of the faithful line of *Shem,* by them propagated to their Hebrew posterity; and through that posterity, during their various migrations and dispersions over the east, diffused through the Gentile nations, among whom they sojourned. I must again take permission to assert it as my solemn belief—a belief founded upon long and elaborate investigation of this important subject, that the Indian, as well as all other triads of Deity, so universally adored throughout the whole Asiatic world, and under every denomination, whether they consist of *persons, principles, or attributes deified,* arc only corruptions of the Christian doctrine of the *Trinity.*[2]

To Adam in a state of innocence, many parts of the mysterious economy of the eternal regions were, by the Divine permission, unfolded; nor did his mind, at the fall, lose all impressions of those wonderful revelations, which

---

2. Vol. iv. 418—19.

had been gradually imparted to him; for the remembrance of his past enjoyments and forfeited privileges, doubtless formed one afflicting part of his punishment. It was in that happy state, when man's more refined and perfect nature could better bear the influx of great celestial truths, that the awful mystery was revealed to him, and it came immediately from the lips of that *Divine Being*, the mighty Αυτο Θεος or *self-existent*, who, by his *holy word* created all things, and animated all things which he had created, by that energetic and pervading *spirit* which emanated from himself. It was at that remote period, that this holy doctrine was first propagated and most vigorously flourished, not in the school of Plato, not in the academic groves of Greece, but in the sacred bowers of *Eden*, and in the awful school of universal nature, when *Jehovah* himself was the instructor, and *Adam* the Heaven taught pupil. With these holy personages that compose the Trinity, he freely conversed during all the period that he remained in a state of innocence, while the refulgent glory of the Divine *Schechinah*, darting upon him its direct, but tempered rays, encircled with a flood of light, the enraptured protoplast, formed in the image and similitude of his Maker. But as he saw the radiance of the Divine Triad in innocence with inexpressible joy, so when fallen from that state of primaeval rectitude, he beheld it with unutterable terror; especially at that awful moment, when the same luminous appearance of Deity, but arrayed in terrible majesty, and darting forth severer beams, sought the flying apostate, who heard with new and agonizing sensations, the majestic voice of *Jehovah Elohim*, literally the *Lord Gods*, *walking in the garden in the cool of the day.*[3]

Dr. Allix informs us, that the Jewish cabalists constantly added to the word *Elohim*, the letter jod, being the first letter of the name Jehovah, *for the sake of a mystery*, as well as according to one of the most respectable commentators on the Pentateuch, the Rabbi Bechai, to show that there is a divinity in *each person*, included in the word.[4]

An extended period had elapsed since Malachi had sounded the prophetic trumpet. Impatient piety glowed with intense fervor, and expectation was on the wing to meet the promised Messiah. At length the long-wished for period of his advent arrived; nor was the awful event, in which were involved the eternal interests of the human race, ushered in amidst darkness and silence. An angel purposely descending from Heaven, announced the incarnation, not of another angel, for that surely were unnec-

---

3. Ibid. 431.
4. R. Bechir, in Genesis 1-10.

essary, but of the Son of the highest, of whose kingdom there should be no
end; and pointed out the manner of his conception, by the overshadowing
of that Schechinah, who, according to the Talmudic Jews, had squally the
key of the womb, of death and the grave,   equally (?)

At the period of his birth, a bright chorus of angels welcomed that birth
in expressive hallelujahs; and guided by the refulgent constellation, that
now first illumined the eastern hemisphere, the Chaldean Magi with reverence hastened to pay homage to that Messiah, to whom, it is said, *"the kings
of Tarshish and the isles shall bring presents, and the kings of Sheba and
Seba should offer gifts."*[5]

Arrayed in the venerable garb of the ancient prophets, and adhering to
the same austere diet, which should have roused the attention of the Jews,
the messenger John appeared his august herald, and a solemn voice was
heard amidst the recesses of the desert, *"prepare ye the way of the Lord,
make strait in the desert an high way for our God."* He was initiated by the
baptizing hand of that celestial messenger, into the sacred office which he
condescended to assume, and received the most solemn and public attestation possible, of his Divine emanation from the eternal fountain, as well
as by the audible voice of Jehovah, giving the everlasting benediction to
his beloved Son, as in the *Holy Spirit* visibly descending in the form of that
auspicious bird which brought to Noah the first tidings of Almighty wrath
appeased. The Jews, had not their expectations been totally blinded during the ceremony of this Divine unction, might there have seen two notable texts relative to the Logos, in their national Scriptures, strikingly
fulfilled— *"O God, thy God hath anointed thee, with the oil of gladness
above thy fellows."*[6] And that in Isaiah—*"And the Spirit of the Lord shall
rest upon him."* [7]

It was thus that the Baptist not only saw, but bore public record that *he
was the Son of God*—and on this occasion I cannot refrain from citing the
words of Dr. Allix—"The three persons in the Godhead, did there so conspicuously manifest themselves, that the ancients took thence occasion to
tell the Arians, *go to the river Jordan, and there you shall see the Trinity."*[8]

---

5. Psalm 72:10.
6. Psalm 45:7.
7. Isaiah 11:2.
8. Ibid. 501

The Chaldee Targum, on these words of Job, "the spirit of God hath made me, and the breath of the Almighty hath given me life,"[9] hath brought into the text, the second person in the trinity, as well as the third—his words are, *spiritus Dei fecit me, et verbum omnipotentis susten-tavit me*—that is, "the spirit of God hath made me, and the word of the Almighty hath sustained me."

Rabbi H. Hagaon, who lived 700 years ago, said, there are three lights in God; the anevit light or kadmon, the pure light, and the purified light; and these three make but one God.[10]

Rabbi Hakadosch, so highly celebrated for his piety as to have the title of Holy conferred on him by his nation, has this remarkable sentence: *pater Dens, filius Deus, spiritus sanctus Deus, trinus in unitate, et unus in trini-tate*; that is, the Father is God, the Son is God, and the Holy Spirit is God, trinity in unity, and unity in trinity—and the Hebrew sentence from which this is translated, is composed of the mysterious forty-two letters, forming according to the Cabalists, another of the names of God.[11]

On Genesis 18:1-3, "And the Lord appeared unto him in the plains of Mamre: and he sat in the tent door in the heat of the day; and he lifted up his eyes and looked, and lo! three men stood by him; and when he saw them he ran to meet them from the tent door and bowed himself toward the ground, and said, my Lord if now I have found favor in thy sight, pass not away, I pray thee, from thy servant."

Philo says, this whole passage contains a *latent mystical meaning*, not to be communicated to every one, and that according to this mystical sense, here was denoted ὁών, the great Jehovah, with his two Δυναμεις, of which one is called θεος, and the other Κυριος.[12]

The same author, in his *Dissertation de Cherubbim*, page 86, speaking of the eternal *Ens*, or ὁών, asserts, that "in *the one true God* there are two supreme and primary Δυναμεις, or powers, whom he denominates *goodness* and *authority*; that there is a *third and mediatorial power* between the two former, who is the *logos* or *word*.

The word Jehovah indicates the unity of the essence : Elohim points out, that in this unity there is a plurality existing, in a manner of which we can

9. Job 33:4.
10. Ibid 525.
11. Kerch. Odep. Egypt, com iii. 246.
12. Philo *judxis de sacrificiis abelis et Caini* 108.

at present have no clear conception, no more than we have of other parts of the mysterious economy of the invisible world.[13]

The letter ' or Jot, which is the first letter of the sacred name, denotes the thought—the idea of God. It is the ray of light, say the enraptured Cabalists, which darts a lustre too transcendent to be contemplated by mortal eye; it is a point at which thought pauses, and imagination itself grows giddy and confounded.—"Man," says Basnage citing the rabbis, "may lawfully roll his thoughts from one end of heaven to the other, but they cannot approach that inaccessible light, that primitive existence, contained in the letter Jod."[14]

From what other reason could the Gentiles have given such names to their pretended Gods. Mercury was called Triceps; Bacchus, Triambus; Diana, Triformis; and Hecate, Tergimina; Jupiter had hid three-forked thunder; Neptune his trident, and Pluto his three-headed Cerberus. Hence the triangle and the pyramid came to be numbered among the most frequent and esteemed symbols of Deity.[15]

It is my humble, but decided opinion, that the original and sublime dogma inculcated in the true religion, of a Trinity of hypostasis in the divine nature, delivered traditionally down from the ancestors of the human race, and the Hebrew patriarchs, being in time misapprehended, or gradually forgotten, is the fountain of all the similar conceptions in the debased systems of theology, prevailing in every other religion of the earth; of a doctrine thus extensively diffused through all nations; a doctrine established at once in regions distant as Japan and Peru; immemoriall acknowledged throughout the whole extent of Egypt and India; and flourishing with equal vigor amidst the snowy mountains of Thibet, and the vast deserts of Siberia. There is no other rational mode of explaining the allusion, or accounting for the origin.[16]

In the Oracles of Zoroaster the first, (supposed to be the grandson of Ham and great grandson of Noah,) though many of them are forgeries; yet many of them bear the marks of the genuine remains of Chaldaic theology; that theology which, according to Proelus, as cited by Mr. Stanley, was revealed to man by the awful voice of the Deity himself. In these oracles we find such singular expressions as these: "Where the *paternal monad* is,

---

13. Ibid 559.
14. Hist. of Jews, 193.
15. Ibid 617.
16. Ibid 620.

that paternal monad amplifies itself, and generates a duality." After declaring that the duad thus generated sits by the monad, and shining forth with intellectual beams, governs all things; this remarkable passage occurs, "for a triad of Deity shines forth throughout the whole world, of which a monad is the head." In a succeeding verse of this section we are informed, "for the mind of the Father said, that all things should be divided into *three*, whose will assented, and all things were divided." Immediately after follows a passage, in which the three persons in the Divine essence are expressly pointed out by appellations, "and there appeared in this triad, *virtue*, and *Wisdom*, and *Truth*, that know all things." This is answerable to the *Kather* (virtue), the *Cochma* (wisdom), and *Binab* (intelligence, or Spirit of truth), of the Hebrews.[17]

In the next section, under the title *"The Father and the Mind"* it is expressly said, the *Father* perfects all things, and delivers them over to *the second Mind,* that second Mind whom the nations of men commonly take for the first.—Under two minds is contained the life-generating fountain of souls, and the artificer who, self-operating, formed the world; He who sprang first out of that mind. In order next to the eternal mind, I Pysche dwell, wanning and animating all things.[18]

Kircher gives the following extract from Hermes Trismegistus' books, "There hath ever been one *great intellectual light*, which has always illuminated *the mind*; and their union is nothing else but the *Spirit*, which is the bond of all things."[19]

Orpheus asserts, (as is abridged by Timotheus, a Christian writer) the existence of an eternal incomprehensible Being; the Creator of all things, even of the aether itself, and of all things below that aether—That this supreme *Demiurgos* is called *Light, Counsel* and *Life.*

Timotheus concludes his account by affirming, that Orpheus in his book declared, that all things were made by one God-head in three names, and that this God is all things.[20]

It is remarkable through all antiquity, the humor of dividing every thing into *three*, displayed itself; and whence, except from the source of revelation, could this general but mutilated tradition of a triune-God have originated. The *Fates*, those relentless sisters, who weave the web of human life,

---

17. Ibid 630 to 634.
18. Ibid 636, 638.
19. Ibid. 690, and cites Oedep Egypt, tom iii. 578.
20. Ibid. 701. 702.

and fix its inevitable doom, were *three*—the *Furies*, the dire dispensers of the vengeance of Heaven, for crimes committed upon earth, were *three*—the Graces were *three*, and the celestial Muses, according to Varro, were originally only *three*.[21]

I have not undertaken so much to account for the perversion of this doctrine, as to record and ascertain the fact, of this notion of a triad of Deity, being radically interwoven in the theological codes adopted in almost every region of Asia—Asia, where the sublime system of the true religion was first revealed; where the pure precepts it inculcates were first practised, and where unhappily its leading principles were earliest adulterated. The Almighty hath not left himself without a witness, amidst the degrading superstitions and the false philosophy of the degenerate Asiatics. In the Persian triad, the character of Mithra, the middle god, is called the mediator: Now, the idea of a mediator, could alone originate in a consciousness of committed crimes, as well as in a dread of merited punishment.[22]

Plutarch, an enemy to a triad of Deity says, "Zoroaster is said to have made a three-fold distribution of things; to have assigned the first and highest rank to Oromasdes, who in the oracles, is called the *Father*; the lowest to Ahrimenes, and the middle to Mithras, who, in the same oracles, is called Ton Deutcron Nou, the second mind."[23]

Of exquisite workmanship and of stupendous antiquity—Antiquity to which neither the page of history, nor human traditions can ascend; that magnificent piece of sculpture, so often alluded to, in the cavern of *Elephanta*, decidedly establishes the solemn fact, that from the remotest eras, the Indian nations have adored a *triune Deity*. There the travellers, with awe and astonishment, behold, carved out of the solid rock, in the most conspicuous part of the most ancient and venerable temple in the world, a bust expanding in breadth near twenty feet, and no less than eighteen feet in altitude, by which amazing proportions, as well as by its gorgeous decorations, it is known to be the image of the grand presiding deity of that hallowed retreat: he beholds, I say, a bust composed of three heads, united to one body, adorned with the oldest symbols of the Indian theology, and thus expressly fabricated, according to the unanimous confession of the sacred sacerdotal tribe of India, to indicate the Creator, the Preserver and the Regenerator of mankind. I consider the superior antiquity of the Elephanta

---

21. Ibid. 712.
22. Ibid. 713.
23. Plutarch de Iside et Osiride, page 370

temple to that of Salsette, as established by the circumstance of the flat roof, proving it to have been excavated before mankind had discovered the art of turning the majestic arch, and giving the lofty roof that concave form, which adds so greatly to the grandeur of the Salsette temple—and as Salsette is supposed to be three thousand years old, the Elephanta must have been as near the flood, as the progress of science will allow us with propriety to fix it.[24]

In the Bhagvat-Geeta, the most ancient and authentic book of the Indian divinity, the supreme Veeshnu thus speaks concerning himself, "I am the Holy One, worthy to be known. I am the mystic (triliteral) figure *a u m*; the *Reig*, the *Yajush*, and the *Saman Vedas*."[25]

The Hindoos, says Mr. Sonnerat, adore three principal deities, *Brouma*, *Chiven* and *Vichenou*, who are still but one. He gives a literal translation from the Sanscreet, of a Pouran, thus, "It is God alone who created the universe by his productive power; who maintains it by his all preserving power, and who will destroy (or regenerate) it by his destructive (or regenerative) power; so that it is this God who is represented under the name of three Gods, who are called Trimourtin.[26]

Mr. Foster, in his Sketches of Hindu Mythology, says, "One circumstance which forcibly struck my attention, was the Hindu belief of a Trinity—These persons, are by the Hindus supposed to be wholly indivisible, the one is *three*, and the Three are *One*.[27]

From the previous extensive survey of the various systems of *Eastern theology*, it is evident, that the notion of a Divine Triad governing the Universe, however darkened and degraded through the prevalence of a long series of gross superstitions, was a doctrine that immemorially prevailed in the schools of Asia. From whatever distant source derived, through successive generations, and amidst a thousand perversions, the *great truth* contended for beams forth, with more or less splendor, in every country of the ancient world, and darts conviction upon the mind not prejudiced against the reception of it, by the suggestions of human pride, and the dogmas of false philosophy.

To try the merits of this great cause in the court of human reason, is evidently to bring it before a tribunal incompetent to decide upon so impor-

---

24. Ibid. 736.
25. Ibid. 744.
26. Ibid. 747, 749, and cites Sonnerat's Voy. 1 vol. 259,
27. Ibid. 750, and cites Foster, fol. 12.

tant a question; and is, in fact, to exalt a terrestrial judge, before the eternal judge of all things—yet we are justified in asserting, that this doctrine, though not founded upon reason as a basis, is by no means destitute of its decided support and concurrence. The basis upon which it rests, is far more noble as well as durable; *Divine revelation*, strengthened by the most ancient traditions, and the consenting creed of nearly all the kingdoms of the greater Asia.[28]

In fact, the name and history of Noah and his three sons, are precisely the same in the Sanscreet language, as in the Hebrew bible. In the ancient geographical records of India, we find the whole country denominated after Cush, or Cuth, the eldest son of Ham, its domestic appellation being *Cusha-Dweepa*; and we know that the inhabitants of the northern district were anciently called Cuthaei. We find again *Raamah*, the fourth son of that *Cush*, in the Indian *Rama*, renowned first as a conqueror, and afterwards as a God, throughout the whole extent of that vast region; and we discover his last son, *Nimrod* or *Belus*, in their *Bali*, the *Baal* and *Bel* of their neighbours.[29]

There was another very remarkable symbol of *Taut* or *Mercury*, prevalent in Egypt, as well as in India. It was the letter T, or in other words, the *Cross* or *Crux-Hermis*; in which form we find many of the more ancient pagoda's of India, as *Benares* and *Mattra*, erected; and many of the old Egyptian statues, as is well known to antiquaries, are represented bearing this symbol in their hands, or their breasts. I have elsewhere observed the very singular manner, after which the Latin Vulgate, and according to Lowth, probably the ancient copies of the Septuagint, have rendered the original of that passage in Ezekiel, the 9th chap. and 4th ver.—"Set a mark on the foreheads of the men that sigh, and that cry for all the abominations that be done in the midst thereof;" rendering it in their version, "I will mark them on the forehead with the letter T," which affords room to suppose it was a symbol of a more sacred import than is generally imagined, in the early patriarchal ages.

Now it is a fact not less remarkable, than well at tested, that the druids (in Great Britain) in their groves, were accustomed to select the most stately and beautiful tree, as an emblem of the Deity they adored; and having cut off the side branches, they affixed two of the largest of them to the highest part of the trunk, in such a manner, as that those branches, extending on each side like

28. Vol v. page 1.
29. Vol. vi. 42.

the arms of a man, presented to the spectators the appearance of a huge cross, and on the bark in various places was actually inscribed the letter T.[30]

---

30. Consult Borlase, fol. 108, and the express authorities which he adduces for the truth of this curious fact. Vol. vi. 67.

7

The Character of Christ

Our author proceeds with a declaration, "That nothing he has said, can apply, even with the most distant disrespect, to the real character of Jesus Christ. He was a virtuous and amiable man. The morality he preached and practised, was of the most benevolent kind; and though similar systems of morality had been preached by Confucius and some of the Greek philosophers, many years before; by the quakers since, and by many good men in all ages, it had not been exceeded by [any.]

TO read this passage with attention, is a sufficient refutation of his whole system; as well as an evidence of our author's strange principles, to every person who has read the New Testament, and has made himself acquainted with its effects.

What? Can that man be a virtuous and amiable man—a preacher and practicer of the most benevolent morality, not exceeded by any—and yet in the opinion of this writer, be guilty of imposing on his followers, by assuring them that "He was before the foundation of the world—that he was the first born of every creature—that he was sent of God—came down from Heaven—that he was the only begotten Son of God—that God was his father—that he and the Father were one—that he who had seen him, had seen the Father—that whosoever believed on him, should have everlasting life—that God had so loved the world, that he gave his only begotten Son, that whosoever believed on him, should not perish, but have everlasting life—that he that believeth on him is not condemned; but he that believeth not, is condemned already, because he hath not believed on the name of the only begotten Son of God—that all judgment was committed to the Son—that all men should honor the Son, even as they honor the Father—he that honoreth not the Son, honoreth not the Father who sent him—that the hour was coming, when the dead should hear the voice of the Son of God, and they that hear should live: for as the Father had life in himself, so had he given to the Son, to have life in himself—that the works he did, bore witness of him, that the Father had sent him—the Father also himself had borne witness of him—that if they believed Moses, they would believe in him, for Moses had written of him." He performed miracles—he raised the dead—he foretold things to come—he commanded, and the winds and waves obeyed him. All these things he did, (or at least he endeavoured to persuade his followers that he did them) as an evidence of his Almighty power; and that he had come down from God, and was the Son of God, the Messiah who was to come. He asserted, "That he was the bread of life, that came down from Heaven—that he would raise every believer in him, from the dead at the last day—that no man had seen the Father but himself, who was from God, and that he had seen him—that whoever hated him, hated the Father also." He declared himself to be "The light of the world—that before Abraham, he was—that as the Father knew him, so he knew the Father—that the Father was in him, and he in the Father—that he was the resurrection and the life—that he gave to his people eternal life—that thereafter they should see the Heavens opened, and the angels of God ascending and descending upon the son of man."

He openly declared himself to be the Messiah, expected by the Jews, and spoken of by their inspired prophets, as the Lord of Glory—the Lord our Righteousness—the Father of the everlasting ages—the Prince of Peace.

When John sent two of his disciples to enquire of him, whether he was the Messiah or not, he answered, "Go and show John those things *which ye do hear and see*; the blind receive their sight, and the lame walk; the lepers are cleansed, and the deaf hear; the dead are raised up, and the poor have the Gospel preached to them."[1] Thus appealing to their senses, for all the great essential proofs of Messiahship, as foretold by the prophets in a very few words, and to which they had been eye and ear witnesses.

He promised his disciples to send them the comforter, even the Holy Spirit, after his death, "who should proceed forth from the Father, and should remain with them forever, and guide them into all truth, and show them things to come. He asserted that he knew all things—that he had power over all flesh, and would give eternal life to as many as the Father had

---

1. Matthew, xi. 4, 5.

given him—that he had a glory with the Father before the world was; and though he should be crucified, yet he would arise again on the third day."

These are the doctrines, assertions, declarations, instructions and precepts of Jesus Christ, as made and taught in his own person, and enforced as obligatory on mankind, with the authority and power of a Divine messenger from God. If then he was a virtuous and amiable man, in the opinion of our author, what must be the consequence of his principles, as developed in the Age of Reason? If the devils once believed and trembled, what has our author reason to fear, when his eyes shall be opened by an awful conviction of the truth? He will, I fear, do more than believe and tremble.

If these doctrines proceeded from a virtuous and amiable man, they must be true; and all the sophistry of our author cannot avoid the conclusion; and if true, where will the sinner and ungodly appear! If these doctrines are virtuous and amiable, what can we say to the objects aimed at in this treatise, styled rather ludicrously "the Age of Reason." Is it not on the whole, a collection of the most artful deceptions, hidden under a veil of ridicule; dangerous falsehoods, covered by an easy flow of language; and malicious sneers, made palatable by an attempt at wit and satire, that ever disgraced the pen of a pretender to philosophy, and that on a subject of infinite consequence to the essential interests of mankind ?

True philosophy is the great supporter of the religion of Jesus Christ. He is represented as Wisdom herself, and therefore she will always be justified by her children. This idea is so well expressed by a late learned writer, that no excuse need be made for the following quotation. "Philosophy, so far as the term signifies a knowledge of God's wisdom and power in the natural creation, which is the best sense of the word, is so far from being adverse to true religion, that with all the common evidences of Christianity in reserve, we may venture to meet the philosopher upon his own ground. We have nothing to fear from the testimony of nature; we appeal to it; we call upon every man of science to compare the Gospel which God hath revealed, with the world which God hath created; under an assurance that he will find the latter to be a key to the former, as a noble philosopher has well asserted; and if nature answers to Christianity, it contradicts Deism; and that religion cannot be called natural, which is contradicted by the light reflected upon our understandings from natural things. The Socinian is nearly in the same situation with the Deist, and they may both join together in calling upon nature from morning until night, as the priests of Baal called upon their Deity, but there will be none to answer; and philosophy must put out one of its eyes, before it can admit their doctrines. In short, take any religion but the Christian, and bring it to the test, by comparing it with the state of nature, and it will be found destitute and defenceless.

"The doctrines of our faith are attested by the whole natural world; wherever we turn our eyes, to the Heavens or to the earth; to the sea or to the land; to men or to beasts; to animals or to plants; there we are reminded of them. They are recorded in a language which never hath been confounded; they are written in a text which shall never be corrupted. The creation of God is the school of Christians, if they use it aright."

But if the doctrines of the Gospel are not founded in philosophical truth, as they are not in the *professed* opinion of our Sophist, what can he mean by the acknowledgment, "That the real character of Jesus, was that of a virtuous and amiable man, preaching and practising the most benevolent morality," In truth there is no medium; he was either what he declared himself to be, or he was the worst of impostors and deceivers of mankind, justly deserving every mark of reprobation. But indeed truth and consistency seem to be no part of the creed of the author of the Age of Reason, and the farthest from the principal object of the performance, in whatever point of light you view it.

The excellent Mr. Hartley has made some just observations on this subject. He says—"If we allow only the truth of the common history of the New Testament, or even such a part of the character of Christ, as neither the ancient or modern Jews, heathens, or unbelievers seem to contest, it will be difficult to reconcile so great a character, claiming Divine authority, either with the moral attributes of God, or indeed with itself, upon the supposition of the falsehood of that claim. One can scarcely suppose, that God would permit a person apparently so innocent and excellent, so qualified to impose upon mankind; to make so impious and audacious a claim, without having some evident mark of imposture set upon him; nor can it be conceived, how a person could be *apparently* so innocent and so excellent, and yet *really* otherwise. The manner in which the evangelists speak of Christ, shows that they drew after a real copy; that is, shows the genuineness and truth of the gospel history. There are no direct encomiums upon him; no laboured defences or recommendations. His character arises from a careful, impartial examination of all that he said and did; and the evangelists appear to have drawn the greatest of all characters, without any direct design to do it. And if we compare the transcendent greatness of this character, with the indirect manner in which it is delivered, and the illiterateness and low condition of the evangelists, it will appear impossible that they should have forged it, or that they should not have had a real original before them; so that nothing was wanting but to record simply and faithfully. How could mean and illiterate persons excel the greatest geniuses, ancient and modern, in drawing a character? How came they to draw it in an indirect manner? This is indeed a strong evidence of genuineness and truth."[2]

Our author proceeds in his work, by observing, " That similar systems of morality had been preached by Confucius, some of the Greek philosophers, and lately by the quakers."

As far as Confucius had received the tradition of a Saviour to come, with the blessed fruits of his grace to sinners, from the revelation made to Noah and the antediluvian patriarchs, he may have seen some distant prospect of the Divine system of the Gospel;[3] but as to the Greek philosophers, although some of them now and then, might have struck out some useful principle of true morality, yet few of them, it is believed, ever before bore such glorious company: there can be no more comparison between them, and the benevolent Jesus, than between the wretched enjoyments of a mere earthly sensual life, and the consummate and inexpressible joys of Heavenly glory. Yet even some of them could see excellencies and beauties in the Gospel, that have escaped the critical eye of our pretender to philosophy. Amelius, the master of Porphyry, that great opposer of the doctrine of a crucified Saviour, on reading the beginning of St. John's Gospel, swore by Jupiter, "That the barbarian" (meaning St. John) had hit upon the right notion, when he affirmed that the *Word* which had made all things, was in the beginning, in place of prime dignity and authority with God; and was *that God* who had created

---

2. Hartley on Man.

3. The patriarchal tradition had fortunately been preserved in considerable purity in the family of Confucius; but he perceived with sorrow the degeneracy of China. He claimed no Divine commission, but declared that his doctrines were not his own, but those of the ancients, handed down by tradition.

His system consisted in the simple worship of the God of Heaven, and the practice of moral virtue.—Dr. Hardy's sermon before the society for propagating the Gospel.

Confucius, (who lived about 500 years before the Christian era) the noblest and most Divine philosopher of the Pagan world, was himself the innocent occasion of the introduction of the numerous and monstrous idols that in after ages disgraced the temples of China; having in his dying moments encouraged his disconsolate disciples, by prophesying "in the West, the Holy one will appear." They concluded that he meant the God Bhood of India, and immediately introduced into China, the worship of that Deity, with all the train of abominable images and idolatrous rights, by which that gross superstition, was in so remarkable a manner distinguished.—5th Ind. Ant. 758.

all things, and in whom every thing that was₍ made had, according to its nature, its life and being. That he was incarnate and clothed with a body, wherein he manifested the glory and magnificence of his nature; and that after his death he returned to the repossession of his divinity, and became the same God which he was, before his assuming a body, and taking the human nature and flesh upon him."[4]

Indeed Mr. Hartley asserts, that "The ancient Pagan religions, seem evidently to be the degenerated offspring of the patriarchal revelations; and so far to have been true, as they taught a God—a Providence—a future state—supernatural communications made to particular persons, especially in the infancy of the world—the present corruption of man—and his deviation from a pure and perfect way—the hopes of pardon—a mediatorial power—the duties of sacrifice, prayer and praise; and the virtues of prudence, temperance, justice and fortitude. They were false as they mixed and polluted these important truths with numberless fables, superstitions and impieties. That degree of truth and moral excellence, which remained in them, was a principal cause of their success and easy propagation among the people; for their moral sense would direct them to approve and receive what was fit and useful."

As to the people called quakers, they are a denomination of devout Christians, many of whom do honor to their profession, by copying the example and living according to the precepts of their Divine master, whom this writer terms "A virtuous and amiable man," while he charges his doctrines and precepts with the basest imposition and deception; and it is only in the exercise of that dignified humility which he has taught them, that the quakers will patiently bear the invidious comparison with Chinese and Greek philosophers. This pretender to Common Sense, seems as ignorant of the principled and profession of the people called quakers (though he asserts that he was born in their communion, and I know that he has lived among them) as he is of the Gospel, which they publicly profess to be their hope and confidence. How unhappy is it for a writer, not to understand any part of a subject on which he attempts to instruct his fellow men.

I am well aware that this writer asserts, that Jesus Christ did not write any account of himself, but his history is altogether the work of other people, and that this history is the foundation of my answers.

---

4. Euseb. Praep. Evang. lib. ii. X

But even giving a weight to this assertion, that it does not merit, our author himself has given a sanction to this history, that must support the sufficiency of testimony; since it is from this source alone, he could draw the conclusion, that Jesus Christ was "a virtuous and amiable man, and preached and practised the most benevolent morality," as it is the only one that gives an original account of him or his doctrines.

If we are not to believe the history of any person or country, except it has been written by such person himself, or the chief of that country, our source of information will be small indeed. How few persons since the creation have written their own histories. Where is the instance of a king of England, or France, who have written his own history? Are we yet to be supposed ignorant of the characters and conduct of all the kings of those kingdoms, who, for a thousand years past, have figured on the theatre of Europe? If we should discredit the existence or actions, recorded in the histories of Alexander, Philip, or Anthony, because they had not written their own histories, I believe we should be laughed at by our philosopher himself, for our folly. But nothing appears too extraordinary for the author of the Age of Reason to assert or attempt, if it does but militate against the heart searching doctrines of the Gospel.

If memoirs written by men of good characters, though personally unacquainted with the transactions they relate, and who did not exist till long after the times of which they write, are to receive credit in the world, what return ought our author to meet with, for decrying those written by contemporaries—intimate friends—of the same family—parties to most of the transactions—their eternal all risked on the truth of the facts—and under every possible advantage to know the truth—men of established moral characters—of devout lives, and who sacrificed their ease, comfort, fortune, and even life itself, in confirmation of the facts they relate?—Surely nothing less than at least the universal detestation of every serious Christian.

The denial of the principal events and historical occurrences of the life of Jesus Christ, as recorded by the evangelists, necessarily implies a miracle, equal to the affirmation of them. Is it not equally miraculous, that thousands of Jews, with Gentiles of every nation, language and tongue, whose principles and practices were wholly repugnant to every idea held up by the Gospel, should be prevailed upon by twelve illiterate fishermen, without power, riches, character, influence or abilities, to forsake the religion of their fathers, in which they had been bred with superstitious rigidness, and in which they had lived to advanced life, under all the violent prejudices and attachments peculiar to their day and nation—not only to profess this new religion, but to do it on the express terms of being despised, contemned and exposed to the loss of every thing dear to them, and frequently to death itself, with all the horrors that human ingenuity, whetted by malice and superstition, could invent.

Among these were to be found men of the first rank in life, famous for riches, honor, learning, and every earthly comfort—emperors, consuls, senators, priests, lawyers, scribes and pharisees.

Is it supposeable that men of this character, should unite to hand down to posterity, with the most scrupulous and religious exactness, and from the very moment of the transactions, an account of facts and occurrences known even to themselves to be false, for no other end than to ruin themselves, and impose upon their fellow men.

About one year after the crucifixion, the Christian church was greatly multiplied. We read in the acts of the apostles, that the original number were one hundred and twenty, and that in ten days (the day of Pentecost) after the ascension, there were added to their society, "about 3000 souls." Soon after they amounted to 5000. It was but a short time after that, we again read, that "Believers were the more added to the Lord, multitudes both of men and women." It is again said, that "A great company of the priests were obedient to the faith." Three years afterwards, we are told, "That the churches had rest throughout all Judea, Gallilee and Samaria, and were edified, walking in the fear of the Lord, and in the comfort of the Holy Ghost, were multiplied." About seven years after the crucifixion, St. Peter was miraculously sent to the Gentiles. One year after this, "A great number believed and turned to the Lord." "Much people were added to the Lord—the apostles, Barnabas and Paul, taught much people." This was generally in Syria. The next year, it is said, "That the word of God grew and multiplied." Afterwards, not exceeding three years, we are told, that on the preaching of Paul, "A great multitude of both Greeks and Jews, believed." Afterwards, the apostles were charged with being persons "who had turned the world upside down." In less than thirty years after the crucifixion, the disciples were greatly multiplied throughout all Greece, and besides, we read of converts at Rome, Alexandria, Athens, Cyprus, Cyrene, Macedonia, and Philippi. It had also spread throughout Judea, Gallilee, Samaria—the lesser Asia—the islands of the Aegean Sea, and the coast of Africa. And about this time the apostles inform Paul, "That many thousands (literally myriads) 'were in Jerusalem who believed." Add to these, the testimony of Pliny, Tacitus, Justin Martyr, and Tertullian.

This was all done by the preaching of twelve illiterate fishermen, not only without the power of the Jaw or the sword, but in opposition to them both, with no other weapons but reason and argument, under the recent knowledge of the facts they related, then prevalent among the people.

Surely a belief that reasonable men would act so absurd a part, requires a degree of evidence superior to that of any miraculous fact contained in the Gospel history. Thus, in the words of a noted author, "The existence of the sacred volume is a miracle, unless we allow the truth of the Scripture miracles."

But more of the evidence of the truth of the sacred writings hereafter, in its proper place.

8

Resurrection & Ascension of Christ

Another important objection of the Age of Reason, to the Gospel Revelation, is on account of the resurrection and ascension of Jesus Christ, as related by the Evangelists, which our author asserts " was the necessary counterpart of the story of Christ's birth. His historians having brought him into the world in a supernatural manner, were obliged to take him out again, in the same manner, or the first part if the story must have fallen to the ground.—The wretched contrivance, with which this latter part is told, exceeds every thing that went before it.—The resurrection of a dead person from the grave and his ascension through the air, is a thing very different, as to the evidence it admits of, to the invisible conception of a child in the womb.—The resurrection and ascension, supposing them to have taken place, admitted of public and ocular demonstration, like that of the ascension of a balloon, or the sun at noon day, to all Jerusalem at least.—A thing which every body is required to believe, requires that the proof and evidence of it, should be equal to all and universal: and as the public visibility of this last related act, was the only evidence that could give sanction to the former part, the whole of it fails to the ground, because the evidence never was given.—Instead of this, a small number of persons, not, more than eight or nine, are introduced, as proxies for the whole world, to say that they saw it, and all the rest of the world are called upon to believe it."

THE objections to the resurrection and ascension of Jesus Christ, been now first made; or had no solid and conclusive answers been given to them when made, this reasoning of our author, with the unfounded observations and objections to those well established facts, might have been

passed by, without the imputation of rash and malicious misrepresentations.—But after the able and masterly manner in which this subject has
been investigated and cleared up to every candid inquirer after truth, by
some of the best pens in every age of the church, and lately by the famous
Gilbert West; with whose writings (which do him immortal honor) the author of the Age of Reason, may *possibly* be acquainted, no tolerable excuse
can be given, for the obstinacy and perverseness with which the charge "of
the resurrection being a wretched contrivance exceeding every thing that
went before it," is here made, with the addition of a palpable falsehood, asserted in proof of the charge, viz. "that instead of public and ocular demonstration which those facts admitted of, not more than eight or nine persons
are introduced as proxies for the whole world to say they saw it."

Here again our author refers to the account given of these facts in the
sacred History, by alledging "that not more than eight or nine persons are
introduced to say that they had seen the transaction."—This must refer to
the account given of it by the inspired penmen, and that account is capable
of positive proof to the meanest capacity, who can read the whole narrative
of the resurrection of our Lord and Saviour with its convincing circumstances and confirmations as there related.

For trial of our author's veracity, we must there refer to the sacred writings, as delivered to us by the Evangelists.

These give us a plain, simple, unadorned narrative of the whole process,
with its consequences.—They tell us, that the subject of this extraordinary
and supernatural occurrence, was condemned and executed as an enemy to
God and man, in the most cruel manner by his inveterate enemies, who
were previously made acquainted with his predictions, as well of his death
and the manner of it, as of his resurrection from the dead, and particularly,
that it should take place on the third day after his crucifixion.

Here then was every advantage, an enraged and malicious enemy, who had
the authority and power of an absolute and despotic government on their
side, to prevent or detect imposition, could wish or desire. Accordingly the
chief priests and pharisees, the religious rulers of the country, apprehending
an intention in his followers to promote a deception among the people relative to the fulfilment of his prediction, take the most proper measures that
could be devised, to obviate the evil and prevent the possibility of their being
imposed upon. And this they did, as if directed by the providence of God to
establish and confirm the evidence of the great facts, beyond contradiction,
which of all things these leaders of the Jews most dreaded.

They not only have a ponderous stone rolled to fill the door of the sepulchre, where the body of our Lord was deposited, to prevent his being easily removed, but that the event might be rendered impractical, or the fact, if it should be attempted, prevented and the authors exposed and punished; they affix their own seals to the stone, so that it could not be stirred by any force without breaking them. And, lest all this should not be sufficient to prevent eleven poor unsupported fishermen from accomplishing their purpose, against the power of the government, they obtain a guard of Roman soldiers, known to be then under the best discipline in the world, to watch and guard the sepulchre, thus secured, against any sudden attack; for the Jews tell Pilate, "that they remembered that this Deceiver, while he was yet alive said, that after three days I will rise again."

Is it reasonable to suppose, that the chief priests and pharisees, after having carried their enmity so far against this supposed enemy to their religious hierarchy and the Roman government, for which they now pretend great concern, saying to Pilate, "If thou let this man go, thou art not Caesar's friend;" and on whose guilt of character they had pledged themselves and their posterity, by preferring a murderer? I say, is it reasonable to suppose, that these people, thus circumstanced, would have now risked their influence with the Roman governor, as well as their popularity with the people, by suffering it to remain possible to have the body of Jesus stolen away, so as to found the idea of his having known things to come, as well as his power over death and the grave? In that event, his party would be greatly increased, and the last error become in their apprehension worse than the first! The measures they took show, that they acted with prudential caution, with wisdom and decision, like men of the world, under the influence of all these motives.

And who was it that this powerful body of men were afraid of? A set of poor, disheartened, contemptible disciples, who, at the first capture of their Master by the civil officers, affrighted out of their reason, and concerned alone for their own safety, fled and left him in the hands of his bitterest enemies, and to suffer the most ignominious death. Nay, they had not even the courage to come forward, and act the part of friends on his trial, (which was allowed by law to the connections of the basest malefactor, and had long been the practice in the Jewish courts of justice) by declaring the manner of his life and daily conduct, as testimony in his favor, to counteract the testimony adduced against him, inconsistent with such a regular habit of conduct. This indeed, however criminal in the disciples, was fulfilling the ancient prophesy of Isaiah, in these remarkable words: "He was led as a sheep to the slaughter, and like a lamb dumb before his shearers, so he opened not his mouth: in his humiliation, his judgment was taken away, and who shall" (or rather, there was no one to) "declare his manner of life; for his life was taken from the earth."

Having taken all these precautions against so cowardly a set of weak and timid disciples, with the advantage of knowing the day on which the predicted event was to take place, the rulers of the Jews thought themselves (as on their principles they certainly were) perfectly secure.

But it was not a sepulchre secured by stones and seals, guarded by frail mortal men, or aided by death and hell, that could detain the Lord of life and glory. He burst the bands of death asunder, and rose from the dead early on the third day. The discovery was first made by two or three defenceless women, of the number of his followers, who coming at the rising of the sun, when no suspicions of any improper designs would take place; and having no apprehensions of his resurrection, intended to embalm his body in order to preserve it from putrefaction, according to the manner of the Jews:—so little did they know of the great designs of Providence, or of the power of their crucified Saviour, over the bonds of death.

It being now day, and their designs lawful, open, and public, their only difficulty was the removing of the stone to gain admission into the sepulchre. They did not find the guard asleep, or alarmed at their thus coming openly on a lawful and pious errand. There was no stir—no suspicions of the body having been previously stolen away—the stone was securely sealed—the guards remained in perfect ease and security at their posts, not suspecting the great event that had taken place.

"Twice had the sun gone down upon the earth, and all as yet was quiet at the sepulchre; death held his sceptre over the Son of God. Still and silent the hours passed on. The guards stood by their post. The rays of the midnight moon gleamed on their helmets and on their spears. The enemies of Christ exulted in their success. The hearts of his friends were sunk in despondency and sorrow. The Spirits of Glory waited in anxious suspense to behold the event, and wondered at the depth of the ways of God. At length, the morning star arising in the east, announced the approach of light; the third day began to dawn on the world; when on a sudden, the earth trembled to its centre, and the powers of Heaven were shaken; an angel of God descended; the guards shrunk back from the terror of his presence, and fell prostrate on the ground. His countenance was like lightning, and his raiment white as snow. He rolled away the stone from the door of the sepulchre, and sat upon it. But, who is this that cometh forth from the tomb, with dyed garments from the bed of death? He that is glorious in his appearance, walking in the greatness of his strength? It is thy prince, O Zion! Christian, it is your Lord! He hath trodden the wine press alone. He hath stained his raiment with blood; but now, as the first born from the womb of nature, he meets the morning of the resurrection. He rises a conqueror from the grave. He returns with blessings from the world of spirits. He brings Salvation to the sons of men. Never did the returning sun usher in a day so glorious! It was the jubilee of the universe: the morning stars sang together, and all the sons of God shouted aloud for joy."[1]

It was now indeed that the Roman soldiers, notwithstanding all their courage and intrepidity, astonished at so awful a sight, became as helpless as dead men: they could make no opposition to the inquiries of the sorrowful Mary Magdalen and her disconsolate companion, to whom the angel spoke in the mildest terms of complacency, requesting them not to be afraid, as he knew their errand was to seek Jesus of Nazareth; and he assured them that he was sent to inform them, that Jesus was not in the sepulchre, but was risen from the dead; and to give them fall conviction, he bade them approach and see the place where the Lord had lain, for that he had been sent to roll away the stone for that purpose.

This is a plain simple account of this all-important event; and it bears all the marks of truth, especially when supported by the story told by the soldiers to the high priest and pharisees, together with the subsequent measures, which they are said, by the sacred historians, to have adopted to prevent the ill effects of the first impression of so remarkable a phenomenon, that the soldiers should have said, "That while they slept, his disciples came and took away the body." If they were really asleep, how did they know that any person took the body away? Their assertion then, had they made it, was nothing more than a conclusion drawn by themselves, without evidence, from finding the body gone when they awaked from sleep. But how it was removed, it was impossible for sleeping men to know. Besides, the disciples, in taking away the body, must have only deceived others; they could not have deceived themselves; and of all men, they must have acted the most absurdly, to lay down their lives in support of facts they knew to be false.

Here again, it requires the belief of a miraculous fact, to disbelieve the miracle of the resurrection of our Lord and Saviour.—There can be no pos-

---

1. Scots Preacher.

sible cause assigned, why men, simple in their manners, honest and upright in their lives, and totally cut off from every temporal advantage, should voluntarily bring on themselves the hatred and detestation of their government and fellow-citizens, by asserting and steadily professing through their whole lives a fact which they knew of their own knowledge to be false, and finally to seal the truth of it with their blood. Add to this, that they should within a few days of the transaction, be able to convince thousands of their countrymen of all ranks and characters, under every advantage of examination and detection, of the truth of what they asserted, so as to lead them, also, to forsake every personal advantage and expose themselves to contumely and reproach for the sake of him who was the great object of this miraculous event, and that with his express declaration before their eyes, " that they should suffer persecution for his sake."

Had the story, said to be told by the soldiers, been true, or even so related by them to the chief priests and pharisees, what would have been the probable consequences?—Indeed it is not likely that disciplined soldiers, would have voluntarily acknowledged themselves guilty of a crime, for which they must according to the laws of war, have suffered death; to wit, sleeping on their post, when having an important charge. But, could it have been proved upon them, is it probable, that the enraged and exasperated priests and pharisees, who so cruelly persecuted the man Christ Jesus to death, preferred a base murderer, to one in whom the Roman governor could not find any fault, should pass by unpunished, so aggravated a crime, by which all their care and foresight were wholly frustrated.—Had these soldiers been punished for this breach of duty, would not the opposers of the Christian faith, immediately on the promulgation of its doctrines in the first age of the resurrection while they were persecuting the church on every side, have adduced the record of such punishment in proof of the deception and fraud, especially when its advocates at the moment, expressly charged the authors of this persecution, with the wicked subterfuge of persuading the soldiers to make this excuse, and promising to save them from the punishment that would otherwise necessarily have followed the confession.

We have many answers of the Jews and Heathen, controverting the principles and doctrines of the Christian revelation, but never has it been yet asserted, that any of these soldiers were either tried or punished for this crime. When Peter was arrested by Herod, and delivered into the custody of four quaternions of soldiers, they used all possible care to secure him, by putting him in chains, and sleeping one on each side of him; yet when the angel delivered him in the night from their power, and he was not to be found in the morning, did the report of the soldiers, that he escaped while they slept, excuse them? No; they had not the priests and pharisees to cover their negligence, and to screen them from punishment. "When Herod had sought for Peter and found him not, he examined the keepers, and commanded that they should be put to death."[2] This was the natural consequence of military discipline, and it could not on principle be forgiven.

Had the testimony of the resurrection rested here, perhaps it might have been less complete—but the history proceeds, and informs us, that, as the women were hastening with the joyful news to the disciples, behold, Jesus himself in person, meets and converses with them. This information being communicated to the rest of his disciples, who had yet no belief in an actual and immediate resurrection of the body of their Redeemer, two of them ran off to the sepulchre to examine for themselves, and not meeting with any opposition, the soldiers being fled, and the stone being removed, they found the grave-clothes lying in the sepulchre, and the body gone; they return with a kind of doubting satisfaction, notwithstanding their late unbelief. On the same day, Jesus appeared again to two other of the disciples, as they were going to Emmaus, and made himself known to them by the manner of his breaking bread at supper.

Afterwards, at a meeting of the disciples, Jesus personally came and stood in the midst of them, and showed his hands and his side: he then ate and drank with them, to prove his actual presence, that they might have time to recover from any sudden surprise occasioned by his first appearance. But notwithstanding this convincing evidence of the fact, Divine Providence so ordered it, to increase the testimony to its full amount, that Thomas, one of the twelve disciples, should be absent. To him the other disciples, in the fullness of their joy, relate the complete evidence afforded them of the resurrection of their master; and assure Thomas of the pleasing and ocular demonstration of this mysterious fulfilment of his gracious promise.

Thomas had providentially something of the incredulous temper of the author of the Age of Reason. He thought that he was not bound to believe on the rational testimony of another—He was so far from being prepared for this occurrence, by an expectation of the resurrection, or by a credulous mind in favor of the event, that he did not hesitate with warmth to deny the fact; and supposing his brethren to have been imposed upon by their too

---

2. Acts, 12, 19.

easy credulity, declared with a decision of temper bordering on obstinacy, that no evidence should have any effect on his mind, to convince him of what he thought impossible, unless he should have the sensible demonstration afforded him, of putting his finger into the print of the nails, and thrusting his hand into his side, being determined, in a matter of so great consequence, not to trust his own sight, which he supposed might be deceived. To such obstinate incredulity, the mourning disciples could only oppose a melancholy silence, pitying Thomas's want of faith and confidence in their united testimony.

Here then was every qualification for unbelief, that could be desired by the most obstinate and profane infidel, even though it should be our author himself. And happy would it be for him, had there been but one Thomas of this perverse character. Here was no weak credulity, or fond acquiescence, in what the mind eagerly desired.

A few days afterwards, the disciples being again convened, and the unbelieving Thomas one of the company, the risen Saviour, with infinite condescension, not only to the obstinate Thomas, but to all who should ever after imitate his unbelief and repentance, surprised them a second time with his sudden appearance in the midst of them; and in testimony of the reality of his resurrection and omniscience, at once addresses himself to Thomas, and mildly reproves him by saying, "Reach hither thy finger, and behold my hands; and reach hither thy hand, and thrust it into my side; and be not faithless, but believing."

Thomas, having thus received satisfaction to every doubt, is not only fully convinced of the resurrection of his master, but of his knowing the thoughts of his heart, and the words he had spoken in secret. In extacy and astonishment, therefore, he cries out under the deepest conviction, "My Lord and my God!" Jesus then replied, "Thomas, because thou hast had this condescending evidence of my resurrection, thou hast believed in, and acknowledged my divinity, blessed shall they be, who have not seen, and yet shall believe," May God Almighty, of his infinite mercy, grant, that another unbelieving Thomas may be yet added to the triumphs of the cross, though it should be that despiser of the Gospel, the author of the Age of Reason himself.

Jesus Christ continued to give many other evidences of the reality of his resurrection, by repeatedly appearing to his disciples, and instructing them in their all-important mission, during the space of forty days. Particularly he appeared to seven of them on the sea shore, as they were fishing, when he dined with them again. In fine, during this period, he frequently met with them, and freely conversed about the great plan of his mediatorial kingdom; foretelling what should happen to them in the world, in consequence of their fulfilling his commandments—and, at last, in presence of about five hundred brethren, he ascended up towards Heaven before them all, till a cloud received him, and prevented their sight.[3]

Among many things which he had foretold his disciples, and afterwards accomplished, and is still at this day bringing to pass in confirmation of the faith of his followers, was the promise of the Holy Spirit, who should descend upon them, when he should return to his father. Just before his ascension, he ordered them to remain at Jerusalem, till this divine promise should be realized. This event only remained to be fulfilled, to complete the certainty of his resurrection and Divine nature, to his disciples and followers, throughout the world.

They accordingly remained together till the day of Pentecost, or fifty days after the Passover, or ten days after the ascension, when this glorious confirmation of all their hopes was made good to them, attended with all that evidence, that is thus arrogantly demanded by the sceptical mind of our author, including the public and ocular demonstration, to all Jerusalem at least. And as the *"public visibility of this last related act,* is the only evidence that could

---

3. Acts 1:3. "To whom also he showed himself alive after his passion, by many infallible proofs, being seen of them forty days, and speaking of the things pertaining to the Kingdom of God."

First Corinthians 15:5–8. "And that he was seen of Cephas, then of the twelve. After that he was seen of about 500 brethren at once, of whom the greater part remain at this present, but some are fallen asleep. After that he was seen of James, then of all the apostles, and last of all he was seen of me also, as one born out of due time."And did he rise?

Hear O ye nations! hear it, O ye dead!
He rose ! He rose! He burst the bars of death;
Lift up your heads, ye everlasting gates!
And give the King of Glory to come in.
Who is the King of Glory? He who left
His throne of glory for the pang of death.
Lift up your heads, ye everlasting gates!
And give the King of Glory to come in.
Who is the King of Glory? He who slew
The rav'nous foe that gorg'd all human race!
The King of Glory, he, whose glory fill'd
Heaven with amazement at his love to man:
with Divine complacency beheld
Pow'rs most illumin'd, wilder'd in the theme.
—YOUNG.

give sanction to the former part, the whole is (on our author's own principles) fully confirmed, because of the certainty of this fact.

This happened by a sound from Heaven, as a rushing mighty wind, that filled all the house where they were; and there appeared cloven tongues of fire, sitting upon each of them. These unlettered and ignorant men, as to human learning, immediately gave full and miraculous evidence, to all the city of Jerusalem, of the reality of their master's resurrection, and of the fulfilment of his promise in the heavenly gift, by their publicly speaking before all men, with great fluency, in all the different languages of the several countries in the neighborhood of Judea.

Here then, I repeat it with confidence, *"was evidence equal to all—of public and sensible demonstration, like that of a balloon's ascending, or the sun at noon-day"* at least to the inhabitants of Jerusalem and the sojourners there, and the surrounding nations. This was not done in secret, or before eight or nine witnesses; but the apostles *immediately* began to publish the Gospel, and this wonderful work of God, in confirmation of the resurrection, to the citizens of Jerusalem, in presence of strangers of all the surrounding nations; Parthians, Medes, Elamites, Messopotamians, Cappadocians—those of Pontus in Asia: Phrygians, Pamphylians, Egyptians, Lybians, Cretans, Romans, and Arabians; who were either Jews or proselytes, and happened to be at Jerusalem, attending on the solemn festival of Pentecost, for the purpose of religious worship. Every one, in his own language, was taught, and that with astonishment and wonder, the great things of the resurrection of Jesus Christ, and bore witness to the mighty power of God, which had raised him from the dead.

It is difficult for persons at this day, to form a proper idea of the number of people, who usually attended at Jerusalem at the passover, when all their males were obliged to appear before the Lord. The particular account of the last Passover ever held in that devoted city, just before the Romans besieged and so completely surrounded it, according to our Lord's prediction, that few or none could escape, will enable the reader to form some judgment of their numbers. Josephus records, that the number that perished in the siege, and were taken prisoners, amounted to upwards of thirteen hundred thousand souls.

This notable miracle, therefore, having been performed so soon after the Passover when it may fairly be presumed, that great numbers of the people, both Jews and proselytes, from every part of the country and of the surrounding nations, were yet remaining in Jerusalem, gave as full and general conviction of its truth, as the nature of the case could admit.[4]

These strangers then, who were thus made acquainted with the power of God, and the glad tidings of the Gospel, carried the first news of these glorious truths to all their different countries, and prepared the way by laying the foundation of the subsequent work of the apostles.

The evidence of the resurrection of the Son of God, did not end here, however public and notorious it may have been. More than has been required by our author, was done by the mercy and goodness of God, that no excuse or pretence for unbelief might be left to those who despise the grace of the Gospel, which offereth Salvation to all men. This miraculous gift was not a sudden and mere temporary afflatus of the Spirit, and so an evidence to those of Jerusalem only, who were personally witnesses of the great event: but it became a durable and permanent qualification of the mind, enabling the apostles of our Lord, in their subsequent progress through every nation, to repeat the miracle, by preaching the Gospel among them in their own language, that thereby the reports of those, who were witnesses of the fact at Jerusalem, might be confirmed, and witnesses to the power of the resurrection, increased wherever they went. Thus it seems, as if the condescension of a merciful God, to the weakness and frailty of his offending creatures, knew no bounds. To raise the proof to demonstration, and remove every possibility of doubt or cavil, from the mind of the sceptic, this extraordinary and miraculous power was not only continued to them during their lives, but they were enabled, by the imposition of their hands, and by prayer, to communicate it to thousands of others, of every nation and language; so that they became with their disciples, a continued and miraculous proof of the truth of the resurrection, throughout the then habitable world, that carried with it such conviction, as could admit of no rational contradiction.

So far then, from this great and all essential event, the very foundation and corner-stone of the Christian system, being confined to the testimony of eight or nine persons, as is most falsely and maliciously charged upon us, by the author of the Age of Reason; it is supported by the testimony of hundreds, who had seen and conversed with the blessed and risen Saviour, after his resurrection, and beheld his ascension to glory. Thousands and tens of thousands also, who bore witness to the supernatural fulfilment of his promise, as the consequence of his resurrection and ascension. It is also

---

4. The strangers or proselytes in Judea, in the beginning of Solomon's reign, were 153,600 men, fit to be employed in building the temple. Reas. of Christianity, 17.

supported by the complete proof of the same event, in the sending of the Holy Spirit, who should be a witness of him, in confirmation of the glorious facts, and which, as before observed, was continued during the lives of the apostles; and many of their converts, attended with the power of working miracles in their own persons, to the conviction of multitudes in every nation and language in the Roman world, many of whom also received the like gift of the Spirit, till the evidence was full, by the completion of the sacred cannon, and the well established experience of the church of Christ.

This was the case, in a special manner, among the Jews at Jerusalem, where the first Christian church was established; it being but a few days after this miraculous descent of the Spirit, and at Peter's first sermon, that no less than three thousand souls were converted to the belief of the resurrection in one day. And, on his second sermon, which was preceded by the miraculous healing of the lame man, who sat at the gate of the Temple begging alms, the number of men only amounted to five thousand.[5]

These things, therefore, instead of being confined to the knowledge of a few, were so public and popular, that the high priest and his council, within three or four days after, could say, "Did we not strictly com mand you, that ye should not teach in this name! and behold *ye have filled Jerusalem with your doctrines*, and intend to bring this man's blood upon us.

The apostles did not confine their doctrines founded on the resurrection of Jesus Christ, to a few chosen friends; but immediately on the crucifixion of their master, a few days after his ascension, when the Holy Spirit, as has been shown, was miraculously given to them, they boldly *told the chief priests, and the whole council of Jerusalem*, "The God of our fathers raised up Jesus, *whom ye slew and hanged on a tree*; him hath God exalted with his right hand, to be a prince and a Saviour; to give repentance unto Israel, and forgiveness of sins; and *we are his witnesses* of these things, and so is *also the Holy Ghost, whom God hath given to them who obey him.*"

Did the Sanhedrin, or great council of the Jews, undertake to deny these facts, and to charge the apostles with falsehoods? No; they did not dare so to do—the facts were fresh in the memories of all the people, and the testimony of the Holy Spirit could not be denied. Hear, on this occasion, Gamaliel, one of their greatest lawyers, and of the chief council, "Take heed to yourselves, what ye intend to do as touching these men: let them alone: if this counsel or this work be of men, it will come to naught;

---

5. Acts, ch. ii. v. 14. ch. iv. v. 4.

but if it be of God, ye cannot overthrow it, lest haply ye be found even to fight against God; and to him they all agreed." This is not the language of men who knew the facts declared by the apostles to have been founded in falsehood and misrepresentation.

Add to this, the many instances of the apostles foretelling the state of the church, and the effect that the preaching of the Gospel would have on the hearts and conduct of men, down through the several ages of it to the present day; which by its precise fulfilment in every age, and being at this moment fulfilling before our eyes, and not in a small degree by the author of the Age of Reason himself; adds no inconsiderable weight of testimony, both internal and external, to the apostle's credibility, and the certainty of the facts related by them.

Under one branch of this fulfilment, a familiar and frequent instance, will give the completion of the rest. The apostles minutely detail the effects which the preaching of the Gospel, or rather the receiving of it, would have on the sentiments and tempers of men, by the effectual operation of the Spirit of God on their hearts. Examine the divine work, as exhibited in the lives and practices of many real converts to religion at this day. Behold the unhappy man, brought up in vanity and folly—his life a scene of drunkenness and debauchery—no consideration of character—parents—wife—children, or the most influential connections, can withdraw him from the infatuating habits of sinful pleasure. He is proof against every earthly consideration and argument.

Providentially he hears the Gospel in such a manner as to reach his heart. He is roused from his lethargy—alarmed at his awful situation, he implores the mercy of Heaven—he seeks—he strives—he knocks—he takes it as it were by a holy violence. His heart is renewed—his life is changed—he at once becomes a new man—he is sober and chaste—he is prudent and industrious—a useful citizen—a good father—an affectionate husband—a kind and benevolent friend. In short, he forsakes all his former follies, and becomes a valuable member of civil society. The simple doctrines of the risen Saviour, have miraculously wrought in him an effectual change, which all the powers and allurements of the world had failed to do; and that precisely in the way and manner, and with the minute circumstances foretold by Jesus Christ and his apostles, 1800 years ago. And, what is equally remarkable,these effects are produced on Jew and gentile—bond and free—European and American—the philosopher and the savage—all—all, when brought to the knowledge of the true God in Jesus Christ, speak the same language—produce the same fruits, and talk of the same happy effects, arising from the blood of a crucified Saviour. In this way alone, then, can our author's doctrine be true, that " the way of God is open to all men alike."

The following quotation, from an author of credit, will command respect— "In the beginning of the second century, the Christian church increased and flourished in a marvellous manner; and though it wanted all human help—though it had all the force and policy of the world bent against it, growing by opposition and oppression, and overbearing all the powers of earth and hell—whereunto then shall we liken the kingdom of God and its wonderful increase, or with what comparison shall we compare it? There is indeed some resemblance of it, in the increase of the seeds and leaven which our blessed Lord so often made use of to illustrate it; but there is nothing parallel to it in the history of all the religions, which have obtained among men, from the beginning of the world to this day—and, therefore, as this shows that the original was from Heaven, and that the hand of Omnipotence has all along guided and preserved it; so one would imagine, at this time of day, it would have prevented such absurd and ridiculous objections, founded in the ignorance and obstinacy of those, who are too indolent to inquire into its real merits. But our consolation is, that the wise and good receive from it a full assurance of hope, that the same Divine Providence will continue to protect and defend it, until we come to Mount Zion, and to the city of the living God—the heavenly Jerusalem—and to an innumerable company of angels—to the general assembly and church of the first born, whose names are written in Heaven—to God the judge of all—to Jesus the mediator of the new covenant, and to the spirits of just men made perfect." Even the famous Mr. Gibbon, whom no one will accuse of partiality to the Gospel, can testify, "that within fourscore years after the death of Christ, the humane Pliny laments the magnitude of the evil, which he vainly attempted to eradicate. In his curious epistle to the emperor Trajan, he affirms, that the temples were almost deserted—that the sacred victims scarcely found purchasers, and that the superstition, (meaning the Christian religion) had not only infected the cities, but had even spread itself into the villages, and the open country of Pontus and Bithynia."[6] Again, several Roman citizens were brought before the tribunal of Pliny; and he soon discovered, that a great number of persons of every order of men in Bithynia, had deserted the reli-

---

6. 2d Vol. Gibb. 374.

gion of their ancestors. His unsuspected testimony may in this instance obtain more credit, than the bold challenge of Tertullian, when he assures the proconsul of Africa, that if he persists in his cruel intentions, (of persecuting the Christians) he must decimate Carthage; and that he will find among the guilty, many persons of his own rank; senators and matrons of noblest extraction, and the friends and relations of his most intimate friends. And about forty years after, the emperor Valerian, in one of his rescripts, evidently supposes, that senators, knights, and ladies of quality, were engaged in the Christian sect."[7]

It is upon the foregoing plain narrative of facts, attended with this convincing testimony of the mighty power of God, that our author, pretending to the advantage of Reason and Common Sense, impiously and blasphemously asserts, that" The story (of the resurrection) so far as it relates to the supernatural part, has every mark of fraud and imposition stamped upon the face of it; and that the Christian mythologists, calling themselves the Christian church, have credited their fable, which for absurdity and extravagance, is not exceeded by any thing that is to be found in the mythology of the ancients."

This author, throughout his performance, seems to have taken leave of all pretensions to modesty and decorum, or he certainly would have paid some respect to the learning and wisdom of multitudes of Christian writers and professors, who have so long and so ably defended the Christian system, against the many attacks of more formidable, as well as more modest and decent adversaries, than our author; yet he ought to have credit for the following very extraordinary concessions, amidst all the puerile objections to the Gospel history—"That no one will deny or dispute the power of the Almighty, to make such a communication if he pleases:" and afterwards, "That such a person as Jesus Christ existed, and that he was crucified—that he preached most excellent morality, and the equality of man, and that he was a virtuous reformer and revolutionist."

Observations of this kind have added some weight to the arguments in favor of revelation. "Thus wisdom has not been denied the testimony even of enemies: a testimony of which indeed it did not stand in need: but which being extorted by the irresistible force of truth, may well be esteemed as a confirmation of its general evidence: since they, whose wish and whose interest was to deny it, yet were compelled, if not to receive it wholly, yet

---

7. 3d Vol. Gibb. 360

to acknowledge it in part; and thus like Pilate, they pronounced him righteous whom they condemned; and like Judas, confessed him innocent whom they betrayed."[8]

It is an extraordinary fact, that almost every modern infidel writer, is forced to acknowledge and bear testimony, to the virtuous character of our blessed Lord, and to the excellence of that morality which he taught, while they despise his doctrines, and treat all his pretensions to Deity, and his being the Son of God, as the effect of the most artful deception, and deliberate fraud. Thus their inconsistency with themselves, shows that it is the purity of his doctrines, and the holiness of his character, to which they are enemies, in contradiction to all their professions and practices. In addition to the example of our author, I will select one other, whose celebrity among unbelievers, is well established, and to whom our author may attend with more pleasure, than to a Christian writer. I mean the famous *Rousseau*. Hear then this champion of the enemies of Jesus Christ crucified, when instructing his pupil Emilius, and let his testimony have its due weight.

"I acknowledge to you," says Rousseau, "that the majesty of the scriptures astonishes me, and the sanctity of the Gospel fills me with rapture: look into the writings of the philosophers, with all their pomp and parade: how trivial they appear, when compared to this sacred volume. Is it possible that a book so simple, and yet so sublime, should be the work of man? Is it possible that he, whose history it contains, *should himself be a mere man?* Is the style that of an enthusiast, or of a sectary inflated with ambition? What sweetness, what purity in his morals? What force, what persuasion in his instructions? His maxims, how sublime! His discourses, how wise and profound! Such presence of mind, such beauty and precision in his answers! Such empire over his passions! Where is the man, or the philosopher, that knows how to act, to suffer and to die, without weakness or ostentation? Plato, in his picture of the imaginary just man, covered with all the opprobriousness of guilt, and worthy every reward of virtue, gives us an exact representation of Christ: so striking is the resemblance, that all the fathers saw it; and indeed there is no possibility of mistaking it. What prejudice, what blindness, to compare the offspring of Sophronisca, to the Son of Mary! how immense the difference between these two! Socrates dying without pain and without ignomity, found it easy to support his character to the very last; and if his life had not been honored by so gentle a death, we

8. White's Sermons, 4.

might have doubted whether Socrates, with all his understanding, was any thing more than a sophist. You will say he invented a system of moral philosophy: others had practised it before his time; he only related what they had performed, and drew lectures from their example. Aristides had been just before Socrates told us what justice was. Leonidas had sacrificed his life for his country, before Socrates had made the love of our country a duty. Sparta was sober, before Socrates commended sobriety Before he had given a definition of virtue, Greece abounded with virtuous men. But of whom did Christ borrow that sublime and pure morality, which *he, and he only,* taught both by word and example? From the centre of the most extravagant fanaticism, (meaning Judea) the highest Wisdom made itself heard, and the vilest of nations was honored with the simplicity of the most heroic virtues. The death of Socrates, philosophizing coolly with his friends, is the easiest that can be desired: that of Christ expiring in the midst of torments, abused, scorned, detested by a whole people, is the most dreadful that can be apprehended. Socrates taking the poisonous draught, returns thanks to the person, who, with tears in his eyes, presents it to him. Christ, in the midst of the most exquisite torture, prays for his bloody executioners. Yes, if Socrates lived and died like a philosopher, *Christ lived and died like a God.*

"Shall we say that the evangelic history was invented at pleasure? My friend, inventions are not made after that manner; and Socrates' history, of which no body entertains a doubt, is not so well attested as that of Christ. Upon the whole, it is removing the difficulty further back, without solving it; for it would be much harder to conceive, that a number of men should have joined together to fabricate this book, than that a single person should furnish out the subject to its authors.

"Jewish writers would never have fallen into that style, or that system of morality; and the gospel has such strong and such inimitable marks of truth, that the inventor would be more surprising than the hero. Yet notwithstanding all this, *this same Gospel abounds with things so incredible and so repugnant to reason, that it is impossible for any man of sense either to conceive or admit them.*"[9]

How literally is the Scripture fulfilled. "And he said, go and tell this people, hear ye indeed, but understand not; see ye indeed, but perceive not; make gross the heart of this people; make their ears dull, and close up their

---

9. 2d Vol. Emilius, 36. Lond. edit. 1763

eyes, lest they see with their eyes, and hear with their ears, and understand with their hearts, and be converted, and I should heal them."[10]

However absurd the conclusion of this famous writer, and the general conduct of the opposers of revelation may be, yet their concessions certainly yield the question, and give up the dispute. For if Jesus Christ was the person whom they describe, then he ought not to be suspected of deception and falsehood. What he said and taught concerning himself, and what he endeavoured to persuade others to, must have been consistent with truth, at least in his own ideas.

Most of his miracles were such objects of sense, that he could not have been deceived himself, by enthusiasm or other false principle. They all come within the first two rules, laid down by an excellent writer of the last century, relative to the proof of ancient facts, on which he justly challenges all the enemies to revelation, as to every other system but that of the bible, viz. First—"That the matters of fact shall be such, as the reality of them may be ascertained by external evidence." Second—"That they shall be performed publicly." Thirdly—"That not only public monuments shall be maintained in memory of them, but some external deeds should be performed." Fourthly—"That such monuments, deeds or observances, shall be instituted and commence from the period in which the matters of fact shall be transacted."[11]

Jesus Christ walked upon the waters—he healed the sick, openly and publicly, before all the people, by a word, and often at a distance—he raised the dead at his first approach to them—he cast out devils, and once permitted them to enter into a herd of 2000 swine, which were near at hand—he rebuked the winds and the waves, and they obeyed him—he fed multitudes with a few loaves and small fishes. He therefore could not mistake these events, or be deceived by an enthusiastic temper of mind; but the miracles he wrought, and the predictions he declared, must have been honestly intended as evidences, conclusive evidences, of his divine mission, and for the good of mankind; the truth of which he sealed with his blood, premeditatedly and deliberately, with his own foreknowledge, having frequently forewarned his disciples, and declared to his enemies, that such would be the issue of his ministry.

Yet, notwithstanding these concessions of our author, and the express declarations of our divine Redeemer, during his mission on earth, and which are recognized by the chief priest in his request to Pilate, for a guard

---

10. Isaiah, ch vi. v. 9.
11. Lesslie.

of soldiers; the author of the Age of Reason, with no inconsiderable degree of self-importance, adds, "The resurrection of a dead person, and his ascension through the air, is a thing very different as to the evidence it admits of, to the invisible conception of a child in the womb. The resurrection and ascension, supposing them to have taken place, admitted of public and ocular demonstration, like that of the ascension of a baloon, or the sun at noonday, to all Jerusalem at least."

After attending carefully to the facts relative to these extraordinary and supernatural events, can the observations of our author be rendered consistent with common candour, or the necessary love of truth in a writer, who presumes to set himself up as a corrector of religious systems? Did not the public declaration of Jesus Christ, foretelling his death and resurrection; did not the earth quake at his crucifixion; the preternatural darkness—the rending of the rocks, (to be seen at this day)—and that of the veil of the temple—the rolling away of the stone from the sepulchre, in presence of an armed band of soldiers; and his appearance first to the women and his disciples—then to five hundred brethren at once, with the after descent of the Holy Spirit, agreeably to his predictions while living; and the public attestation of the whole transaction by the miraculous gift of tongues—did not all these afford evident and sensible demonstration of the truth of the resurrection? Add to this, that these facts were immediately declared, as the facts on which the advocates of a crucified Jesus depended, as full proof of their doctrines. They were then capable of immediate contradiction and refutation, had they not been known to be true, which the amazing progress of the Gospel in Jerusalem itself, the theatre of all these transactions, within one month of the events taking place, fully confirms.

Did not then all this give, with double evidence, demonstration equal to that required by this incredulous author, not only to all Jerusalem, but to the surrounding nations before mentioned? Was not the supernatural evidence of the gift of tongues, being continued to the apostles during their lives, a standing demonstration of the truth of the important facts they promulgated? Was not the demonstration such as to induce these strangers to say to each other, "Are not all these which speak, Gallileans, and yet hear we every man in his own tongue wherein he was born, the wonderful works of God." And what rendered this testimony to the resurrection of Jesus Christ, even superior to that of a balloon rising in the air, and must convict our author of acting contrary to every rational principle, is, that the apostles not only were thus endued with the gift of tongues, and of working miracles themselves, but actually communicated the power to others, in all the churches of their planting.[12]

What greater evidence could have been desired? Is not this evidence sufficient to convince every man, of a truly humble and teachable temper of mind? And if so, who art thou, O child of the dust, that darest to prescribe degrees or forms of testimony to thy Maker? Does thy belief add any thing to the happiness of him who made thee? Or does thy unbelief render him less supremely blessed? Put thy hand on thy mouth, and thy mouth in the deepest dust, and cry with tears of penitential contrition, guilty—guilty, before the Lord thy Creator!

Would our author have had the Saviour of the world to have remained on earth to this day, for the purpose of convincing him of the truth, and thus saving him against his will? For although Christ had appeared after his resurrection to every man in Jerusalem, nay even to all the then world, on the principle advanced in the Age of Reason, our author would not have been obliged to believe, because he himself had not seen him. But, if the divine Saviour should even now appear to him, as he did to another unbelieving Thomas, and show him his hands and his sides, I have as great doubts of his assent to the truths of the Gospel, as the disciples had of the Jews, who refused equal evidence, afforded them in infinite mercy by the benevolent Jesus, before they proceeded to the last awful act of deliberate iniquity, by which they voluntarily entailed the vengeance of Heaven on them and on their children. Both had the same reason for resisting the Gospel, because their deeds were evil. There is indeed one solemn difference between them—our author is an apostate from the truth, and that after having attempted to preach this very Gospel to others, as the glad tidings of Salvation. This the Jews have not in the black catalogue of their sins.[13] Did not the divine Redeemer, in the beginning of his mission, yield such sensible demonstration of his Almighty power, as wrought conviction in devils and evil spirits? His first miracle was at a public marriage feast, where he turned water into wine. Before his incomparable sermon on the Mount, he healed great numbers of all manner of diseases, in presence of multitudes. When he entered into a city or village, how did the people at large flock to him "with their sick and diseased, laying them in

---

12. Vide 1st Romans 11; 2 Corinthians 12:13, Galatians 3:2, 5; 1 Corinthians 12 and 14..

13. It is said in the life of Thomas Paine, that he once professed to be a Methodist preacher.

the streets, beseeching him, if they might but touch the borders of his garment, and as many as touched him were made whole." The widow's son was raised to life in the presence of multitudes attending him to the grave, when Christ accidentally met them; and Lazarus, after being buried four days, was resuscitated before many of the Jews, who went with his sisters to the sepulchre; this was well known to the whole body of Jews, and for which their council was desirous of punishing Lazarus with death. Jesus raised the ruler's daughter to life, before a number of people playing on minstrels and making a noise, as was common in that country at the death of people of note. These people had very much the temper of our author; for upon Christ's assuring them of her life, they laughed him to scorn. It was very common for the people at large, of all characters and ranks, to bring their lame, their blind, their dumb, deaf and maimed, and cast them openly and publicly in presence of all the people, at Jesus's feet, and he healed them *before them*. He cast out an impure spirit in the midst of the congregation of the Jews. At one time they brought to him a man sick of the palsy, lying on a bed, to whom Jesus, with divine authority, said, "Son, be of good cheer, thy sins be forgiven thee."

This not being an object of sense, so as to be ascertained by external evidence, the scribes who were present charged him with blasphemy: the benevolent Jesus, to leave them without excuse as to his divine power, and to establish a fact not an object of sense, by one that was capable of the testimony of their senses, said to the sick man, "Arise, take up thy bed, and go into thine house." This the man immediately did; and the multitude convinced by so extraordinary a fact *done in their presence*, "marvelled and glorified God." After this, will any one wonder at the success of the Gospel, under the preaching of the apostles, among a people thus informed of the facts on which their doctrines were founded? At another time Jesus healed another paralytic, and commanded him to walk, in *presence of the pharisees and doctors of the law*, the most bitter of his enemies; as he did a dumb man, possessed of an evil spirit, *before the scribes and pharisees*. When he healed the woman of her issue of blood, the multitude pressed greatly upon him. Did he not feed five thousand at one time, and four thousand at another, besides women and children, in a miraculous manner? A great number were present, when he restored sight to the two blind men near Jericho. It is a remarkable confirmation of the Almighty power of the blessed Jesus, that in no one instance, among the thousands that were brought to him, did he ever fail in accomplishing the cure.

To prevent all suspicion of a combination between him and the diseased, did he not permit the devils to go into the herd of 2000 swine, by which they all ran into the sea, and were destroyed? By this he gave as full and notorious evidence of his absolute power over those infernal spirits, as any one could have, "of the ascension of a balloon, or of the sun at noon-day." Was not this testimony complete, and conclusive to all the inhabitants of that region, especially to those who were present and those who owned the swine? and yet there is no reason to believe, that they became converts to the religion of the meek and humble Jesus, but rather that their opposition to him was increased; for they "besought Jesus to depart from them." Was not this whole territory instructed by this visible operation of divine power over the spirits of darkness and the rulers of the wickedness of this world, whose real existence and subjection to the divine government, were thus undeniably taught in the most convincing manner; and yet by so plain and public a miracle, were those, whom we may call type of our author, wrought upon to believe?—No, as we before have observed, they besought the Saviour of mankind," to depart from them;" and, as a just judgment for their unbelief, "he went into the ship, and returned back again."

An objection might have been raised by infidels, that the diseased were employed to carry on an imposture; but with the swine, all objections of this kind are obviated.

Even after the Jews had determined to put the innocent Jesus to death, did he not heal the lame and the blind in the temple, before the scribes and pharisees, his greatest enemies? At the crucifixion, was there not darkness over the whole land for three hours, as we have before observed, when the rocks were rent, and when the veil of the temple was rent in twain from top to bottom.

What greater evidence of Almighty power, could even the sceptical mind of our author require, than these repeated acts of Omnipotence? And yet did the chief priests, scribes and pharisees, believe on him? Or did they, for these very acts, crucify the Lord of Glory? Could all these benevolent acts of mercy, and instances of unlimited power, have been exceeded in weight of evidence, by the public appearance of Christ himself in the Sanhedrin, after his resurrection? Would not the same persons, who refused to believe his miracles and his heavenly doctrines before his death, and who, being unable to deny them because of their publicity, attributed them to the power of Baalzebub, the prince of devils? Would they not, on such an appearance after his resurrection, as some unbelievers have since, have alledged that this appearance was that of a phantom, and not a reality? Did not his apostles publish these important facts, and charge the Jewish government with their unbelief and the crime of murder, immediately in their presence, and before all the people, who were witnesses to many of these facts? These the rulers did not attempt to deny, but charged the benevolent author with being possessed by an evil spirit? Pharaoh hardened his heart more and more, as the demonstration of the Almighty power under which Moses acted, increased to his view; so did the Jews; and so I suspect our author, with most of his brethren in unbelief of the present day, would do again, under the like circumstances.

I have not forgotten that our author asserts, "That it is impossible for us now to know, who were the authors of these historical facts; or that the books in which the accounts are related, were written by the persons whose names they bear," What then? Does the want of the knowledge of the author of a history, render the facts reported doubtful, if supported by good authority ? The conclusion is false; but we deny the premises from which it is drawn. The authors are as well known, and better vouched, than the writers of the books called Cicero's Orations, or Caesar's Commentaries.[14] Even our author himself, undertakes to give the character of Jesus Christ—an account of his life, death, and doctrines; yet it is impossible for him to have any other source of the knowledge of these facts, but the sacred writings, which he declares "have every mark of fraud and imposition."

As well might he deny the existence of such a place as Rome, because he had never seen it. He acknowledges the possibility of the whole system of Revelation, if it had pleased the Almighty to give it; yet rejects the evidence of his having given it, because it was not given to him. "Divine communications, miracles and prophecies, are agreeable to natural religion, and even seem necessary in the infancy of the world. Since God is a being of infinite justice, mercy and bounty, according to natural religion, it is reasonable to expect, that if the deficiencies of natural religion, or the inattention of mankind to the footsteps of his providence, were such at any time, as that the world was in danger of being lost in ignorance, irreligion and idolatry, God should interpose by extraordinary instructions, by alarming instances of

---

14. Shall we say, that the evangelic history was invented at pleasure? My friend, inventions are not made after that manner; and Socrates' history, of which no body entertains a doubt, is not so well attested as that of Christ. Jewish writers would have never fallen into that style, or that system of morality; and the Gospel has such strong and such inimitable marks of truth, that the inventor would be more surprizing than the hero. Rosseau's Emilius, vol. ii. 86.

judgment and mercy, and by prophetic declarations of things to come, in order to teach men his power, his justice and his goodness, by sensible proofs and manifestations. We must not say here, that God could not suffer this, but inquire from history, whether he has or not."[15]

Vain and arrogant mortal! examine every part of thine own life, and unbeliever as thou professedst thyself to be, behold how thine existence from day to day, depends on thy living by faith, even in thy frail fellow-men. Arguments, such as have been mentioned, are too shallow and contrary to every man's experience, to be admitted in things of such real importance.

Our author must have been very ignorant, even of the English writers on this subject, or he would have attempted to show, that their elaborate reasonings and researches, were mistaken or inconclusive.

Is it possible that he could have published such a parade of declamation against the writers of the sacred history, and so solemnly denied the authenticity of the books of the Old and NewTestament, had he read the learned and laborious investigation, of the candid and instructive Lardner, in his credibility of the Gospel history; as well as a number of other learned writers in the English language, who have so accurately traced up the sacred writings to their original authors, with incomparable clearness and certainty. The investigations of these learned critics, cast more light on and give greater evidence of the truth of these books, and their undoubted authenticity, than can be had of any other writings of antiquity.[16] Even the unbelieving Thomas, and the persecuting Saul, are among the proselytes to the truth, and propagators of these doctrines; for the confirmation of which, they also work miracles, and perform the most wondrous acts, in which they themselves could not have been deceived; and all this under the certain expectation of suffering the most fearful and cruel deaths on account of these doctrines, which finally took place.

It is acknowledged, that these doctrines contain the purest morality ; and they universally profess the utmost detestation of falsehood, even though it should be the means of saving life.

---

15. Hartley on Man.

16. The miracles of Christ were publicly appealed to by his apostles, a few days after his ascension—they are transmitted down to us by eye-witnesses and contemporary writers, in well authenticated books, and they are supported by the most credible testimony; that of a number of plain honest men, who sacrificed all worldly advantages, and life itself, in attestation of what they advanced And we are to consider in these witnesses, their competency to judge of the facts—their integrity and benevolence to mankind—not their learning, station, or opulence.—Newcomb, 320

After the fatal end of others, and with their cruel sufferings in full view, under the deep impression of sharing the same fate, we find members of the Jewish Sanhedrin, scribes, and pharisees, giving up all the temptations of the present life; and after them, senators, counsellors, princes, and other great men among all nations, enlisting into the service of a crucified, but risen Master; and that, while the evidence was fresh in every man's mind, and proofs were at hand to be resorted to, had facts been asserted contrary to the truth.

Thus we find, from the labours of twelve poor, illiterate, despised fishermen, the Gospel, contrary to all human expectations and conclusions, but agreeably to the positive predictions of Christ and his apostles, in their lowest state of humiliation, spreading itself from Judea as a centre, throughout the habitable world, from Britain to the farthest India.

"The reception which Christ, his fore-runners, and followers, with their doctrines, have met with in all ages, is an argument for the truth and genuineness of the Scriptures. This evidence does, as it were, embrace all the others, and gives a particular force to them; for it will be a strong confirmation of all the evidences for the Jewish and Christian religion, if we can show that the persons to whom they have been offered, have been influenced by them as much as there was reason to expect, admitting them to be true, and far more than could be expected, on supposition they were false. The most illustrious instance of this, is the victory which the Christian miracles and doctrines, with the sufferings of our Saviour and his followers, gained over the whole powers, first of the Jewish state, and then of the Roman empire, in the primitive times; for here all ranks and kinds of men, princes, priests; Jewish and heathen philosophers; the populace, with all their associated prejudices from custom and education; with all their corrupt passions and lusts; with all external advantages of learning; power, riches, honor, and in short with every thing but truth, endeavoured to suppress the progress that Christ's religion made every day in the world, but were unable to do it. Yet still the evidence was but of a limited nature; it required to be set forth, attested and explained by the preacher; and to be attended to, and reflected upon, with some degree of impartiality by the hearer; and therefore, though the progress of it was quick, and the effect general, yet they were not instantaneous and universal. However, it is very evident, that any fraud or false pretence, must soon have yielded to so great an opposition, so circumstanced."[17]

---

17. Hartley on Man.

Every profession of Christians, must indeed acknowledge, that the whole stress of the Christian cause, rests on the truth of our Lord's resurrection; and that therefore, all proper methods of convincing the world, was necessary upon the occasion. "These were certainly used," (says an eminent writer) "by the good providence of God, without our Lord's appearing to his mortal enemies, the rulers of the Jews. But allowing it had been consistent for him to have done so, yet the unbelieving Jews, especially the chief priests and rulers, were of all men the most unworthy to have had an extraordinary mode of conviction afforded them.

They had already despised the evidence that had been given them; and not only so, but maliciously imputed the plainest miracles that ever were wrought, to the power and operation of the devil. They also attributed one of the greatest of miracles, which he wrought in his life time, the raising of Lazarus from the dead, after he had lain in the tomb four days, to an evil power, and for which they threatened to put him to death."

It is true, that our author endeavours to justify his unbelief, by saying more than once, "that he is not obliged to believe a revelation, on the report of another; and, as Thomas would not believe without actual and sensible demonstration, neither will he."

The Christian system forces no man's will. The consequence then is plain—it is positive—it is unavoidable in any other way. If the Gospel is true, *"He that believeth, shall be saved; but be that believeth not, shall be damned."* These are the words of the judge of the quick and the dead. Our author has made the awful choice. His eternal state depends on the certainty of this revelation, which he will not believe on the report of others, however well vouched.

"If men will believe upon reasonable motives, they have sufficient means of Salvation allowed them; but if they will not believe without an immediate personal revelation, they are never like to have that in this world; but in the next, God will reveal himself with terror and vengeance upon all the workers of iniquity. God doth, both by nature and revelation, provide for the necessities, the welfare and happiness, but never for the humours and peevishness of men: and those who will not be saved but according to some new way and method of their own, must be miserable without remedy.

But if God should vouchsafe to make some immediate revelation of himself to these insolent offenders and blasphemers of his name and authority, how can we be assured that they would be converted? Would they not rather find out some pretence to persuade themselves that it was no real revelation, but the effect of natural agents, or of melancholy, or of a disturbed imagination? For those who have so long, not only rejected (that were a modest thing) but derided and reviled Moses and the prophets, nay the apostles and our Saviour himself, would not believe, though one should arise from the dead."[18]

This extraordinary principle of conduct in a rational creature, with regard to things of eternal consequence, and to whom life and immortality are offered by one, who claims a right to affix his own terms, is not peculiar to the infidelity of our author. Neither is it the first time that this resolution has led its votaries to destruction; although they have acknowledged that the doctrines they are required to believe, contain the purest and most benevolent morality. One at first sight would imagine that the sporters of this sentiment, thought, that by their belief, the teachers of our holy religion, were to be personally gainers; and that the teachers were as ambassadors for Christ, beseeching them to be reconciled to God, on account of some private benefit or emolument to themselves; and that the inestimable boon, was to be conferred on the teacher instead of the pupil.

Alas! let me ask this profound philosopher with all his boasted reason, who is to be the sufferer in consequence of his resolute determination, not to believe any revelation from God, on the well attested report of others, and not, unless it is made to him personally—and what is that revelation, which he is determined to reject with so much obstinacy? Take his own words for an answer, which I again repeat, "a morality of the most benevolent kind, ever taught to man and never exceeded by any."

Can our author give any rational assurance, that even if God should thus condescend, it would work conviction in his sceptical mind and produce a firm belief in the doctrines of the Gospel. For my own part I must confess, that from his present temper and disposition and judging from the conduct of his predecessors in unbelief, in the time of our Lord and his apostles, I am fully convinced, he would not, and that the same obstinate mind would raise equal objections from other quarters to avoid conviction. An additional reason to those already mentioned for this conclusion is, that although our author has agreed, that Jesus Christ was "a virtuous character and preached the purest and most benevolent morality," yet let me ask, has he conformed himself in his life and conduct to the moral precepts and excellent practices of Jesus Christ, which he thus gives credit to, as pure,

18. Reasonab. of Christianity, vol. i. 18.

amiable and benevolent. If he has not, which I believe, from my personal knowledge of the man, he will not even pretend to, I must in my turn indulge a principle of unbelief, that he would even submit to a revelation from God, made personally to him, if it did not fall in with his carnal ideas and worldly expectations, unless it should also be attended with the convicting influences of the spirit of God, to whom all things are possible.

Far be it from me to indulge an uncharitable temper towards any man, however we may differ in opinion; but I consider myself founded in this conclusion by the experience of ages, and particularly by the conduct of many persons, under similar circumstances, recorded in sacred history for our instruction. Did not Nebuchadnezzar receive ocular demonstration, *"equal to the ascending of a Balloon, or the sun at noon-day"* when he cast Shadraeh, Meshach and Abednego into a fiery furnace? *when* beholding the contempt which was put on all the effects of his rage and fury by the living God, *he was* constrained to cry out "blessed be the God of Shadrach, Meshach and Abednego, who hath sent his angel and delivered his servants that put their trust in him; and hath changed the king's commandment and yielded their bodies rather than they would serve or worship any God save their own God; therefore I make a decree, that every people, nation and language which shall speak any thing amiss against the God of Shadrach, Meshach and Abednego, shall be drawn in pieces and their houses made a dunghill: because there is no other God that can deliver after this sort."—And yet notwithstanding this extraordinary and supernatural demonstration of the power of the God of Shedrach, Meshach and Abednego, was not the prophet afterwards sent to Nebuchadnezzar, with this kind exhortation, "to break off his sins by righteousness and his iniquities by shewing mercy to the poor?" What was the consequence? Did he not despise all these convictions arising from the long suffering goodness of God and still boast "of his power and the honor of his majesty," despising the judgments and warning of heaven, till "being driven from among men to dwell with the beasts of the field, and to eat grass, as oxen, and become wet with the dew of Heaven till seven years should pass over him;" and till by this heavy indignation of the wrath of God, he became humbled by the bitterness of contrition and repentance? and was led to declare, "now (after all I have justly suffered) I Nebuchadnezzar praise and extol and honor the king of Heaven, all whose works are truth and his ways judgment, and those that walk in pride he is able to abase."

Thus was Nebuchadnezzar brought to reason and to act like a rational creature: and it affords a very useful lesson to our author, if he will but hearken to the divine teachings of the spirit of God therein. But it may turn out with him as it did with Nebuchadnezzar's successor, who disregarded all this ocular demonstration to all Babylon, and the thousand kingdoms of Nebuchadnezzar for seven years.—Hearken for a moment to the language of Daniel to Nebuchadnezzar's grandson Belshazzar, an abandoned prince. "O king! hear thou! the most high God gave unto Nebuchadnezzar thy father, a kingdom, and majesty, and honor, and glory: and for the majesty that he gave him, all people, nations and languages, trembled and feared before him: whom he would he slew, and whom he would he kept alive; and whom he would he set up, and whom he would he put down; but when his heart was lifted up, and his mind hardened in pride, he was deposed from his kingly throne, and they took his glory from him: and he was driven from the sons of men; and his heart was made like the beasts, and his dwelling was with the wild asses; they fed him with grass like oxen, and his body was wet with the dew of Heaven, till he knew that the most high God ruled in the kingdom of men, and that he appointeth over it whomsoever he will. And thou his son, O Belshazzar, hast not humbled thine heart, *though thou knewest all this*, but hast lifted up thyself against the Lord of Heaven; and they have brought the vessels of his house before thee; and thou and thy lords; thy wives and thy concubines, have drank wine in them; and thou hast praised the Gods of silver and gold, of brass, iron, wood and stone, which see not, nor hear, nor know; and the God in whose hand thy breath is, and whose are all thy ways, hast thou not glorified."[19]

Happy will it be for our author, if the severest judgment of God, even to eating grass like an ox, should be inflicted upon him; provided it should be so sanctified, as to prevent the last awful sentence, "Thou art weighed in the balance, and art found wanting." Alas! every day's experience proves the fact, "that for spiritual truth, there must be a spiritual sense; and the scriptures call this sense, by the name of *Faith*; and teach that all men have it not; and that where it is, it is the gift of God."[20]

If a gracious God, in his infinite mercy, for the sake of what his only beloved Son has done and suffered, thinks proper to place offending man in a state to be saved, by making known to him his will, and the terms of access to him, by which he shall finally attain to everlasting life; and this revelation

---

19. 5th chap. Dan. 18th to 23d ver.
20. Jones.

is made through the medium of chosen witnesses, who have laid down their lives in support of their mission; and they offer rational proof of these facts, such as is more than sufficient to convince the mind in any human inquiry: and yet if one, who is to be solely benefitted by these offers, obstinately and perversely refuses his assent, and insists on greater or different testimony, before he will accept the terms of grace and mercy; ought he not as a rational being, to consider seriously, before it is too late, what is most likely to be the issue of this unreasonable conduct? Is not the final destruction of such a person sure and irretrievable? Art thou stronger than the Almighty; or is there any appeal from his righteous judgment ? Can a plea of the want of further or different evidence, excuse in the day when thou shalt appear before his awful tribunal, to render a reason why thou hast not believed on his only begotten Son, whom he hath sent into the world, with such proofs of his divine mission, as he has thought proper as a sovereign God to give, and which it became every sinner, who was earnestly seeking after truth, to have received with gratitude and thankfulness.

Go on, Sir, in your determination, with unbelieving Thomas of old, that you will not believe till you receive conviction in your own way; but be not deceived into the expectation of Thomas's gratification, as you stand in a very different predicament; but fear greatly, lest all conviction be withheld, till everlasting destruction shall work it in you, to your eternal shame and reproach.[21]

In fine, "there can be no acquiescence in authority, by assenting to a proposition, whose truth we perceive from the reason of the thing—To such a proposition we should assent, though it were affirmed by the most fallible man; nay, though he was not a man of truth; and consequently in the case of religion, it would be no manner of proof, that we acknowledged the supreme authority and infallible veracity of God. This acknowledgment can only appear, by our assenting to a proposition made to us by God, whose truth we do not perceive by any evidence from the nature of the thing; for then we act upon the simple authority of God's affirmation; and our assent is an explicit acknowledgment of his absolute veracity."

---

21. "There is a degree of evidence and of influence, to which we are not entitled. When a person acts against conviction, and turns from the light, God does not always leave him in that state of twilight, but adds to his blindness, and brings on a tenfold darkness. When people pervert their best gifts, they will be farther corrupted to their ruin; and those who are guilty of wilful and obstinate folly, will be doomed to judicial infatuation. Bryant Obs. 379.

This short abstract of the resurrection and ascension of our divine Redeemer, as recorded by the evangelists, and the observations that have naturally arisen out of the subject, are fully sufficient to satisfy any candid mind, of the imposition, in point of facts, of our author's statement and inferences from the Christian theory, and the principal event on which it is acknowledged to rest; and which, if the imposition has any effect, involves the everlasting interests of those who are thus deceived.

And now may we not, with great propriety, retort on our author his own unguarded language, "that his observations have every mark of fraud and imposition stamped on the face of them;" and may add, that they are apparently designed to mislead the young and unwary mind, into the fatal vortex of scepticism and infidelity.

Had my plan and leisure permitted, it might here have been shown, how fit and proper this glorious scheme of Salvation, founded on the resurrection and ascension of Jesus Christ, was to the distressing necessities of the ruined posterity of Adam. Nay we might have gone farther, and proceeded to explain the advantages of it, not to our race alone, but to all the inhabitants of the spiritual world—that such is the infinite and incomprehensible nature of the great, supreme, self-existent Jehovah—the Being who necessarily is—that finite beings, however exalted in their nature or rank, cannot bear to contemplate the ineffable and unveiled glory of the divine essence, but through some medium, by or in which, they might behold the divine image, in a manner consistent with their finite natures. That this was done from the beginning, through or by the eternal Logos, or divine Word, under a visible form, in which he mediately governs and directs the whole system of created intelligences, agreeably to the rules of eternal order.

That angels and men having sinned, and thus introduced a principle of disobedience into the creation of God, which must have proved of the most dangerous consequence to the whole extent of being; God of his infinite love and mercy, to prevent the awful catastrophe, determined to show to all worlds, his infinite disapprobation and abhorrence of sin.

It might well be expected indeed, that our author, with his incredulous temper, would have laughed at this doctrine of original sin, and the defection of angels; but on his own system, let him otherwise account in a rational manner, for the universal prevalence of evil, both in the moral and natural world—the sufferings of infants, with those of the best of men—the fury of animals and their devouring each other—the disregard and inattention in men to the great First Cause; and the blasphemies of those who presumptuously deny the existence of any God but nature.

Speaking with the humility and reverence which becomes such imperfect creatures in pronouncing on the inscrutable operations of God, we have reason to believe, that the disapprobation and abhorrence which the Supreme Governor of the universe must necessarily entertain for all sin, could not have been shown with conviction to the celestial ranks of angels and archangels, and the whole universe of intelligent beings, so well in any other way, as by the incarnation, death and resurrection of the Logos, or only begotten Son of God. The divine nature cannot be capable of anger, wrath or vengeance, which are predicable of it, merely in a metaphorical sense, to adapt language to the finite capacities of mortal man, and therefore the effects of this unnatural breach of order, or disobedience to the righteous law of a holy God, were manifested in the most striking and expressive manner, by the humiliation and sufferings of the sacred humanity of the Son of God, as a voluntary substitute for the offending creature. This, though apparent to man, only in their external infliction, were well known to the whole intelligent world of spirits, in his inward derelictions and desolations when forsaken on the cross, and which are well calculated to affect their pure minds to all eternity.

The suffering Messiah known to the whole angelic host, as lying in the father's bosom from eternity, and as the great object of their love and adoration from their first existence; and who alone was capable of knowing and contemplating the Divinity in his pure essence, and who had seen the Father, being the express image of his person, and who thought it no robbery to claim an equality with God:—this glorious being, becoming an expiatory sacrifice and propitiatory victim for the sins of the world, magnified the law of God; demonstrated his infinite justice and love to being in general, and made it known to the universe, when he declared, "That God so loved the world, as to give his only begotten Son, that whosoever should believe in him should not perish, but have everlasting life." All this fully proved the infinite wisdom of the amazing plan, designed to subdue all things to, and keep them in the love of order and obedience, discovering to men and angels "the exceeding sinfulness of sin," and the awful consequences of it, ever when the sacred humanity of the eternal Son of God was to be the victim, as a substitute for the aggressor.

We might have shown further, that as far as we can see, if it had not been for this divine scheme of redemption, the sinless inhabitants of the numberless worlds of spirits, would not have been made acquainted with the horrible nature of transgression, or have been so well confirmed in an universal, invariable and absolute principle of obedience. Thus it was, "that Mercy and Truth met together, and that Righteousness and Peace have kissed each other." "The astonishing scene, probably, remains still deeply imprinted upon the minds of celestial spirits, and may to all eternity be an everlasting proof of the wisdom and sanctity; the justice and goodness of God."

It might have been added, that no sooner had the awful scene of man's defection taken place, and the dark cloud of destruction overwhelmed our guilty parents, than the love of God, "who delighteth not in the death of the sinner, but would rather that he should repent and live," made known this only possible mode of restoration to his favor; and perpetuated the blessed revelation, "by typical observances wherein men should kill a kid, a lamb, a dove, or an unspotted male, the first born of some animal, as an emblem of the innocent, suffering Messiah—this repeated afterwards every year on a solemn day—once every month on the first day—once every week on the seventh day—and twice every day, morning and evening, became a living memorial, and emblematic record of this supernatural divine mystery."[22]

But alas! this would have been a dry subject, and unintelligible language, illy suited to the taste or comprehension of our author, however his urgent necessities might require the inestimable knowledge of these glorious truths.

Let us, therefore, return to our answer, and again take notice of an objection of our author, which has been already mentioned, but which is deserving of a more particular attention.

---

22. Philoioph. Prill.

9

Authenticity of the Books of the New Testament

After acknowledging the character of Jesus Christ, as already stated,
our author thinks to strengthen his opposition to our holy religion, and
to gain credit to his infidelity, among those, who are not in the habit of
inquiring with accuracy for themselves, by assuring the world, "That it
is impossible now, to know who were the authors of this story of the res-
urrection and ascension; as it is to be assured, that the books in which it
is related, were written by the persons whose names they bear. The best
surviving evidence is the Jews, and yet they say it is not true."

OUR author thus discovers once more, either an extreme ignorance of
what the advocates for Christianity have written on this subject; or a
determination to pass upon his unlearned readers, assertions which he
knows to be unfounded in truth.

It must again be repeated, that most of the books of the New Testament,
and particularly the four evangelists, are better vouched, and have greater
evidence of their authenticity, than any ancient profane history. The writers
of Caesar's Commentaries, Cicero's Orations, the Aeneid, or the Iliad, are
not so well ascertained and authenticated as those of the Gospels, the acts
of the apostles, and of divers other books of the New Testament.

They have been verified by the church, and its learned advocates, from
the times of the apostles to the present day, with as much accuracy and precision as the nature of the thing, and the circumstances of the times, would
admit of. "The absurdity of atheism has been exposed; and the atheist driv-
en from the field he had the presumption to call his own, even by the very
weapons which he chose for his defence. Deism in all its forms, has been
examined and detected; all its illiberal cavils have been replied to; all its

haughty pretensions confounded; and even the pertinent and momentous objections, to which the best informed and best disposed of its advocates, sometimes had recourse, have been weighed with impartiality, and refuted by argument. Those tenets, which rash and superficial inquirers had supposed to be destitute of foundation, have been expressed with greater precision, supported by stronger proofs, and recommended by new illustrations. Objections, which from their minuteness, might otherwise have been neglected, have now received the most satisfactory answers; and doubts, which from their obscurity, and from the modesty of those in whose minds they arose, might have remained unresolved, have been openly examined and fairly removed. In short, every part of the great fabric of religion, has received some distinct support or illustration, which has added to the strength and beauty of the whole system."[1] Thus where iniquity has most abounded, grace has abounded also.

The excellent Dr. Lardner, to whom I am so much indebted, has with incredible labor, and the soundest judgment, given such a complete and candid statement of the evidence on this subject, as to amount to demonstration. To his invaluable work on the credibility of the Gospel history, for the purpose of shortening these observations, I refer every serious inquirer after truth. He justly observes, that from the quotations of Iraeneus, Clemens Alexandrinus, Tertullian, and other writers of the second century; of Origen in the third, and Eusebius in the fourth, it appears, that the greater part of the books which are now received by us, and are called canonical, were universally acknowledged in their times, and had been so, by the elders and churches of former times—and the rest now received by us, though they were then doubted of or contradicted, were well known and approved by many."[2]

It is to be suspected, I acknowledge, that our author has never been concerned in looking into the evidence on which the theory of the Christian church is founded, whatever he may have done with regard to the heathen mythology. To those who know him as well as I do, it will

---

1. White's Serm. 15—16.

2. The epistle to the Hebrews, the second epistle of Peter, the second and third of John, those of James and Jude, and the book of the Revelations, being published a considerable time after the greater part of the other portions of the New Testament had been written and received as authentic histories, and inspired oracles by all the churches, were not all at once embraced throughout the whole extensive body of Christians. In tome places, therefore, they were at first received with doubt, till their evidence, and the circumstances of their publication, were thoroughly examined, since which time they have become universally adopted.

arise to more than suspicion. If it had been otherwise, he would hardly thus have forfeited the celebrity he has obtained as a man of reading and observation, by betraying to the world that he had gained it, by superficial harangues on popular topics, that required little more than the suggestions of a knot of friends, who might easily supply his indolence and inattention, for purposes they esteemed of great public importance: or perhaps with great truth it may be said, that he has contented himself with barely copying from the Royal Infidel of Prussia, the apostate of Fernay, or the more modern Boulanger; all of whom have done the same from Bolingbroke, Morgan and Tindal, of the last century, whose objections to revelation were the repetitions of many who had gone before them.

The assertion then of our author, is like a bow shot at a venture. He may plead that he knew no better; but this is a poor excuse for misleading his readers, who might depend on his character as an author; and shows a very daring spirit, that will measure the truth by his own weak and uninformed standard.

For the information then of those who doubt of this important matter, among whom our author may properly be included, I will venture to collect a very short abstract of the testimony on which we found our belief.

The difficulties attending the investigation of very ancient books, as to their authors and authenticity, might well excuse a research further than the times of those historians, who have treated the subject as a system; which generally does not happen till many years after the original transactions have taken place: and even then the general reputation among people of information and character, and the tradition of the times, in most cases are taken for the best evidence of which the nature of the thing is capable. But as the present dispute is of the utmost importance to the souls of men, I shall ascend to the highest source from whence the necessary proof proceeds.

The Bible is a word which has been in general use, among Christians, as including those writings which are held as of divine authority. That part of it called the New Testament, or the Gospels, which gives us the history of the life and death of Jesus Christ, and teaches the doctrine of Salvation as delivered by him and his disciples, consists of the four evangelists, the acts of the apostles, the epistles, and the revelation to St. John.

It is a collection of books written by the several persons, whose names they bear, as is asserted by Christians in general, but denied by our adventurous author, even in the eighteenth century.

In addition to the proof, we shall presently adduce, "the excellence of the doctrines contained in the scriptures, is an evidence of their divine authority. This is an argument which has great force, independent of other considerations. Thus let us suppose, that the author of the Gospel that goes under St. Matthew's name, was not known, and that it was unsupported by the writers of the primitive times; yet such is the unaffected simplicity of the narrations, the purity of the doctrines, the sincere piety and goodness of the sentiments, that it carries its own authority with it. And the same thing may be said in general of all the books of the Old and New Testament; so that it seems evident, that if there were no other book in the world besides the Bible, a man could not reasonably doubt of the truth of revealed religion—"the mouth speaks from the abundance of the heart." Men's writings and discourses must receive a tincture from their real thoughts and designs; It is impossible to play the hypocrite in every word and expression. This is a matter of daily observation, that cannot be allied in question; and the more any one thinks of it, or attends to what passes in himself or others—to the history of the human thoughts, words and actions, and their necessary mutual connections, the more clearly will he see it. We may conclude, therefore, even if all other arguments were set aside, that the authors of the books of the Old and New Testaments, whoever they were, cannot have made a false claim to divine authority. But there is also another method of inferring the divine authority of the Scriptures, from the excellence of the doctrines contained therein; for they contain doctrines concerning God— a Providence—a future state—the duty of man, &c. far more pure and sublime than can any ways be accounted for, from the natural powers of men, circumstanced as the sacred writers were. To set this in a clear light, let any one compare the several books of the Old and New Testaments with the contemporary writers amongst the Greeks and Romans, who could not possess less than the natural powers of the human mind; but might have had over and above some traditional hints, derived ultimately from revelation. Let him consider whether it be possible to suppose, that Jewish shepherds, fishermen, &c. should both before and after the rise of the heathen philosophy, so far exceed the men of the greatest abilities and accomplishments in other nations, by any other means than by divine communications. Nay, we may say, that no writers, from the inventor of letters to the present time, are equal to the penmen of the books of the Old and New Testaments, in true excellence, utility and dignity; which is surely such an internal criterion of their divine authority, as ought not to be resisted. And perhaps it never is resisted by any, who have duly considered these books, and formed their affections and actions according to the precepts therein delivered."[3]

We will now proceed to the evidence afforded us from the history of the first and second centuries.

The Lord Jesus Christ was crucified and rose again about the year thirty-three—and the apostles continued in Jerusalem till about the year forty-eight. At the time of Christ's death, and of the first preaching of the apostles, for twenty or thirty years, there was no written system of the Salvation by Jesus Christ. It was preached by him personally during his life, and confirmed by continual miracles, in the presence of all the people, openly and publicly; and finally confirmed by a cruel and ignominious death; and the fulfilment of his promise, by the descent of the Holy Spirit. Afterwards his apostles, being poor and illiterate men, but filled with the spirit, and endowed with the gift of tongues on the day of Pentecost, following his example, taught the people in Jerusalem and the neighboring nations, by word of mouth, confirming their doctrines by undoubted and convincing miracles.

As yet, there was no call for written systems—full evidence attended the apostles wherever they went. But when they began to form and settle churches in every place where they came, the persons whom they appointed to govern and teach in their absence, stood in need of written instructions, as well as written information of the great facts of the Christian history, to which they and their proselytes might at all times recur; and they considered this blessed system as bringing to their knowledge, life and immortality.

The first fifteen years after the crucifixion, the church was mostly confined to Jerusalem; but as churches multiplied fast, throughout the Roman empire, soon after this period, the apostles frequently made use of writing, for the purpose of more general information.

The apostle Paul, a man of learning and of considerable natural abilities, was now added to the number of the apostles by a divine mission; and he first set the example about the year fifty-one, or fifty-two, (eighteen or twenty years after the descent of the Spirit on the apostles) by writing an epistle to the Thessalonians, who had been instructed by him in person; and who received his teachings, "not as the word of man, but as it was in truth the word of God;" and he exhorts them "to read it to the brethren."

---

3. Hartley on Man.

In this manner he continued to write epistles to the different church- es under his care, till they amounted to the number now extant in the New Testament.

The other apostles, as Peter, James and John, followed his example, and wrote the several epistles that go under their names. The Acts of the Apos- tles were written by St. Luke, about the year sixty-two or sixty-three.

The four evangelists in order, are, Matthew, Mark, Luke and John. The first three wrote their Gospels about the same time that the Acts of the Apos- tles were written; and St. John wrote his Gospel about the year ninety-eight.

Clemens says, "And yet of all the disciples of our Lord, only Matthew and John have left us written records; who also, as report says, were necessitated to write; for Matthew having preached first to the Hebrews, and being about going to other nations, did in his own country language pen his Gospel, sup- plying by writing the want of his presence and converse among those who he was now to leave. Soon after, when Mark and Luke had set forth their Gos- pels, John, they say, spent all that time in preaching, and at length came to write for this reason. The three first written Gospels, having been now deliv- ered into the hands of all, and of John himself, they say that he approved of them and confirmed the truth thereof by his own testimony; only there was wanting in writing, an account of those things done by Christ at the first be- ginning of his preaching. And the thing is true, for 'tis evidently conspicuous, that the other three evangelists have committed to writing only those things which were done by our Saviour in one year's space after John the Baptist be- ing shut up in prison. Therefore, they say, that the apostle John being for these causes thereto requested, has declared a Gospel according to him, the time passed over in silence by the former evangelists."[4]

Irenaeus, who was conversant with Polycarp, a disciple of St. John, says, "And all the elders that were conversant in Asia with John the disciple of our Lord, do testify, that John delivered his Gospel to them, for he continued among them till Trajan's time."[5]

In process of time, the primitive Christians, having had these sacred books handed down to them in various copies, authorized by the particular church who had the original in keeping, or from men of established charac- ters among them, determined their being genuine, not by any positive au- thority, or special power universally acknowledged by them, as general councils or other church assemblies; but, as they judged of any other of their

---

4. Euseb. Lib. iii. 42.
5. 2d Book of Heresies, ch. 39.

religious facts, from testimony or tradition. The first was afforded by the contemporaries of the apostles and their companions, who were writers of them; and the last, by the records of the several churches to whom they were respectively written.

"The manner of handing down the Scriptures to posterity, resembles that of all other genuine books, and true histories. The Greeks and Romans, by tradition, always received the principal facts of their histories as true, and never doubted. So have Jews and Christians. These evidences, though traditionary, are sufficient, and afford a real argument, as well as one *ad hominem*, for receiving books so handed down to us. For it is not to be conceived, that whole nations, should either be imposed upon themselves, or join to deceive others, by forgeries of books of facts."[6]

The first publication after the three Gospels and the epistles, which we have on record, is the epistle of St. Barnabas, written about the year seventy-one, in which, though he does not mention the Gospels by name, he alludes to them by a number of quotations, where by it is plain, that he had seen the one written by St. Matthew, and several of the epistles.

The epistles of St. Clement, (the third bishop of Rome, after St. Peter) to the church of Corinth, was undoubtedly written about the year ninety-six. St. Paul mentions him "among his fellow labourers, whose names are in the book of life." In this epistle he expressly quotes the epistle to the Corinthians, and says, it was written by the apostle Paul: besides which, it clearly appears, that Clement had in his hands, the Gospels of Matthew, Mark and Luke; the Acts of the Apostles; the epistles to the Hebrews, Romans, Galatians, Ephesians, Philippians, Colossians, Thessalonians, Timothy Titus, James and Peter. Clement observes also, that St. Peter's hearers at Rome, were desirous of having his sermons written down for their use; they therefore requested Mark to leave them a written memorial of the doctrines they had received from him by word of mouth, which Mark did. When Peter knew what had been done, he was pleased; and confirmed the work by his authority, that it might be read in the churches.

In the year one hundred, Hermas, who is mentioned among others, in the end of the epistle to the Romans, wrote his Shepherd, or Pastor of Hermas, wherein he refers to many passages from Matthew, Luke and John. The Acts, the epistles to the Romans, Corinthians, Galatians, Ephesians, Philip-

---

6. Hartley on Man.

pians, Colossians, Thessalonians, Timothy, Hebrews, James, Peter, John, Jude, and the Revelation.

About seven years after the *Shepherd*, Ignatius, who was ordained in sixty-nine, and as some have alleged, by Peter himself; and who, as Chrysostom observes, conversed familiarly with the apostles, and was perfectly acquainted with their doctrines, wrote seven epistles to as many churches, in which he mentions the epistle of Paul to the Ephesians. He also mentions the Scriptures, as a general name. He plainly alludes to the Gospels of Matthew and John, and possibly to Luke—the Acts of the apostles—the epistle to the Romans, Corinthians, Galatians, Philippians, Colossians, Thessalonians, Timothy, Titus, Hebrews, Peter and John.

About this time, or in one hundred and eight, Polycarp, who were also taught by the apostles, and had conversed with many who had seen Jesus Christ in the flesh, and who had been appointed bishop of Smyrna in Asia by the apostles, in his epistles to the churches, mentions the writings of the New Testament as "the oracles of the Lord," and calls them the Holy Scriptures. He has quotations from the epistles to the Corinthians, Ephesians, Philippians, and Thessalonians—and also from Matthew's and Luke's Gospels. He refers to the Acts of the Apostles, the epistles to the Romans, Corinthians, Galatians, Ephesians, Thessalonians, Colossians, Timothy, Peter, John and Hebrews.

In the epistle from the church of Smyrna, concerning Polycarp's martyrdom, they give the title of Gospel to the history of our Lord by the evangelists, by which they seem also to intend the New Testament in general, and refer to it as a book then in use.

Eusebius, in giving an account of the evangelists in the year one hundred and twelve, says, "Among those who were illustrious at that time, was Quadratus, who, together with the daughters of Philip, is said to have enjoyed the gift of prophecy; and besides these, there were at that time many eminent persons, who had the first rank in the succession of the apostles, who being the worthy disciples of such men, every where built up the churches, the foundations of which had been laid by the apostles; extending likewise their preaching yet farther, and scattering abroad the salutary seeds of the kingdom of Heaven, all over the world. For many of the disciples at that time, whose souls *the divine Word* had inspired with an ardent love of philosophy, first fulfilled our Saviour's precept, distributing of their substance to the necessitous—then travelling abroad, they performed the work of evangelists, being ambitious to preach Christ, and deliver *the Scriptures of the divine Gospels.*"

In the year one hundred and sixteen, Papias, who had been a hearer of St. John, (and a companion of Polycarp) was bishop of Hierapolis in Asia, and wrote five books, entitled, "An Explanation of the Oracles of the Lord." He asserts, that the presbyter John told him, that "Mark being the interpreter of Peter, wrote exactly what he remembered," and that "Matthew wrote the divine Oracles in the Hebrew tongue." He mentions also the epistle of John and Peter, and the Acts of the apostles, and the Revelation.

In the year one hundred and forty, Justin Martyr came to Rome, and presented his first apology to the emperor Antoninus Pius. He also had the celebrated conference with Trypho the Jew, and returned to Rome again, and suffered martyrdom in one hundred and sixty-four. He expressly mentions the Gospels under *the title of Memoirs or Commentaries of the apostles and their companions—Christ's Memoirs*. He also calls them Gospels. He again mentions them as the memoirs of the apostles and their companions, who wrote the history of all things concerning our Saviour Jesus Christ—as the memoirs composed by the apostles, which are called Gospels. Thus he acknowledges the four Gospels; two written by the apostles, and two by their companions, and asserts, *that these Gospels were publicly read in the assemblies of the Christians on the Lord's days, by a person appointed for that purpose.*

Trypho the Jew, in the conference above alluded to, says to Justin, "I am sensible that *the precepts in your Gospels, as they are called*, are so great and wonderful, that I think it impossible for any man to keep them, *for I have been at the pains to read them.*" Justin also mentions the Revelation, as being written by a man from among themselves, by name John, one of the apostles of Christ. He quotes from the Acts of the apostles—the epistles to the Romans, Corinthians, Galatians, Ephesians, Philippians, Colossians, Thessalonians, Hebrews, Peter, and the Revelations.

In the elegant epistle of Diognetus, who wrote in one hundred and sixty-six, he has this remarkable passage—"The fear of the law is celebrated, and the grace of the prophets is known; the faith of the Gospels is established, and the tradition of the apostles is kept, and the grace of the church rejoiceth exceedingly." In this also he refers to St. Matthew, John, the epistles to the Romans, Corinthians, Philippians, Timothy; of Peter and John. He speaks of the law and the prophets; Gospels and apostolical epistles.

In one hundred and seventy-seven, Melito, bishop of Sardis in Lydia, says, "That when he went into the east, he procured an accurate account of the books of the *Old* Testament," from which we may safely conclude, that there was a collection known by the name of the New Testament. One of his works, now lost, was entitled, "Of the Revelation of St. John," so that he might have had that book in his collection of the New Testament.

About the year one hundred and seventy-eight, Iraeneus, bishop of Lyons in Gaul, and disciple of Polycarp, wrote five books against heresies. He is very full as to the truth of the Scriptures. He says, "We have not received the knowledge of the way of our Salvation, by any others than those by whom the Gospel has been brought to us; which Gospel they first preached, and afterwards by the will of God committed to writing, that it might be, for time to come, the foundation and pillar of our faith. After that our Lord arose from the dead, and "the apostles were endowed from above, with the power of the Holy Ghost coming down upon them, they received a perfect knowledge of all things." They then went forth to all the ends of the earth, declaring to men, the blessings of heavenly peace, having all of them, and every one alike, the Gospel of God. Matthew, then among the Jews, wrote a Gospel in their own language; while Peter and Paul were preaching the Gospel at Rome, and founding a church there. And after their decease, Mark also, the disciple and interpreter of Peter, delivered to us in writing, the things that had been preached by Peter. Luke, the companion of Paul, put down in a book, the Gospel preached by Paul. Afterwards, John, the disciple of the Lord, who also leaned on his bosom, likewise published a Gospel, while he dwelt at Ephesus in Asia—and all these have delivered to us, that there is one God, the maker of the Heavens and the earth, declared by the law and the prophets; and one Christ, the Son of God. And he, who does not assent to them, despiseth indeed those who knew the mind of the Lord, but he despiseth also Christ himself the Lord, and he despiseth likewise the Father, and is self-condemned, resisting and opposing his own Salvation, as all heretics do."

He often quotes the Acts of the apostles as written by Luke, the disciple and companion of the apostles, and sums up with this observation. "Nor can they," says he, "pretend that Paul is not an apostle, when he was chosen to this end; nor can they show, that Luke is not to be credited, who has related to us the truth with the greatest exactness; and possibly God has for this reason, so ordered it, that many parts of the Gospel should be declared to us by Luke, which all are under a necessity of receiving, so that all might believe his subsequent testimony, which he has given concerning the acts and doctrines of the apostles; and might have a sincere and uncorrupt of faith, and be saved. Therefore his testimony is true, and the doctrine of the apostles is manifest and uniform, without any deceit; hiding nothing from man, nor teaching one thing in private, and another in public. He expressly quotes twelve epistles of Paul, and takes several verses from the Hebrews. The epistle of Peter, he acknowledges as written by him. Also the epistles of John, the disciple of our Lord. He quotes the Revelations, as St. John's. He generally calls them the divine Scriptures—divine Oracles—the Scriptures of the Lord—evangelic and apostolic writings—the Scriptures of the Old and New Testament—the law and the Gospel. He says the Scriptures are perfect, being dictated *by the word of God, and his Spirit.* He declares that there were four Gospels received by the church, and no more; all which he has frequently quoted, with the names of the writers; as also the book of the Acts, which he ascribes to Luke.

In one hundred and eighty-one, Theophilus, a learned heathen, was converted to Christianity, and published several books. He quoted Matthew's and John's Gospels, as sacred Scriptures. He alludes to Luke, and refers to the epistles of Paul to the Romans, Corinthians, Ephesians, Philippians, Colossians, Timothy, Titus, and the Revelations as written by St. John.

In one hundred and ninety-four, Clement, a presbyter of Alexandria, said to have been a learned man, and an excellent master of the Christian philosophy, bore a noble testimony to the Scriptures in all his writings. He says there were four Gospels, of Matthew, Mark, Luke and John, and takes notice of the reason for writing of Mark's Gospel. He quotes the Acts of the apostles, as written by Luke. He frequently and expressly quotes the fourteen epistles of St. Paul—also the first of Peter and the first of John. He received the epistle of Jude and the Revelation.

Serapion, bishop of Antioch, in the year two hundred, in an epistle to some who had too much respect for a work, entitled, the Gospel of Peter, says, "We brethren receive Peter and the other apostles as Christians: but as skilful men, we reject those writings which are falsely ascribed to them, well knowing that we have received none such.

There will be no need of an apology for inserting the strong testimony of Origen, about the year 250 or 260, whose learning, piety, and strict attention to sacred things, no one will dispute, however they may object to particular doctrines held by him. His testimony is recorded by Eusebius. He says, "I have understood by tradition, there are four Gospels, which, and only which, are to be allowed without contradiction by the church of God, under Heaven. As to the first, it was written by one Matthew, formerly a publican, but afterwards an apostle of Jesus Christ; he published it written in Hebrew, for the sake of those Jews who believed. The second is Mark's Gospel, who wrote it as Peter expounded to him; whom also he confesses to be his son, in his catholic epistle, and in these words—the church which is at Babylon, (meaning Rome) elected together with you, saluteth you, and so doth Marcus my son. And the third is the Gospel according to St. Luke, which is commended by St. Paul. He wrote it for the sake of the heathens. Lastly, St. John's Gospel."

Let me here add the observations of the excellent Lardner, before mentioned, on this subject. "Though many works of the primitive times of Christianity have not come down to us, we have seen and examined a large number of works, of learned Christian writers, in Palestine, Syria, Asia Minor, Egypt, and that part of Africa that used the Latin tongue; and in Crete, Greece, Italy and Gaul: all in the space of one hundred and fifty years after writing the first book of the New Testament. In the remaining works of Irenaeus, Clement, of Alexandria and Tertullian, though some works of each have been lost, there are perhaps more and larger quotations of the small volume of the New Testament, than from all the works of Cicero, (though of so uncommon excellence for thought and style) in the writers of all characters for several ages,—insomuch, that we have reason to think, a late learned and judicious divine,[7] did not exaggerate beyond the truth, when he said, that the facts upon which the Christian religion is founded, have a stronger proof, than any facts at such a distance of time; and that the books which convey them down to us, may be proved to be uncorrupted and authentic, with greater strength than any other writings of equal antiquity.

Even Julian the apostate, acknowledges the Gospels, as written by those whose names they bear. He mentions the evangelists by name, and quotes many passages. He particularly treats of the first chapter of John's Gospel— of Christ being the *Word* of God, and the *Word* being made flesh, and of the acceptation in which it was at that time received.[8]

He plainly confesses, "that those were Peter's, Paul's, Matthew's, Mark's and Luke's works, read by Christians under their names;"[9] and one might reasonably suppose, that Julian, in that early day, knew, at least, as much of this dispute as our author; *and he is at least*, one person who tells us who wrote them.

---

7. Dr. Jeremiah Hunt.
8. Jul. part ii. 327. lib. x. 333.
9. Cyril, book x.

It is not forgotten, that it has been said, that the canon of Scripture was first settled in the council of Laodicea—but this, as most of our author's assertions, will not appear to be the case to any one, who will read their canon for himself. It is therein declared, "That private psalms ought not to be read in the churches, nor any books not canonical, but only the canonical books of the Old and New Testament." Then follows a list of those books that are canonical. The same may be observed on the acts of the third council of Carthage, in these words; "Moreover it is ordained, that nothing beside the canonical Scriptures be read in the churches, under the name of the divine Scriptures."

Surely there is nothing in either of these that will any way justify our author's assertion, "That the canon of Scripture was settled in these or any other councils."

I will take the liberty of adding an extract from the famous Mr, Le Clerc, as immediately applicable to this subject. He says, "We no where read of the council of the apostles, nor any assembly of the governors of Christian churches, convened to determine by their authority, that such a number of Gospels, neither more or fewer, should be received. Nor was there any need of it, since it is well known to all, from the concurring testimony of contemporaries, that the four Gospels are the genuine writings of those whose names they bear: and since it is also manifest there is not any thing in them unworthy of those, to whom they are ascribed, nor any thing at all contrary to the Revelation of the Old Testament, nor to right reason. There was no need of a synod of grammarians to declare magisterially, what are the works of Cicero or Virgil. In like manner the authority of the Gospels has been established by general and perpetual consent, without any decree of the governors of the church. We may say the same of the apostolical epistles, which owe all their authority, not to the decisions of any ecclesiastical assembly, but to the concurring testimony of all Christians, and the things themselves which are contained in them." And another from St. Augustine—"We know the writings of the apostles," says he, "as we know the works of Plato, Aristotle, Cicero, Varro, and others; and as we know the writings of divers ecclesiastical authors, for as much as they have the testimony of contemporaries, and of those who have lived in succeeding ages."

This part of the argument shall now be concluded by another quotation, equally applicable, from the famous Dr. Hartley on Man. "The manner in which the books of the Old and New Testament have been handed down from age to age, proves both their genuineness, and the truth of the principal facts contained in them. 1st. It resembles the manner in which all other genuine books and true histories have been conveyed down to posterity—as the writings of the Greek and Roman poets, orators, philosophers and historians, were esteemed by these nations to be transmitted to them by their forefathers, in a continued succession, from the times in which the respective authors lived; so have the books of the Old Testament by the Jewish nation, and those of the New by the Christians; and it is an additional evidence in the last case, that the primitive Christians were not a distinct nation, but a great multitude of people, dispersed through all the nations of the Roman empire, and even extending themselves beyond the bounds of that empire. As the Greeks and Romans always believed the principal facts of their historical books, so the Jews and Christians did more, and never seem to have doubted of the truth of any part of them. Now I suppose that all sober minded men admit the books usually ascribed to the Greek and Roman historians, philosophers, &c, to be genuine, and the principal facts related or alluded to in them, to be true; and that one chief evidence for this is, the general traditionary one here recited. They ought therefore to pay the same regard to the books of the Old and New Testament, (independent of their divinity) since they have the same, or greater reason for it. It is not to be conceived that whole nations, should either be deceived themselves, or concur to impose on others, by forgeries of books or facts. These books and facts must therefore be genuine and true; and it is a strong additional evidence of this, that all nations must be jealous of forgeries for the same reasons that we are."— "Whoever received the books of the New Testament in ancient times, as genuine and true, must not only have forsaken all sinful pleasure, but exposed themselves to various hardships, dangers, and even to death itself. They had indeed a future glory promised; but this being future, must have been supported with the most incontestable evidences; also, it could have no power against the opposite motives; and both together must so rouse the mind, as to make men exert themselves to the utmost, till they had received full satisfaction—besides which, it is to be observed, that even joy, and the greatness of an expectation, incline men to disbelieve, and to examine with a scrupulous exactness, as well as fear and dislike.—As to those who did not receive them, they would have sufficient motives to detect the forgery or falsehood, had there been any such. They were all condemned for their unbelief; many for their gross vices; the Jew for his darling partiality to his own nation and ceremonial law; the Gentile for his idolatry and polytheism; and the most dreadful punishment threatened to all in a future state.—It may be added, that the persons reproved an the Gospels, and by the apostles, (meaning the five apocalyptical churches and the Nicolaitans) could not but endeavor to vindicate themselves. The books were all of a public nature, and the reproofs particularly so, as being intended to guard others."

We now come to the last part of the assertion of our author, "That the best surviving evidence is the Jews, and yet they say it is not true." Now, if by this it is designed to insinuate, that none of the Jews have acknowledged the facts of the resurrection and ascension, it is not true, as we have already shown. That the present Jews, as a people or nation, deny the doctrines of the New Testament, is not only a fact, but is expressly foretold in those books, that they should do so till the end of the Roman government—and they also foretell other circumstances, attending this once chosen people of God, who are still to be re-united to him, fully convincing to many wise men of the truth of their declarations; such as their dispersed and humiliating state throughout the world; their continuing a separate people, &c. Yet true it is, that very large numbers of Jews, in the first ages of the Christian church, embraced her doctrines, and gloried in the cross. Nay, for many years, the whole Christian church was made up entirely and exclusively of Jews; and every writer, except Luke, concerned in the Scriptures of the New Testament, were Jews, and none other—and at the first prosecution of Peter before the Sanhedrin, the then representative body of the Jewish nation, "they acknowledged, that indeed a notable miracle had been done by the apostles, was manifest to all them that dwelt at Jerusalem, and that they could not deny it," And the consequence was, "that the word of God increased, and the number of the disciples multiplied in Jerusalem greatly; and a great *company of the priests* were obedient to the faith."

The Jews as a people, nevertheless, at this day, as they have been since the time of Moses, are firm believers in revelation, and though they reject Jesus Christ as the promised Messiah, and will not at present have him to reign over them, yet they fully believe in one yet to come, as foretold by Moses and the prophets. Let some of their late learned, judicious, and excellent writers, speak for themselves.— "When we reflect," say they, speaking on the subject of revelation, "on the baneful systems set up in ages past, and in this one too by philosophers—when we see the providence of God, his justice, and even his existence contested—fatality introduced—liberty destroyed—die land marks of right and wrong daringly torn up, or placed with uncertainty, by those pretenders to wisdom—man degraded—all the bonds of society dissolved—vain imaginations and racking doubts substituted in the place of the most comfortable and salutary truths—when we see these things, our spirit is stirred up at all these errors, and we cannot help thinking ourselves happy in being preserved from them by such reasonable and holy laws. O Israel! happy are we, for the things that are pleasing to God, are made known to us; he hath not dealt so with any nation."[10] And again, speaking of the Christian religion, they say, "Those Christians who persecute on account of religion, either offend against truth, or are illy acquainted with their religion. We Jews, can assure them, that the Christian religion does not oblige men to murder one another for paragraphs, no nor for the most important doctrines. The true spirit of their religion, breathes nothing but mildness—he calumniates it, who ascribes to it the mad deeds of blind fanaticism, and the crimes of dark policy. It equally condemns both these. Those Christians confound Christianity, with the abuses made of it. When will those great men deign to reason justly."[11]

The Jews do not even doubt, that the books of the New Testament, were written by the evangelists, who were their countrymen; and Jews as well as they. They do not deny the writings of Paul and Peter, James and John, or any other of the authors of the New Testament; but they suppose them either to have been impostors, or misled and imposed upon: but these very Jews, as a people, and all their sacred writings, profess the same things, in expectation of their Messiah to come, with the like properties, qualities and character.

The foundation of our author's after observations, being thus answered and removed out of the way, I shall pass them by without, and indeed as unworthy of, farther notice. I mean the ridiculous story he has introduced from the poets, about the race of giants making war against Jupiter, and throwing an hundred rocks against him at once; and afterwards being confined under Mount Etna. From this he supposes the story of Satan's making war against the Almighty, took its rise—that Satan was then defeated and confined to a pit, and afterwards let out again, to deceive a woman in the garden of Eden—finally, that Satan obtained a triumph over the whole creation, Jews, Turks and infidels, and even the Almighty himself—with a number of other as profane and blasphemous accounts of the Christian system, originating in his own brain, or the imaginations of heathen poets,

---

10. Letters of certain Jews, 310.
11. Letters of certain Jews, 172.

who were at a loss to account for the phenomena of nature, from the mere light of nature, unassisted by revelation. But these are not to be found, either in the books of the Old or New Testament, or in any theory of a Christian church, ancient or modern. This sufficiently proves, what was before suggested, that our author has undertaken to write on a subject, the first principles of which he has not troubled himself to investigate. He has barely vamped up, in a parade of language, the well answered objections of the Deists of the last, and beginning of the present century. To these our author may claim the merit of adding, the ludicrous and blasphemous reveries of debauchees and drunkards over their cups; thinking thereby to impose on the world such stuff for argument, merely because he has prefaced it with the name of "The Age of Reason;" as if reason consisted in falsehood, ridicule and burlesque.

I shall therefore pass by all this rhapsody of nonsense, and proceed to his observations on the books of the Old and New Testament, beginning with Genesis, and ending with the Revelations.

10

Objections to the
Old Testament Considered

Our author introduces his general observations on the Bible, by endea-
vouring to prejudice the unwary in favor of his objections, by assuring
them, "That although the boldness of his investigations would alarm
many, yet it would be paying too great a compliment to credulity, to
forbear them on that account—that the times and the subject demand
it to be done—that the suspicion, that the theory of what is called the
Christian church is fabulous, is becoming very extensive in all coun-
tries; and that it will be a consolation to such persons, to see the subject
freely investigated."

IT must be evident by this time, to every candid and sincere inquirer after
truth, that if the facts already treated of in this answer be true, there can
be little necessity of further argument, to show the weakness as well as
wickedness of the other observations of the Age of Reason, on the Christian
system; yet, for the sake of those who have not time or inclination to search
into these things, we will proceed, by taking previous notice of the observations above referred to, which he calls bold investigations.

Let me ask this man, who seems so fearful of paying a compliment to
credulity, who it is that he supposes will be alarmed by the boldness of his
investigations? He must, I conclude, mean the weak and ignorant alone.
What has he done to give this apprehended alarm to those who understand
the subject? He has done very little more, than change the style and language of his predecessors, though they have been so fully answered.

Indeed it could scarcely have been credited, before sorrowful conviction
had prevented a doubt, that, at this day of light and knowledge, a man could
have been found, pretending to any character in the learned world, who

would have ventured to talk of the freedom and boldness of investigations, that were to consist wholly of dogmatical assertions on subjects of so great importance, without attempting either argument or proof—and this too, in direct opposition to the unwearied and successful labours of the most learned men of which the world has ever boasted, in answering and confuting the rational and learned objections of men of knowledge and science, who had, (contrary to our author's pretensions) made the professions and doctrines of Christians their long and serious study. These have with great abilities arranged and supported every objection, that could with any propriety be urged against the Christian system, by arguments and reasons founded on the nature and consequences of that system. Mr. Hartley justly observes, that "the true and pure religion of Christ, alone grows more evident and powerful, from every attack that has been made upon it; and converts the bitterness and poison of its adversaries into nourishment for itself, and an universal remedy for the pains and sorrows of a miserable and degenerate world."

The insuperable vanity and unconquerable pride of our author, must have led him to suppose, that his religious dogma's would prove as successful with the ignorant and credulous multitude, as many of his political heresies have done, merely because they were asserted with a licentious boldness, that refused the aid of proof or reason.

We agree with his position, that the times and the subject are very important; and, if he pleases, that infidelity is gaining ground in every part of the Christian world. Is this to be wondered at, when we find infidels in all corners of the land, using every mean and subtle artifice to poison the minds of the young and uninstructed; taking advantage of a season of political disorder and confusion; and impressing them both by precept and example, with an aversion to search after truth, and a love for every vicious inclination.[1]

But under this distressing view of the subject, we would acquaint our author with one important fact; that even this truth, in which he seems so confident, with all its melancholy train of evils, is a confirmation of the doctrines he is endeavouring to subvert, and is an additional proof of the

---

1. The observation of Mr. Gibbon, on the scepticism of the pagan world, at the first propagation of Christianity, may be applicable here.—"The contagion of these sceptical writings, had been diffused far beyond the number of their readers. The fashion of incredulity was communicated from the philosopher to the man of pleasure or business; from the noble to the plebian; and from the master to the menial slave, who waited at his table, and who eagerly listened to the freedom of his conversation."—Vol. ii. 355.

divinity of the sacred Scriptures; the evidence in whose favor is increased even by our author himself.

Hearken to what these divine writings said on this subject, under a prophetic spirit, almost two thousand years ago, when the Christian system was in its infancy, and under the apparent direction of a few poor, despised, obscure and illiterate fishermen. "Now the Spirit speaketh *expressly*, that in the latter times, some shall depart from the faith, 'giving heed to seducing spirits and doctrines of devils, speaking lies in hypocrisy, having their consciences seared as with a hot iron. And there were false prophets among the people; even as there shall be false teachers among you, who privily shall bring in damnable heresies, even denying the Lord that bought them, and bringing on themselves swift destruction. *And many shall follow their pernicious ways*, by reason of whom the way of truth shall be evil spoken of— whose judgment now of a long time, lingereth not, and their damnation slumbereth not—but chiefly them who walk after the flesh, *in the lust of uncleanness, and despise government*—presumptuous are they—self-willed, they are not ashamed to speak evil of dignities—but these, as natural brute beasts, made to be taken and destroyed, *speak evil of things they understand not*, and shall utterly perish in their own corruption, and shall receive the reward of unrighteousness. Spots are they, and blemishes, sporting themselves with their own deceivings, while they feast with you." And again: "This second epistle, beloved, I now write unto you, in both which, I stir up your pure minds by way of remembrance, that ye may be mindful of the words which were spoken before by the holy prophet; and of the commandment of us, the apostles of the Lord and Saviour—knowing this first, that there shall come in the last days, scoffers walking after their own lusts, and saying, where is the promise of his coming."

As to the consolation that is to be afforded to the doubting inquirer, it can never arise from any free investigation of the subject by our author; for, so far from attempting to examine into the books called the Old and New Testament, he acknowledges in page 39 of his pamphlet, that he kept no Bible, and that he could not recollect enough of the passages in Job, on which he was descanting, to insert them correctly.

What idea must this vain man have of his readers, or could he suppose that his own character was as great a secret to some of them, as it appears to be to himself.

He seems confident that whatever he says, however ridiculous or absurd, will be taken for truth; and that he will be considered as an able investigator of doctrines and truths, of which, in the same breath, he confesses himself ignorant. Surely his advocates and proselytes must have a mean opinion of their own understandings, thus to become the dupes of so vain an imagination.

But to proceed. He sets out according to his established practice, with asserting a number of palpable falsehoods relative to the Bible; and then, considering them as proved facts, he argues against the authenticity of their divine origin.

He declares, without hesitation, *"That, beginning with Genesis, and ending with the Revelations, we are told these books are the word of God; but who told us so; nobody can tell, except that we tell one another so."*

This extraordinary introduction to his immediate attack on the Bible, containing the Old and New Testaments, leaves us at a loss to determine, which is with him most predominant, falsehood or ignorance. Conscious of my own fallibility and liableness to error, 1 am sorry to treat any of my fellow-men, even with a seeming harshness; but in so important a controversy, one in which the essential interests of mankind are so deeply involved, truth requires plainness without abuse, and clear deductions without deception, or flattering the person of any man. I appeal to the judgment of even the candid enemies of revelation, on this charge of wilful perversion of historic truth, contained in the above declaration.[2]

Is it not well known to our author, as it is to all the world, that the Christian church and its advocates, for near eighteen hundred years, have unequivocally declared the whole Bible to be the word of God: and that the Jews for twice that period, have published to all mankind, that they consider the Old Testament in the same point of light.

And can it be possible, after the many judicious and instructive works of the learned in the knowledge of antiquity for so many years past, added to the invariable testimony of a whole nation from its origin to this time, attended with public monuments, rites, feasts, and other memorials of the great events of their religion, with the profession and practice of all denominations of Christians, that any man, who calls himself a philosopher, can with the appearance of truth say, *"That nobody can tell who told us that the Bible was the word of God."* The charge is not a denial of the Bible being the

---

2. "A season there is, when inactivity were a crime, and public admonition, even at the hazard of personal comforts, rises into indispensable obligation: to those at least who are desirous that their Master should not be ashamed of them at his second coming."
WAKEFIELD

word of God, but of our knowledge of the authors who wrote and published it as such. That this writer should not understand it—that he should deny the conclusive nature of the testimony by which it is said to be proved to be the word of God; and that he should impiously reject its doctrines as not coming from God, though acknowledged by him to be a pure morality, is not at all surprising with his present temper of mind; but that he should, against such a host of evidence, positively assert, that nobody can tell who originally published the Bible as the word of God; and has since supported and shown, by irrefragable and convincing arguments, that it is so, is a degree of vain confidence, scarcely credible to any one unacquainted with the personal character and history of our author.

In stating the history of this business, he falsely charges "the church mythologists, with determining by vote, out of a collection made by them, which of the collection should be the word of God;" and that "it is a matter altogether of uncertainty to us, whether such of the writings as now appear under the name of the Old and New Testaments, are in the same state in which those collectors say they found them, or whether they added, altered, abridged, or dressed them up." We have already adduced proof of the falsity of this charge, when applied to the New Testament. We shall now show it is still more absurd when applied to the Old.

Our author must have been wholly unacquainted with the evidence adduced in support of the divine authority of the Old Testament; and therefore cannot be justified in attempting to shake the faith of the unlearned, and to impose on mankind in general by his presumptuous and positive declaration; for he must have proceeded on principles known to him at the time to be unfounded in truth.

He could not have been ignorant, that the books of the Old Testament, had been the sacred books of the Jews, and received by them as a divine revelation, and the word of God, for some thousands of years, and that without doubt or dispute. That the Jews are a people more jealously scrupulous of their religious principles, and the facts on which they are founded, than any people on earth; even to the numbering of the lines, words and letters, of the copies of their sacred writings.

"When corruption in worship and manners, and many superstitious usages grew up among the Jews, they were (says Dr. Worthington) obliged to devise an oral law, to be handed down by oral tradition, to countenance those corruptions and innovations, which law they afterwards collected into a body, and committed to writing. But the *Mishna* had been needless and superfluous, durst they have incorporated their traditions with the Scriptures. As they have not done this, in a case in which they were most tempted to do it, there is less room to suspect their having wilfully corrupted them in other respects. So scrupulously vigilant were the Jews in preserving the Scriptures, that the Masorites numbered not only the sections, but even the words and letters, that no fraud or inadvertency might corrupt the least jot, of what they esteemed so sacred. If a word happened to be altered in any copy, it was laid aside as useless, or given to a poor man to teach his children by, on condition it was not brought into the synagogue. The prince was obliged to copy the original exemplar of the law, laid up in the sanctuary, with his own hand; and every Jew was to make it his constant discourse and meditation, to teach it to his children, and wear part of it on his hands and forehead."[3]

Under these circumstances, there can be no human writings or historic facts handed down to us from antiquity, with half the evidence of their truth and certainty. Therefore, when our author asserted, "When the church mythologists established their system, they collected all the writings they could find, and managed them as they pleased," he must have known that he contradicted the clearest and most unequivocal testimony, that ever was produced in support of any ancient books, yet known to the world.

"The Jewish synagogues, in all countries, were numerous; wherever the apostles preached they found them; they were established by the directions of the rabbis, in every place where there were ten persons of full age and free condition. Accordingly the jealous care with which the Scriptures were preserved in the tabernacle, and in the temple, was not more calculated to secure their integrity, than that reverence which afterwards displayed itself in the dispersed synagogues, and in the churches consecrated to the Christian faith."[4]

The language in which they were written, is a great evidence in their favor, as has been often observed by the best authors. It is that of an ancient people,

---

3. Vol. i. 136-140.

4. Grey's Key to the Old Test. 13—16.

There were three celebrated universities of Jews in the provinces of Babylon, viz. Nabordia, Pompeditha and Seria, besides several other places famous for learning. *Buxtorf's Tib. ch. vi. Lightfoot's Harm.* 335.

In Egypt, the Jews had a temple like that of Jerusalem, built by Onias, and continued 343 years, till the reduction of Jerusalem by Titus.

The Jews at that time, (says the Talmud) were double the number in Egypt, that they were when they left it under Moses. *Joseph Antiq. lib. xiv.*

who had but little intercourse with any of their neighbors; and even if they had, they generally spake languages similar to their own; of course, it was not in so great danger of changing, as modern languages which *are mingled together by so many political, literary, and commercial relations.*

Yet some changes must have passed between Moses and Malachi, a space of many hundred years. The Biblical Hebrew corresponds to this criterion. The style is too greatly diversified to have been the work of one jew, or any set of contemporary Jews. If false, there must have been a succession of impostors in different ages, which is altogether inconceivable. The Hebrew language ceased to be spoken as a living language, soon after the time of the captivity, and therefore it was impossible to forge any thing in it, after it became a dead language.

There was no Hebrew grammar till many ages after, and it is impossible to write in a dead language without a grammar. All the Jewish Scriptures must, on these principles, have been as old, at least, as the Babylonish captivity, and as all could not have been written in the same age, some must have been more ancient. The simplicity of their style; the delivery of the several narrations and precepts without hesitation; the authority with which the writers instruct the people; are all circumstances peculiar to those who have both a clear knowledge of what they deliver, and a perfect integrity of heart. These are sentiments on this subject, collected in substance from the Treatise on Man,[5] but they are so forcible and conclusive as to entitle them to the full consideration of every reasonable mind.[6]

How carefully and designedly does our author confound Jew and Christian, under the general name of church mythologists. He had objected to the Christian revelation, the want of the testimony of the Jews, *"who were the only surviving witnesses of the original transactions relating to their religion:"* and now, sensible of the weight of Jewish testimony with regard to the Old Testament, he keeps them out of sight, and seems to suppose their origin to have been that of the church mythologists, whom he sets to voting

---

5. Hartley's

6. It deserves to be remarked, that impostors would probably never have ventured on the many and fearful denunciations which the prophets make against the nation of Israel, for their disobedience to the institutions of God. If they had not proceeded on the authority of a law already established and held sacred among them, or on the clearest evidences of their own sacred character, would not the indignant people have detected the imposture, rejected their prophetic mission, and spurned from them men whom they would have considered only as insulting them by their reproaches and threatenings, without the sanction of Heaven?

which books of a collection made by them, should be the word of God. He may indeed have been so unacquainted with ecclesiastical history, as to have supposed Jew and Christian to have been contemporary at their origin; or that they were the same church; but if so, he should have been the last man, to have undertaken to write on the subject.

No one at this day, not even our author, will deny that such a man as Moses did exist; or that he was the great leader and head of the Jewish commonwealth, at their departure from Egypt to the land of Canaan.

This great people have it among them, handed down from generation to generation, as an indisputable fact, that this Moses was the author or writer of the Pentateuch, which contains the first five books of the Old Testament, and is the foundation and sum of all the rest.

If by this it is understood, that Moses himself wrote every word and letter, as now found in our Bible, it is not what is asserted. Moses, by command of God, kept an exact register of all the public transactions, *"which was laid up before the Lord, under the tare of the priests and Levites;"* and this was continued throughout their generations, as appears from the whole tenor of their history. From this register, as the great source of all their historical facts, their judges, prophets, kings and priests, were to make copies for their instruction, to be read in their synagogues, and to be the rules of their conduct.[7]

These copies were made out, generally, by the priests and scribes, who were of the Levites, and sometimes by their prophets, as Samuel, Nathan, Gad, Ezra and Nehemiah, who had the chief hand in the government of the people, and that in all ages of the Jewish commonwealth; and this being always done by public authority, a few notes of explanation might have been added from time to time, no ways interfering with the original text—such as, *"Now the man Moses was very meek above all the men upon the face of the earth.—And it remaineth there to this day.—The place was called Eshcol, because of the cluster of grapes which the children of Israel cut down from thence.—And again, the Canaanite was then in the land;"* together with the accounts of the deaths of Moses and Joshua at the end of the respective books, and the like. But as these were always done under public authority,

---

7. Mr. Hartley supposes the Pentateuch consists of the writings of Moses, put together by Samuel with a very few additions. Samuel also collected Joshua and Judges—he wrote the book of Ruth, with the first part of the book of Samuel, The latter part, and the second book, were written by Nathan and Gad. Kings, Chronicles, Ezra, and Nehemiah, were collected and written by Ezra and Nehemiah. Esther by some eminent Jew, perhaps Mordecai. Job is uncertain, &c.

and by their holiest men, who were prophets under divine inspiration, no injury was ever considered, as done to the integrity of these books, especially as the original was a sacred deposit in the ark of the covenant. Indeed Maimonides, the famous Jewish writer says, that Moses himself wrote out twelve copies of the law, with his own hand, one for each tribe, besides that which was laid up in the side of the ark; and the rabbis teach, that every Jew was obliged to have a copy of the Pentateuch by him.[8] And Ezra and Nehemiah are said to have brought three hundred copies of the law into the congregation assembled, at their return from captivity.[9]

It was from this example, perhaps, that the practice among the eastern nations arose, of keeping public registers of all important transactions. This is mentioned in 2d Esther, xxiii. when Mordecai had saved the king's life: "It was written in the book of the Chronicles, before the king." And in the 6th chap. v. 1, it is said, "That on that night could not the king sleep; and he commanded to bring *the book of records of the Chronicles*, and they were read before the king."

God expressly enjoined it upon Moses to keep records of what he had commanded him, in 17th Exod. 14th ver. when Amalek and his people were beaten, in the first battle that the Israelites had, after leaving Egypt. "And the Lord said unto Moses, Write this for a memorial in a book, and rehearse it in the ears of Joshua." So when Moses, with the Israelites, had encamped on Mount Horeb, and the law was given to them, the ten commandments were written by God on two tables of stone, and put into the ark; hence it

---

8. Maim. Pref: in seder: Zeraim, fol. 3. Reas. of Christ. 176.

9. Drav. de Trib. liv. iii. chap. i. Reas. of Christ. 176.

There is now no doubt, that Ezra, upon his return from the captivity of Babylon, undertook the settlement of the canon of the Old Testament, by collecting the inspired books of their prophets into a body, and revising and publishing them in one volume, as we have them at this day. That after he had finished it, he had it approved by the grand sanhedrim of the Jewish nation, and published by their authority. Nehemiah, their last (inspired) historian, and Malachi their last prophet, both cotemporaries with Ezra, assisted him in forming this new edition of the Old Testament. Ezra went further, and compared the several copies then extant together, and corrected all the errors which had crept into them through the negligençe or mistakes of transcribers. He changed the old names of several places that were grown obsolete, and instead of them inserted such new ones, as the people were better acquainted with. He filled up the chasms of history, and added in several places, what appeared to be necessary for the illustration, connection and completion of the whole. And lastly, be wrote every book in the Chaldee character, which since the captivity, the people understood much better than the Hebrew. *1 Stack. Hist, of Bib. Introd. 11, & c.*

Ezra was also a prophet and a scribe, ready in the law of Moses—the Jews looked upon him as another Moses—they call him the second-founder of the law. *Lewis Antiq. Heb. lib. viii*

was called the ark of the covenant—the ark of testimony—and which, together with the rest of the law given at the same time, Moses was to teach the people throughout all their generations. This could not be done, but by making them matter of record, from which copies might be taken, for the instruction of their future generations.

When Aaron, Nadab and Abihu, with the seventy elders, were ordered to go up to the mountain, Moses left them at the foot of it, and went up alone to speak with the Lord: he returned with the words of the Lord to the people: "then Moses wrote all the words of the Lord, and rose up early in the morning, and builded an altar under the hill, and twelve pillars, according to the twelve tribes of Israel; and he took *the book of the covenant*, and read it in the audience of the people."[10] And after he came down from the mountain with all the commandments of the Lord, and the second pair of tables of stone, he was again commanded to write what he had received—"And the Lord said unto Moses, write thou these words, for after the tenor of these words, I have made a covenant with thee and with Israel."[11] And afterwards it is said, "And Moses wrote the law, and delivered it unto the priests the sons of Levi, who bear the ark of the covenant of the Lord, and unto all the elders of Israel."[12] When Moses recapitulates the several journies of the people in their presence, he says, "That he wrote their goings out according to their journeys, *by the commandment of the Lord*."[13]

Moses not only wrote the book of the law, and put it into the side of the ark, while the two tables of stone were put into the ark itself, but he also "commanded the priests, and all the elders of Israel, saying, at the end of every seven years, in the solemnity of the year of release in the feast of tabernacles, when all Israel is come to appear before the Lord thy God, in the place which he shall choose, thou shalt read this law before all Israel, in their hearing—gather the people together, men, women and children, and the stranger that is within thy gates, that they may hear, and that they may learn and fear the Lord your God, and observe to do all the words of this law."[14] Here is every mark of honest integrity that could have been expected, and every mode of preserving this book unadulterated, that publicity could have suggested—and what renders imposition less possible, was the com-

---

10. Exodus 24:4-7.
11. Exodus 27:34.
12. Deuteronomy 9:31
13. Numbers 23:2.
14. Deuteronomy 31:10-13

mand to "study this book constantly—to bind it for a sign upon their hands, and frontlets between their eyes; to teach it to their children, speaking of it when they sat in the house, and when they walked by the way, and when they lay down, and when they rose up—to write it upon the door posts of their houses, and upon their gates."[15]

In describing the acts and duties of a king, when the people should thereafter desire one, it is ordered, "That when he shall sit upon the throne of his kingdom, he shall write a Copy of this law, in a book, *out of that which is before the priests and Levites,* and it shall be with him, and he shall read therein all the days of his life."[16] So necessary was the knowledge of the law to good government, that it was not only to be kept with religious care by the principal officers of the government, and read in the ears of the people; but it was essentially necessary that it should be of easy access to the people at large, that they might know and understand it—copying a sufficient number for three millions of people, being not an easy task. Therefore God commanded, that, when the congregation should pass over Jordan, where they were to inherit the land and become a great nation; and of course many must live at a great distance from the tabernacle, where the book of the law was kept, end read to the people every Sabbath day, "they should set up great stones, and plaster them with plaster; and should write upon the stones, all the words of this law, very plain."[17] And afterwards it is commanded, "When all Israel is come to appear before the Lord thy God, in the place which he shall choose, thou shalt read the law before all Israel, in their hearing;" and again he is commanded to write his song and teach it to the people, which he accordingly did.[18]

We read throughout the Old Testament, in almost every period of the the Jewish state, "of the law of the book of Moses—the law of the Lord—the book of the covenant—the book of the Chronicles of the kings of Israel—the book of the Chronicles of the kings of Israel and Judah—the book of the Acts of Solomon—the Chronicles of king David—the book of Samuel the Seer—the book of Shemaiah, the prophet;" and many others.

It is expressly recorded in Joshua, that he built an altar, and performed the directions and commandments as written *in the book of the law of Moses,* after his passing over Jordan, and taking the cities of Jericho and Ai, by

---

15. Deuteronomy 11:18-20.
16. Deuteronomy 17:18—19.
17. Deuteronomy 27:2—8.
18. Deuteronomy 31:11—19—22.

writing on the plastered stones, *"A copy of the law of Moses, which he wrote in the presence of all the people."* And when the elders, and officers, and judges, with the people, were placed half over against Mount Gerizim, and half over against Mount Ebal, as had been commanded; "Jo-shua *read all the words of the law,* the blessings and the cursings, according to all that is written in the book of the law; *there was not a word of all that Moses commanded, which Joshua read not before all the congregation of Israel."*[19]And just before Joshua's death, he made a covenant with the people, "and Joshua wrote these words in the book of the law of God."[20] This was all done immediately after the death of Moses, while the whole congregation were complete witnesses of all the transactions related to them.

In a word, we find Moses commanded by the Lord, to write the law and the commandments, with the goings out of the people, and indeed all the public transactions, in a book. We find him actually executing this commandment, for it is written, " And it came to pass, when Moses made an end of writing the words of this law in a book until they were finished, that Moses commanded the Levites, which bore the ark of the covenant of the Lord, saying, *take this book of the law,* and put it in the side of the ark of the covenant of the Lord your God, *that it may be there for a witness against thee."*[21]

In the time of his successor, we find him reading it publicly to all the congregation. Throughout the administration of the judges and reigns of their kings, we find it kept in the temple, while copies are in every principal man's hands, and referred to on every occasion, and usually read in the ears of all the people, from day to day.

The judgments of God are constantly said to be inflicted on the nation for not walking after the law of the Lord, as given by Moses the servant of the Lord. In the reign of king Josiah, only 600 years before the Christian sera, the book of the law was found in the house of the Lord, and he read all the words of it to the people.[22] This is repeated in the times of Ezra and Nehemiah.[23]

David appointed certain of the Levites "to minister before the ark of the Lord, *and to record,* and to thank, and to praise the Lord God of Israel."[24]

---

19. Joshua 8:30.
20. Joshua 26:34.
21. Deuteronomy 31:24.
22. 2 Kings 23:2.
23. Jeremiah 8:8.
24. First Chronicles 16:4.

"Josephus asserts, that from the death of Moses to the reign of Artax-erxes, the prophets, who succeeded that legislator, wrote the transactions of their own times. This assertion is confirmed by the sacred writers who mention the names of many prophets, as having recorded the affairs of the Jewish nations."[25] It is therefore very probable, that the book of the law, in Moses hand-writing, was preserved, till the return of the captivity from Babylon, besides the copies that were preserved by Daniel, Nehemiah, Ezra, Zechariah, and the other prophets, whose inspiration,ability, and known integrity, have always been confidently trusted in by the Jewish nation.

In fine, the Jews as a people universally acknowledge the fact, that Moses was the writer of the Pentateuch, and that from his day to the present time—their fasts, feasts, and all their religious services, as well as their ancient and modern historians, all agree, without a dissenting voice, in this account of their sacred books. Eben Ezra is said to be a single exception—he lived in the twelfth century, and supposed that the Pentateuch, as now in our Bible, was written about the time of the Kings, but he always acknowledged their authenticity and divine authority, and that they contained faithful accounts of the transactions of Moses.

This people, at the time when Moses brought them out of Egypt, con-sisted of near three millions of souls. He writes his history, for this very people, from time to time, as the facts happen. In one instance, it is said that he wrote it the next day. We find him reading his works to the people, *as the commandments of the Lord*, immediately after the events, when they must have been fresh in every man's memory. His audience were those who ac-companied him out of Egypt, and he relates the several extraordinary and miraculous occurrences, as happening in their presence, and before their eyes. Facts, for the truth of which, not a few special witnesses chosen for the purpose, but the whole congregation were vouchers, and vouchers the most authentic, having themselves, either as actors or spectators, been partakers in them. "The Lord our God made a covenant *with us* in Horeb.—The Lord made not this covenant *with our fathers*, but *with us, even us,* who are all *of us here alive this day.*—The Lord talked *with you, face to face,* in the mount, out of the midst of the fire, I stood between *the Lord and you* at that time, to show you the word of the Lord; for ye were afraid by reason of the fire, and went not up into the mount."[26] And again, "And know ye this day; for I speak not with your children, which have not known, and which have not

---

25. An attempt to a version of 12 Minn. Proph. 5 of preface.
26. Deuteronomy 5:2-6.

seen the chastisement of the Lord your God—his greatness—his mighty hand, and his stretched out arm, and his miracles and his acts which he did in Egypt unto Pharaoh the king, and unto all his land, &c. &c. But *your eyes have seen all the great acts of the Lord which he did.*"[27] Here could be no possible means of deception, neither could any valuable end be answered by it. These great miracles were done before the whole congregation—every individual passed through the Red Sea—every individual saw the pillar of cloud by day, and the pillar of fire by night. So many thousands could not have been slain for their disobedience, and so many thousands cured by looking to the brazen serpent, without the knowledge of the whole congregation. Their clothes not wearing out, and their shoes continuing for forty years, must have been facts, in which they could not have been deceived, and which Moses dared not to have asserted, if they had not been known to be true, by the whole people. The manna[28] from heaven, and the quails that served them for meat, were in their own nature facts of public notoriety, *"equal to the ascending of a balloon, or the sun at noon-day"* and of which every common man was an adequate judge; and it was impossible to have deceived such a body of men for the space of forty years together. Could the chief priests and scribes for several hundred years have been deceived, respecting some of the manna of the wilderness in their keeping, and laid up in the tabernacle as a standing memorial to future generations of the wonderful works of the Loud in their favor?

The supplying of three millions of people in a wilderness, surrounded by the most savage and inveterate foes; was a task not in the power of mortal man, in Moses's circumstances, without divine and supernatural aid: yet all will allow, that the Israelites did migrate from Egypt to Canaan, and did overcome the inhabitants of the land.

Let our adversaries seriously consider the difficulty modern governments experience in supplying a few thousand men with food and clothing, in a most plentiful country, with the advantage of money and friends; and then say what must have been Moses's fate, with his numerous hosts, suddenly

---

27. Deuteronomy 11:2-7.

28. This was not such manna as we are now acquainted with, and if only used in medicine—but it was like a very small round grain, fit for nourishment, and so hard as to be ground in mills or beaten in a mortar—Numbers 9:8. Yet it was melted by the sun, bred worms, and stunk if kept over night, except the night before the Sabbath, on which day it never fell at all—yet, when to be preserved as a standing memorial of the divine mission of their leader, and the supernatural origin of their whole system of government, to the conviction of future generations, it was durable as marble.

fleeing from a tyrant, through an inhospitable wilderness, surrounded with warlike and implacable enemies, if he had depended alone on human exertions. Had Moses been a mere adventurer, would he have travelled through the wilderness, by so circuitous a route, morally certain of being starved to death, and thereby risked his own life and character, as well as the lives of his people, for no apparent end; or would he not have taken the shortest way possible, to a land that flowed with milk and honey, and desperately invaded the nations of Canaan, as he did after forty years wandering in a wilderness? Would any man deserving the character of being the general of so great an army, and who had designed an imposition on his people, ever jealous and given to insurrection, have told them soon after their entering the wilderness, in order to take the shortest route to the Elysium of their hopes, *"that only two of them by name, should ever enter into that happy land, which he had so often assured them was specially designed by heaven for them*; but that for their spirit of insurrection against him their leader, they should wander about and perish in that dismal wilderness during a march of forty years,"* when the promised land was less than the distance of one month's march by the shortest way.

Could the mountains of Horeb have appeared on fire for forty days, and the people not have been sensible of the fact? Or could they have borne with any degree of patience, to have heard Moses, from time to time, appealing to their personal knowledge, in proof of these miraculous transactions, and upbraiding them with acting contrary to the convictions that these supernatural acts of their God should naturally produce; and threatening them with the divine vengeance for their unfaithfulness, if they had not been convinced by their own consciences, that they were strictly true. *"And all the people saw the thunderings and lightnings, and the noise of the trumpet, and the mountain smoking; and when the people saw it, they removed and stood a far off; and they said unto Moses, speak thou with us, and we will hear; but let not God speak with us, lest we die"*[29]

Was it possible for the people to have been imposed upon, when they were told of the cloud that covered them by day, and the fire that led them by night. *"The cloud of the Lord was upon the tabernacle by day, and fire was on it by night, in the sight of all the house of Israel, throughout all their journeyings."*[30] "Whether it were two days, or a month, or a year, that the cloud tarried upon the tabernacle remaining thereon, the children of Israel

---

29. Exodus 20:8-19.
30. Exodus 40:38.

abode in their tents, and journeyed not; but when it was taken up, they journeyed."[31] Can it be imagined that this great people were deceived, when they were told that they finally succeeded according to the divine predictions, in conquering the kingdoms of Canaan, driving out the inhabitants before them, passing over Jordan dry shod, and possessing a land flowing with milk and honey; and this all foretold to their great ancestor, hundreds of years before.

If then the whole nation of the Jews, without exception, from their first founder to this day, received the Pentateuch as written by Moses—if they have preserved it with the greatest care—if all the neighboring nations surrounding Judea, have for the same length of time, assented to this fact, and indeed confirmed it by their conduct, as for instance, Ptolemaeus Philadelphus, king of Egypt, sending to Jerusalem, at a great expense, for a commission of seventy of their elders to interpret this important book into the Greek language. If all the other books of the Old Testament have been written by the greatest and best men of this nation, apparently under divine inspiration, as is now more fully proved by the truth of their prophetical declarations, and all in a supernatural conformity with the books of Moses. If public and religious fasts and feasts, with other rites, have been established in commemoration of the leading facts of this history from the earliest times to the present day; then let me ask in what light must our author be viewed by the judicious reader—or who is he, and from what source has he drawn his extraordinary knowledge, that he should at this day, more than three thousand years since the times of Moses, deny the fact admitted by all nations acquainted with the Jewish history, that the Pentateuch was written by him, and published as the commandments and word of God, and that without offering any reasons, but such as have been often substantially and conclusively answered and confuted?

At this time of day, it would have been sufficient to have held up the difficulties attending the language in which the Old Testament was written, as well as our ignorance of the particular manners, habits and customs of so ancient a people, as answers to those puerile objections brought by our author; but learned men, both of Jews and Chriftians, have condescended to enter into the merits of the weakest objections of infidel writers, and fully obviated every difficulty. Yet our author, with great self-sufficiency, and without pretending to be able to read the original, so as to have any knowl-

---

31. 9th Numb. 22.

edge of the peculiar situation of the nation at the time of this history, most arrogantly pronounces, *"That we have no other external evidence or author-ity for believing those books to be the word of God, than the vote of the church mythologists"* A very modern Jewish author, of good credit, has observed, that "Moses has been the acknowledged author of the Pentateuch, (and his laws observed accordingly) from Moses to Joshua—from him to the time of the Judges—to David and Solomon, and during the existence of the first temple. By those Jews carried captive to Babylon—by those who returned from thence with Ezra; and by those who staid behind in Chaldea, Assyria, and other eastern provinces—by the Jews who have resided from time im-memorial in Cochin, and have had no intercourse with any other Jews, till the Dutch went there for trade (within two centuries). By the Jews of Spain, who were carried captive there at the destruction of the first and second temples, and dispersed over the globe. By Josephus—by the compilers of the Mishna and the Talmud—by that great luminary, Maimonides, who lived in the eleventh century, and who drew up the articles of the Jewish faith; the first of which is on the great degree of the prophecy of Moses; the eighth on the belief that the law is from God; *i. e. we are to believe all the law which we now have, is the very same law given to Moses, and that be received it all from the mouth of God; the historical part as well as the preceptive*; and therefore he is called in Hebrew, a *scribe*, because he acted as one, who wrote from the mouth of another; for which reason we seldom or ever find him speaking in his own person, but as one who is copying from a book, or from what another is rehearsing to him."[32] To this regular chain of testi-mony, may be added, that of the Samaritans and Karaites, who were early taught the Jewish religion by priests sent to them by the Affyrian king, for that purpose.

Dr. Priestley says, " There can be no doubt but that the canon of the Old Testament, was the same in the time of our Saviour, as it is now; nor could it have been corrupted materially after the return of the Jews from the Bab-ylonish captivity, on account of the sect of the Samaritans, which took its rise about that time; for these people professed the same regard to the sa-cred books with the Jews themselves, and were always at variance with them about the interpretation of the Scriptures. The Samaritan copy of the Pen-tateuch is now in our hands, and excepting some numbers, in which the different copies and translations of all ancient writings are peculiarly sub-

---

32. Levi's Answer to Paine.

ject to vary, and a single text in which Mount Gerizim and Mount Ebal are interchanged, it is the very same with the Jewish copy. Not long after this, the books of the Old Testament, beginning with the Pentateuch, were translated into Greek, and dispersed by means of the Jews, into almost every part of the known world.

If we go farther back into the Jewish history, we shall be unable to pitch upon any time, in which any material change in the sacred books could have been attempted with the leaft prospect of success. It was one of the most earnest instructions of Moses himself, that the book of the law, a copy of which was lodged in the ark, should be the subject of constant reading and meditation in every Israelitish family; and it was expressly appointed that it should be read publicly every seven years, at the feast of tabernacles ; and the Levites who were dispersed through all the twelve tribes, were particularly appointed to study and explain it to the rest of the nation; and notwithstanding the times of defection and idolatry, they were never entirely without prophets, and even many thousands of others, who continued firm in the worship of the true God, and therefore must have retained their regard to the sacred books of the law.

On the whole, the Jews have, no doubt, acted the part of most faithful, and ever scrupulous guardians of their sacred books, for the use of all the world in the times of Christianity.

After the last of the prophets, Malachi, they admitted no more books into their canon, so as to permit them to be read in their synagogues, though they were written by the most eminent men in their nation; it being a maxim with them, that no book could be entitled to a place in the canon of Scriptures, unless it was written by a prophet, or a person who had communication with God.

That the Scriptures of the Old Testament have not been materially corrupted by the Jews since the promulgation of Christianity, is evident from the many prophecies still remaining in their Scriptures, concerning the humiliation and sufferings of the Messiah, in which the Christians always triumphed, when they disputed with the Jews."[33]

Our author proceeds to examine the internal evidence contained in the books themselves; though he has made it pretty clear, that he is as totally unacquainted with their spirit and meaning, as the aborigines of North America—but here, as if at a loss how to begin, he starts off from

---

33. Instit. of Nat. and Rev Relig. 297

his subject, to give us his ideas of *revelation*, that he may apply them to the books in question.

He says, "Revelation is a communication of something which the person, to whom that thing is revealed, did not know before. For if I have done a thing, or seen it done, it needs no revelation to tell me I have done it, or seen it, nor to enable me to tell it or to write it—revelation therefore cannot be applied to any thing done upon earth, of which man is of himself the actor or the witness." This definition is exactly characteristic of our author—suffer him to ftate positions at his pleasure, and consider them as proved principles or axioms, and put implicit faith in his conclusions, and he is able to prove any thing, however absurd, that will suit his purpose.

The true idea of revelation, in the scriptural sense, which is the subject of consideration, is, God's making known himself and his will to mankind, in a special manner, besides what he has made known by the light of nature or reason, from his works of creation and providence. Now this may be done expressly * and positively by an immediate divine communication; or it may be done by a history of God's dealings with any people, nation, or sect of men, whom he chooses to set forth as a pattern or example to the rest of mankind; attended with rational evidence of God's being the immediate author of such revelation.

As has before been hinted, when Adam first awoke into existence, and beheld *"the fair creation"* around him, is it supposable that he would have been able, from the powers of his reasoning faculties, to have discovered his various relative duties, without any supernatural communications. He must have been confounded by the sight of every thing around him, being totally ignorant of their nature, properties, uses and qualities. He must have remained ignorant of even the necessities of his nature, and of the common mode of supplying them for a long time, till experience had taught him—every beast of the field must have alarmed him, and every tree of the forest put him in fear—the storm and the tempest must have terrified him with the expectation of immediate dissolution, and the thunder and lightning must have petrified him with horror. A divine communication therefore became absolutely and essentially necessary to him; as necessary as his existence, by which alone it could have been supported.

Even our author admits (page 8) the power of the Almighty, to make such communication if he pleased.

If then it should thus please him, and he should do it, attended with sufficient evidence to convince the human mind of its being from him, and it should be of such a nature as to relate to the whole human race, then I presume he will not deny, but acknowledge, that every man is obliged, by the laws of his nature, to obey the divine mandate. This then closes the circle, and brings the dispute back to its true principle. Has God given this evidence to mankind, or has he not ? We presume, without assuming too much, that this has fully appeared, so as to convince every honest man.

It can hardly be imagined, that, when God had thought proper in his infinite goodness, to make man a rational and immortal being, on purpose to know, love and adore him, and to receive the first spring of all his happiness from the contemplation of his being, attributes and works, that he should then have left him, *in his present state of frailty, weakness and ignorance*, to the mere light of nature, which the experience of almost six thousand years has shown to be wholly insufficient, to keep men even from destroying each other; without affording any other visible tokens of his presence, or communicating any further knowledge of himself, than might be drawn from ignorant reflections on the stupendous works of creation.

Had this been the case, man in his best estate would have been left imperfect indeed; and as a most excellent writer has observed, before me, " without such divine revelation, the case would have been with him, as with one that is born blind; who, whatever other evidence he may have of the being of a God, wants the most convincing of all, that is, the wonders of an Almighty power, and incomprehensible wisdom, conspicuous in the frame of nature, and the visible parts of the creation. Thus in like manner, to whatever such sense men, who have only reason for their guide, may attain of the mercy and goodness of God; whatever they may observe in the course of his providence to confirm them in the belief of it; whatever hopes they may entertain of it from a general notion of the divine nature; whatever desire they may have of it, from a sense of their own misery; yet they want that evidence of it, which alone can satisfy and compose their doubtful and distracted minds, and that is, certainty ; or, which is the same thing, revelation; by which, and nothing less, that certainty is to be obtained."

Without some aid of this kind, and under a full view of the prevalence of natural and moral evil in the world, who could determine whether this world is under the immediate government of the Supreme Being, or not ? Or whether man shall exist after this life ? It is divine revelation alone that hath brought life and immortality to light, with certainty and demonstration.

Were not four thousand years of trial, sufficient to convince even infidelity itself? If you look to the people at large, or the common herd of mankind, you behold them sunk in error and superstition—given up to the most irrational and brutal conduct.[34] If you have recourse to the higher ranks of life, let the most learned and sagacious philosophers of antiquity answer for themselves.

Cicero, famous throughout the learned world for his inquiries after truth and investigations into his own nature, moral faculties, and future expectations, gives us the sum of all their knowledge, that could be acquired without revelation. In his Tusculan Questions, lib. i. he assures us, when speaking of the soul, " That whether it was mortal or immortal, God only knew." And in the same work, " he devoutly wishes that the immortality of the soul could be proved to him." So that with all his knowledge, and after all his researches, he was not able to determine a fact, on which the whole happiness of the rational creature for time and eternity, must depend. It was this uncertainty about divine things, that led him " to allow men to continue in the idolatry of their ancestors, and to conform themselves to the religion of their country, in offering such sacrifices to different Gods, as were by law established."[35]

And again, in his Treatise of the nature of the Gods, he says, " As many things in philosophy are not sufficiently clear, so the question concerning the nature of the Gods, which is in itself the most interesting and necessary for the regulation of religion, is attended with peculiar difficulty. And so various and discordant are the opinions of the most learned, on tins subject, that it affords a good argument for the academies, to withhold their assent to propositions that are uncertain, and to maintain that ignorance is the foundation of philosophy"—" with respect to the question, the greater part held, *what is most probable,* viz. that there are Gods. But Protagoras doubted of it, and Diagoras of Melos, and Theodoras of Cyrene, held that there are none: and of those that supposed there are Gods, their opinions are so various, that it is difficult to enumerate them."

Plutarch, in speaking of superstition, in his tract oft that subject, says, " Men were not at first made atheists, by any fault they found in the Heavens, or stars, or seasons of the year, or in those revolutions or motions of the sun

---

34. "We have already seen, how various, how loose, and how uncertain were the religious sentiments of Polytheists. They were abandoned almost without control to the natural workings of a superstitious fancy. The accidental circumstances of their life and situation, determined the object as well as the degree of their devotion ; and as long as their adoration was successively prostituted to a thousand Deities, it was scarcely possible that their hearts could be susceptible of a very sincere or lively passion for any of them." Gibb. vol. ii. 355.

35. Cicero de Leg. lib. ii. n n

about the earth, that make the day and night; nor yet by observing any mistake or disorder, either in the breeding of animals, or in the production of fruits. No; it was the uncouth actions and senseless passions of superstition, her canting words, her foolish gestures, "her charms, her magick, her freakish processions, her tabourings, her foul expiations, her vile methods of purgation, and her barbarous and inhuman penances and bemirings at the temples. It was these, I say, that gave occasion to many to affirm it would be far happier, if there were no Gods at all, than such as are pleased with such fantastical toys; who thus abuse their votaries, and are incensed and pacified with trifles."

Gibbon, speaking of some of the most able of the heathen philosophers, having, from the nature of the soul, deduced an argument of its immortality, and also its past eternity, says, " A doctrine thus removed beyond the senses and the experience of mankind, might serve to amuse the leisure of a philosophic mind; or in the silence of solitude, it might sometimes impart a ray of comfort to desponding virtue, but the feint impression which had been received in the schools, was soon obliterated by the commerce and business of active life. We are sufficiently acquainted with the eminent persons who flourished in the age of Cicero and of the first Caesars; with their actions, their characters, and their motives, to be assured that their conduct in this life was never regulated by any serious conviction *of the rewards or punishments of a future state.* At the bar and in the senate of Rome, the ablest orators were not apprehensive of giving offence to their hearers, by exposing *that doctrine* as an idle and extravagant opinion, which was rejected with contempt by every man of a liberal education and understanding."[36]

Examine the laws of Lycurgus, so famous throughout the heathen world. Did he not establish, in some measure, a community of wives, or something very much like it. His practice of obliging the youth of both sexes to exercise in the most active and violent games, undressed and in a state of nature, without regard to the natural modesty of the sex, and against every principle of even natural religion, is a reproach to human nature.

The best of the heathen sages knew nothing of the love of God to man—of his grace to repenting sinners, and the divine aid yielded to him for his attaining to and persevering in virtue and holiness of life—God's hatred to sin, and the absolute necessity of holiness and purity of heart, to those who are to become heirs of a happy immortality, were doctrines wholly unknown

---

36. Vid. Cicero pro Cluent. ch. 61.—2d Gibb. 296.

to the learned heathen—although they had some confused notion of a future state, yet it was such as consisted merely in a vain imagination concerning shades and spectres; the resurrection of the body never once entered their thoughts. It was reserved for revelation alone to make known the great things of another and better world, as well as to explain the otherwise difficult enigma of this.

The great apostle Paul takes notice of the insufficiency of human wisdom, when he says, " For after that, (or since) in the wisdom of God, the world by wisdom knew not God, it pleased God by the foolishness (or simplicity) of preaching, to save them who believe."[37]

Our author will, I doubt not, readily hearken to Mr. Gibbon, whom we have already quoted, as a witness not suspected of an unfair bias towards revelation. Speaking of the decline of the Pagan religion, about the fourth century, he says, " Some Deities of a more recent and fashionable cast might soon have occupied the deserted temples of Jupiter and Apollo, if in the decisive moment the wisdom of Providence had not interposed a *genuine revelation, fitted to inspire the most rational esteem and conviction*, whilst at the same time it was adorned with all that could attract the curiosity, the wonder, and the veneration of the people. "[38]

Let our author himself become a witness of the insufficiency of the revelation he speaks of, and confines himself to *"He has seen the fair creation— a world furnished to our hands, that cost us nothing. He has seen the sun that is lighted up by the power of the Creator, and he has been blessed by the rain poured down by the same Almighty hand"* What, let me ask him, have been the returns he has made to the great author of these mercies; or how have his gross feelings been exercised towards his beneficent Creator ? Has a life of forgetfulness of God, immorality of conduct, an abuse of the mercies of God, and a disregard to laws human and divine, discovered that all this mighty light of nature, has led him in gratitude and admiration to adore and love the great First Cause of all his mercies?—Let him put his hand on his heart, and answer as in the presence of God for himself.

But if we turn from a few individuals, of professed learning and deep investigation, to the people at large of every nation and language in the heathen world, who enjoyed all the benefits and advantages of our author's *word of God* in the creation, and to whom he asserts, "The way to God was equally open," what opinion can we form of their morals from their practices? Do we

---

37. 1st Cor. chap. i. 21.
38. Gibb. 2d Vol. 375.

not find them encouraging a spirit of revenge—commending suicide as a virtue—recommending fornication as a proper remedy against a greater evil—asserting the expediency of men having their wives in common—teaching the lawfulness of unnatural incest and lust. The Cynics laying aside all natural restraints of shame and modesty—the Stoics encouraging the most filthy and obscene language, so that their own philosophers could not help observing, " That the most notorious vices were screened under the name of philosophy; and that they did not labor to maintain the characters of philosophers by virtue and study, but concealed very vicious lives under an austere look, and an habit different from the rest of the world."[39]

Consonant to this is the representation in the 14th chap. Wisdom of Solomon, 23rd verse and onwards— "For while they slew their children in sacrifices, or used secret ceremonies, or made revellings of strange rites they kept neither lives, nor marriages undefiled any longer; but either one slew another traitorously, or grieved him by adultery. So that there reigned in all men without exception, blood, manslaughter, theft, dissimulation, corruption, unfaithfulness, tumults, perjury, disquieting of good men, forgetfulness of good turns, defiling of souls, changing of kind (or sex), disorder in marriages, adultery and shameless uncleanness. For the worshipping of idols (not to be named) is the beginning, the cause, and the end of all evil."

And Dr. Priestly justly observes, " Without revelation the degree of reason that God has thought proper to give to man, is so far from being sufficient for his moral instruction, that the most intelligent of the heathens, those who thought and reflected the most, as we may judge by their refinement in metaphysics, mythology and theology, as the Egyptians, Greeks, and Hindoos, have erred the most widely, having given into more absurd superstitions, than the most stupid of mankind."[40]

But let us attend to the character of Moses, the writer of these books, as it is acknowledged that a revelation said to come from God, is a mark of favor and respect to the persons who are made the instruments of communication. Such revelation should be supported—BY THE PERSONAL CONDUCT OF THE PERSON TO WHOM MADE THE SUBJECT MATTER OF THE REVELATION—AND THE ATTESTATIONS ATTENDING IT IN CONFIRMATION OF THE TRUTH.

As to the first, that there was such a person as Moses, who was a Hebrew, brought up at Pharaoh's court; a very wise man—and the great leader of the

39. Quintil. Inst. lib. i. pref.
40. Priestley's Corrupt. 272.

people of Israel, is a fact already shown, and so well established by historians of all characters, that even our author condescends to acknowledge and confirm it.

Moses is also taken notice of, as the founder of the Jewish nation, after leading the Hebrews, to the number of near three millions of souls, from Egypt to the land of Canaan, in a very extraordinary manner. His personal character seems to answer every particular that might be expected from a person favoured by the Supreme Being with extraordinary and supernatural communications.

It is agreed on all hands, that the court at which he was educated, was the most learned and polite of all the then nations of the earth. That he was instructed in all the learning of the Egyptians, who were then considered as the chief depositaries of all religion. That he was remarkable for his meekness, temperance, and justice.

He was in a special manner attached to the service of one great Almighty Being, and an irreconcilable enemy to every species of idolatry. He declared and taught openly and explicitly, that he was sent of God; and he appealed to the many miracles that he wrought publicly before the whole Egyptian court, for the truth of that mission. That the institutions of divine worship, which he enjoined on his countrymen, were not of his own devising, but that he received them from God, who had given his people visible and sensible manifestations of his divine presence at the time. Of course all his conduct was both moral and religious ; and during the long and severe trial of forty years, he was acknowledged by that numerous and discontented people, as blameless.

Neither in his doctrines or ceremonies did he aim at his own aggrandizement or advantage; but he preferred his brother, when singled out *himself* by God, as a special messenger to Pharaoh.

When establishing a permanent priesthood, the chief of which was to be clothed with more than royal power and dignity, he prefers his brother Aaron and his family, notwithstanding his unworthy behavior in the case of the golden calf, *passing by his own family.* And when declining in years, and in the prospect of sudden death, though in sight of the promised land, he nominates as his successor, Joshua, the son of Nun, of the tribe of Ephraim; passing by his two sons and his own tribe, for whom he makes no public provision.

Throughout his whole history, he not only does not hesitate to record his personal errors and mistakes, but gives a correct account even of his crimes, and the divine displeasure, and the punishment of them. He records the opposition of his brother—the revolt of Aaron's sons, with their destruction and that of their families.

His whole life manifested the most exemplary piety towards God; and, though under the most trying circumstances, the purest justice and strictest impartiality to those whom he governed.

2dly. *The subject matter of the revelation.* It was in all respects worthy the majesty of a God to impart and the necessities of man to receive.

The state of the world, by reason of the prevalence of idolatry and a total perversion of all former divine revelations, whether immediate and personal, or by the works of creation and providence, was most deplorable.

The one only living and true God was not known or acknowledged, except by a few individuals here and there scattered through the world. Mankind, to speak in general terms, were overwhelmed in the most superstitious idolatry, and devoted to practises of the most wicked and immoral tendency. They had lost sight of every true principle of conduct towards their great Creator, and were at a loss how to establish any general rule of moral obligation, whereby men might be led to perform their duty to God or their neighbor.

The amazing number of gods and demi gods, who were made objects of solemn worship, totally destroyed all rational ideas of the real great first cause of all things, who ought to have been the sole object of all divine honor. Some distant idea may be formed of the awful situation to which men were reduced at the time of Moses's mission, from a contemplation of the character and conduct of the author of the Age of Reason and his contemporaries at this day of light and knowledge, who pretend to substitute, what they call the worship of nature and reason, and other unintelligible jargon of the like kind; instead of him who liveth for ever and ever.

In this state of the world, what could be more worthy of God, than a revelation of himself—the being that is—the self-existent being—I am that I am? of the origin of the world in which we live, and of the beginning of the creation of God?—Of the first state of man at his formation?—his purity, innocence and state of perfect happiness?—of his intercourse with his creator?—Of his general knowledge of, and dominion over other parts of the creation? of the obligations laid upon him, enjoining obedience to the will of his creator, with the worship and homage that he required from his creatures?—Of the fell of man? his penitence? expulsion from Paradise, the seat of innocence and happiness? and of the sad and deplorable consequence of the first transgression, all naturally and evidently flowing from so awful a breach of his duty ?

Then follows what could never have entered into the human mind to have conceived of, without a divine revelation—an account of that door of hope, opened to our despairing first parents, in the redemption of their otherwise hopeless race, by a saviour "who should bruise the serpent's head, while the serpent should only bite his heel".

What was there in nature to have dictated a scheme of this kind, or by what means should man by his natural faculties, have ever conceived so wonderful a plan for the restoration of his sinful posterity? This first suggestion, was the sure foundation of a glorious system, that has grown brighter and brighter through every age of the world, and will so continue to the end of it, or rather through the immeasurable of eternity. It was the great fact, that should run, like the web through the woof, and appear in every transaction of the governor of the world towards his fallen creatures through every age, both in his natural and moral government. "This history expresses an awful and amiable sense of the Divine Being, our creator and judge r shows the heinousness of sin, and mortifies us to this world, by declaring that our passage through it must be attended with labor and sorrow. We find ourselves accordingly, in this state—revealed religion did not bring us into it; nor is this state, an objection to revealed religion, more than to natural, if any such can be shown. Revealed religion goes a step higher than that which is termed natural, and shows the immediate secondary causes, viz. the sin and wilful disobedience of our first parents. And when the account of Paradise—man's expulsion therefrom—and of the curse passed upon him in Genesis; are compared with the removal of that curse, of sorrow, crying, pain and death—with the renovation of all things, and man's restoration to the tree of life and the paradise of God, and his admission to the new Jerusalem in the last chapter of the Revelation, hope and fear quicken each other, and both conspire to purify the mind, and to advance the great design, considered as to its unity."[41]

Here was a revelation of the divine intentions, concerning the children of men during their whole existence, which I must again repeat never did or could have entered into the mind of man to have conceived of, without supernatural aid. Many have been the schemes and plans of priests and philosophers, to establish religion and government among men, but no such idea had ever been formed, but what has arisen from the source declared by Moses. "He plainly divulged the mind of God with regard to his public ser-

---

41. Hartley

vice—all the common practises of life were consecrated by a divine command, and so became acts of religious obedience.

The external worship was loaded with a great variety of rites and ordinances, which, when practised in the true spirit of their institution, became
a sort of continual prayer—their abstinencies a daily mortification—their
ablutions and purifications, symbols of that perfect purity of heart, necessary to prepare us for the divine union—the daily, weekly, monthly, and
annual feasts and sacrifices, were emblems and figures, either of the great
victim to be offered up for the sins of the world, or of the internal sacrifice
of the passions, sensual desires, or spiritual vices, which must be mortified
and destroyed e'er we can be reunited to our first principle.

In short, Moses's whole design, (if he is barely considered as a legislator)
was, to form a nation of true adorers of the Supreme God, that should destroy
idolatry, enlighten the world, subject all nations to the empire of the Most
High, and to make them at once happy and virtuous, wise and religious."[42]

To accomplish this, a divine revelation was absolutely necessary, for the
very reason that the apostle John has expressly assigned. "No man hath seen
God at any time; the only begotten Son, who is in the bosom of the Father,
he hath declared him."[43]

The ten commandments are worthy of God himself, and the moral precepts of the Pentateuch are of the most excellent and beneficial kind: "The
poor, the widow and the orphan are bountifully provided for by a number of
laws, or by counsel equivalent to laws, repeated so often, and enforced with
so persuasive arguments, that they could not fail of producing the intended
effects; they give us a most favorable idea of the benevolence and philan-
thropy of the lawgiver. Brotherly love and good neighborhood are enjoined
or recommended in the strongest terms. The interest of one's neighbor
must be one's own: his landmarks must not be removed; his strayed cattle
must be kept and restored; his fallen beast of burden must be helped up; his
deposits must be faithfully returned, and what hath been stolen from him,
be repaid with indemnification. To a native and even a sojourner, one must
lend without demanding interest, and if a pledge be required, it must be
such as the borrower can give without great inconvenience. The mercenary
is to receive his hire on the day he earns it. Even the slave who has served his

---

42. Philos. Princip.
43. 1st John, 18th vcr.

time, is not to be dismissed empty handed....No one is to be oppressed, or hardly dealt with."[44]

We now proceed to the last test of a revelation coining from God, viz. *"the attestations attending it, in confirmation of its truth."*

As mankind were essentially interested in this all important revelation, it was not left, for its authenticity to the moral character, religious practises, or public authority of Moses. His communications to the Jewish people were attended with such evident marks of the divine power and wisdom, as convinced even the hard and obstinate heart of Pharaoh, though the sovereign of the most powerful and enlightened nation on earth, and that not merely as to his own speculative opinion; but so as to found an important act of government on it, contrary to his former most solemn and resolute determinations, not to part with three millions of laborious and useful subjects, on whom he greatly depended, for the perfecting those immense works of art and curiosity, which he had contemplated as the means of handing down his character, with eclat, to posterity. Moses proved his supernatural mission by prodigies which surpass the force and power of human nature, and were peculiarly adapted to the idolatry and prejudices of that country. They were public, universal as to that and the neighboring nations, and of such a kind, that they could not be impostures, or the delusion of the senses. The consequences that attended them, particularly the deliverance of so great a body of defenceless people, from so mighty and powerful a tyrant, without force, are convincing proofs of their reality and truth. Monuments were erected and feasts instituted from the time in which they were wrought, to perpetuate the remembrance of them, and render their veracity unsuspected to all generations : add to this that they were testified by millions of living witnesses.

Moses's mission and character were also confirmed by miracles and prophetic declarations to the people, which were to take place after his death; and accordingly some of them continued during the whole time of this people possessing a government of their own, and while they conformed themselves to their laws and religious polity, as standing and uncontrovertible proofs of his divine and prophetic authority. Among an hundred, I will confine myself (beside the manna in the temple) to two instances only. While in the wilderness, and before they had succeeded in taking possession of the promised land, with all the certainty of the event as if it had already hap-

---

44. Gedies, pref. xxi.

pened, Moses gives them precise rules for their conduct, when they should inherit the land according to his words; and among others, "that thrice in the year all their males should appear before the Lord, the God of Israel; for," says he, "(in the name of God) I will cast out the nations before thee, and enlarge thy borders; *neither shall any man desire thy land, when thou shah go up to appear before the Lord thy God thrice in the year*."[45]

Here then was a prophetic declaration, of a miracle to exist for hundreds of years, on which no man above an idiot would ever have risked his reputation and the existence of his people, without the fullest assurance of his divine authority. The issue fully proved the certainty of his dependence, and for many hundred years the facts turned out as he had promised them; for during their continuance in a faithful submission to their laws and ordinances, it was never known, that an enemy ever invaded their territory, while their males were thus gone up to Jerusalem, to appear before the Lord; yet it is as well known, that they were surrounded by the most bitter, savage, and revengeful nations, who took every other opportunity to destroy and oppress, them.

The next instance is that of the seventh or sabbatical year, during which, as Moses commanded while yet in the wilderness, their land was to be at rest, they were neither to plough, sow nor reap: "And if ye shall say what shall we eat the seventh year ? behold we shall not sow, nor gather in our increase—then will I command my blessing upon you in the sixth year, and it shall bring forth fruit for three years: and ye shall sow the eighth year, and eat yet of old fruit until the ninth year; until her fruits come in, ye shall eat of the old store."[46]

Here is another prophetic declaration of a miracle, which never could have been ventured upon, by any rational creature, who was not a vain enthusiast, had he not been certain of the promise coming from him, whose Almighty power was equal to the performance of whatever he promised, however difficult. The history of this people proves, that this was fully verified, and it continued a repeated confirmation of the divine origin of their national institutions, every seventh year, and left this stiffnecked people without excuse, in all their obstinate deviations from the path of duty, and rendered them justly liable to the severe punishment, which at the same time was threatened, and afterwards strictly executed upon them.

---

45. ExocL 34th chtp. 23—24.
46. 25th Lcvit. 20—22.

In this part of the proof of the divine mission of Moses, deception was impossible. He was not present to work upon their hopes or fears. He was dead, as were the whole body of the congregation, over whom he had any influence, and who had been personally acquainted with him. It was not a single event in which the people might have been deceived and imposed upon by their enthusiasm or credulity. It was not an event, in the first instance, favorable to their interest. They were to risque their whole crops for two years, and in that their very existence as a people; for if they were deceived or mistaken, nothing short of famine stared them in the face. They were very frequently engaged in wars with their neighbors, they were therefore doubly exposed. Had they doubted the truth of the prediction, they never could have acted so absurd and irrational a part, as to have risked famine and pestilence on a doubtful event. Yet in all their history for a thousand years, there is no instance of their having reason to repent their faith and confidence, in the divine mission of their leader.

Our author, in the case of the resurrection, calls for public, ocular and universal demonstration, or he will not believe. Is there not in the case of Moses, the fullest demonstration, under every idea that he demands it, except that of the revelation being made personally to himself; and yet, is he convinced of the truth by this conclusive testimony ? Or do we not still find him not only denying Moses to be the author or writer of these invaluable books, but also ridiculing every idea of their divine original?

When Moses was first honored by the divine presence as a preparative to his being sent to Pharaoh, it was sufficient that Moses alone should be convinced of the truth of the revelation of the divine will; hence the miraculous burning of the bush, without being consumed; and the voice of God therefrom, went no farther than his own conviction; and had the evidence ended here, no one but Moses would have been bound to believe. Our blessed Saviour himself confirms this conclusion, by saying to the Jews, "Had I not done among you, the works which no other man ever did, ye had not had sin"—that is, if I had not given you evidence of my coming from God, sufficient to convince the human mind, you would not have been to blame for not believing. But when Moses was sent, first to his own people, and afterwards to Pharaoh, in the name of God, the evidence was equal to the nature of the mission.

Moses, conscious of his own insufficiency, and the difficulty of requiring the belief of his nation, without full evidence of his mission, said to God, "But behold they will not believe me nor hearken unto my voice; for they will say, the Lord hath not appeared unto thee." This was rational and proper—God therefore enabled him to prove his mission to them, by casting his rod on the ground, and it became a serpent, and by taking it again, it became a rod, "that they may believe that the Lord God of their fathers hath appeared unto thee." And if this did not work a full conviction, then he was empowered to perform two other miracles, that could not be doubted.[47]

Pharaoh being the head and governor of a nation, the request to let so large a body of the people leave the kingdom at once, was of a more public nature. He ought not to have consented, but upon full, public and convincing testimony, that the demand was made by divine authority. And though he received this, yet he hardened his heart, and rejected the full testimony at first afforded him, till by the repetition of them, they became his severest punishment. The miraculous plagues brought on the court and people of Egypt previous to their convictiori, and the consequent departure of the Hebrews from that house of bondage, need not here be repeated. No one who reads the account, will doubt of the publicity, universality, and unequivocal nature of the testimony.

They were at last suffered to depart for a few days to worship God in the wilderness: but they were no sooner gone, than the Egyptians, with Pharaoh at their head, finding by their manner of going, that they did not mean to return, and knowing that they carried with them much property given to them, under a violent paroxism of fear, repented of their concession, and determined without delay to pursue, overtake, and bring them back.

It now became necessary, that Moses should be able to show more expressly to the multitude of the people at large, some plain and certain evidence of his divine authority, suited to their then peculiar circumstances, and which should so operate on the whole congregation, as to leave no doubt, but that they were acting in what they did, by the commandment of heaven.

The Egyptian king was a mighty monarch, and had at his command a numerous army, with which the Hebrews could not pretend to combat.

Nothing short of the interposing power of Omnipotence could save them. Here was no possibility of deception; no eloquence, no magical art, no intrigues, could now avail against an incensed tyrant, raging with malicious fury against an unarmed people, who were trying to escape by flight from his power.

---

47. 4th chap. Exed. 1st to 10th.

The Red Sea is in their front, without any artificial mode of passing it; and a haughty and powerful enemy in their rear—three millions of souls, men, women and children—no provisions laid up for any length of time—no arms in their hands, or means of defence in their power, equal to their necessities. To God alone, through the mediation of Moses, the great type of him that was to come, could they look. Now was the time to try their faith and constancy—if they had been deceived by an impostor, or had they too credulously believed, without a certainty of Moses's supernatural power, they now stood on the brink of irretrievable destruction. But as it is often the case with the children of God, in the moment of danger, they found a glorious deliverance. Behold the fiery cloud changing its position from front to rear— and while it affords a perfect light to the Hebrews in advance, is total darkness to the Egyptians pursuing in the rear.

At a stroke of Moses's rod, the billows cease to roll—the waters separate, and a passage on dry ground is opened for their escape into the wilderness; which passage, whilst it proves their salvation, becomes a snare and immediate destruction to Pharaoh and his host. "And Moses stretched out his hand over the sea, and the Lord caused the sea to go back by means of a strong *south* wind,[48] (as it is in the Septuagint, and should be rendered) all that night, and made the sea dry land, and divided the waters—and the Egyptians pursued and went after them into the midst of the sea—and Moses stretched forth his hand upon the sea, and the sea returned to its strength early in the morning, and the Egyptians fled against it, and the Lord overthrew the Egyptians in the midst of the sea."[49]

This miraculous deliverance could not be ideal—it was not done in secret—it was not done "*in the presence of eight or nine witnesses, as proxies*

---

48. Both the Alexandrian and the Vatican copies of the Pentateuch, agree that it was a south wind—this wind sweeping along the eastern coast of Africa and Arabia foelix, and driving the waters cf the ocean back from the mouth of the Straits of Bibelmandel towards the Persian Gulph, would naturally, in consequence of the projecting coast of Adel and Cape Guardafui, draw off the waters of the Red Sea, and lower them greatly, and especially if such wind, co-operated with a strong ebbing tide from the coast of Arabia, as was most probably the case. In consequence of these two circumstances conspiring together, all the shoals and banks of the Red Sea would be left bare; and any remarkable shoal running across at the place of the passage, would divide the waters, causing those above to remain as a lake; while those below were falling down towards the straits of Babelmandel.—The return of the tide from the ocean the next morning, restored the waters as before. Let any curious person cast his eye on the globe, and he will see that an east wind would have the direct reverse effect. King's Morsels of Criticism—87.

49. Exodus 14:21-27,

for the whole world." The facts, in Mr. Paine's own words, *"admitted of public and ocular demonstration like the sun at noon-day."* This demonstration was given, and every individual man, woman, and child, (capable of knowledge) who passed through the sea, and found themselves the next morning safe on dry land, while they beheld their enemies perishing in the waters, now closing on all sides of them, were, with the whole Egyptian people, witnesses for Moses that he was sent of God.

Let me here ask, what effect this public demonstration of the divine mission of Moses had on Korah, Dathan, and Abiram—or, to come nearer home, what effect has it had on our author, who calls for it with so much confidence in the case of the resurrection and ascension of our Lord and Saviour Jesus Christ; the evidence of which, take it in all its parts, though equal in point of universality and certainty, yet was necessarily different in the form and nature of the testimony.

Has it commanded his assent ? Does he firmly believe in the divine mission of Moses, or has he impiously considered it as *"a history of wickedness, that has served to corrupt and brutalize mankind and which therefore be sincerely detests."* If this has been the case with him and his brethren in unbelief, when the public demonstration, which they consider as necessary for the confirmation of truth was so clearly and unequivocally given, we may safely conclude, what would have been their conduct and practice, with their present dispositions, had they been eye witnesses of the resurrection and ascension of Jesus Christ.

The effect of this unequivocal evidence of the divine mission of Moses, and the presence of God with him, on hearts unchanged by divine grace, was very manifest from the conduct of many of the Israelites themselves, who but a few days after this *"public and ocular demonstration"* of the divine power and presence, murmured against Moses, and upbraided him with bringing them into a wilderness to perish. Such was, and still is, the nature of man in a fallen state, without the knowledge of God; until by means of sufferings and trials, and a thorough change of heart by the Spirit of God, he is brought to renounce his own wisdom, and to abhor himself in dust and ashes.

It is very certain, from all the light that can be obtained from history, that the five books of Moses were written by him, in his life time; during the actual existence of thousands who had come with him through the wilderness; who had been eye and ear witnesses of most, if not of all the miracles that he records. The young people among them, afterwards actually possessed the land of Canaan, promised to their fathers many hundred years before, viz. by God himself to Abraham, and afterwards by Moses to them in the land of Egypt—their descendants enjoyed it upwards of fifteen hundred years, and lost it again, according to the express predictions of this same Moses, while yet in the wilderness. He also foretold them of events which should take place among them, especially relative to their wickedly desiring a king to rule over them, in imitation of the nations around them, hundreds of years after his death; and also that the Lord would raise up another prophet, to whom they should finally hearken, which has been accordingly done—and some of those events are fulfilling even at this day.

To us who have seen the completion of the awful prediction, one would have imagined no argument would have Been wanting to authenticate the divine mission of the leader of the tribes of Israel, after attending to this solemn declaration of Moses, so many thousand years before it came to pass. "And the Lord said unto Moses, behold thou shalt sleep with thy fathers, and this people will rise up and go a whoring after the Gods of the strangers of the land, whither they go to be among them, and will forsake me, and break my covenant, which I have made with them. Then my anger shall be kindled against them in that day, and I will forsake them, and I will hide my face from them, and they shall be devoured; and many evils and troubles shall befall them, so that they will say in that day, are not these evils come upon us, because our God is not among us—and I will surely hide my face in that day, for all the evils which they shall have wrought, in that they have turned unto other Gods."[50]

Let the last address of the successor of this man of God, to the people whom he had conducted, from the death of Moses to the complete possession of the promised land, being a space of twenty-eight years, have some effect in the proof of the divine mission of his great predecessor, being founded on the personal knowledge of every one to whom he spake; "behold this day I am going the way of all the earth, and *ye know in all your hearts and in all your souls*, that not one thing hath failed of all the good things, which the Lord your God spake concerning you; all are come to pass unto you and not one thing hath failed thereof."[51] This address he prefaces with, "Be ye very courageous to keep and to do all that is written in the book of the law of Moses,"[52] and then he proceeds to enumerate the special miracles

---

50. Deut. 31st chap. 16—18.
51. Josh. 23.—14.
52. Josh. 23.—6

that had been performed in their favor, repeating all the remarkable instances recorded by Moses from his first application to Pharaoh to their
passing over Jordan. So that if there was any design in Moses to deceive the
people, his successor must have combined with him to carry on the deception, and that at the moment of his dissolution.

It must be acknowledged that hitherto, we have considered these historical facts as evidences in favour of Moses, principally as related by himself, and extracted from his own writings: but since these were written for
the instruction of and a memorial to the people themselves, among whom
all the transactions related, were performed, and who were fully capable of
determining on their truth or falsehood; and who with their posterity to
this day, set their seals to the truth of them;[53] to which may be added, the
actual fulfilment of the many predictions contained in them, they must receive great additional weight of testimony, so as to command the belief of
every candid inquirer after truth. "The writings of the prophets bear plain
signatures of their divine authority. Examine the books of the Greek and
Roman sages, and observe what discordant opinions they contain on almost
every point of theology and philosophy; but in the Hebrew prophets there is
a wonderful harmony of doctrine for above one thousand years, unparal-
leled in the writings of any other country History teaches us, that a great
number of their prophecies have been accomplished; and we know that
some of them are accomplishing at this day."[54]

But if we examine into the records of profane History, we shall find
much to support the faith of the servant of God with regard to the leading
facts of the Mosaic Pentateuch.

Profane historians who mention Moses, and his character, seem to be in
part acquainted with his education, his military exploits and his miracles,
especially those plagues he brought on Egypt, and consider him as a famous
magician. In addition to what has already appeared herein, as the attestation of heathen authors to the character of Moses, he is universally consid-

---

52. The Pentateuch is the great repository of the most remote antiquities, religion,
polity, and literature of the Jewish nation; to which, in all their posterior writers, there is
a constant reference or allusion. To them the righteous judge, the reforming prince, the
admonishing priest, the menacing prophet, perpetually and uniformly appealed: on them
the historiographer, the orator, the poet, and the philosopher, endeavoured to form their respective styles: and to rival the language of the Pentateuch was, even in the most felicitous
periods of their state, considered as the highest effort of Hebrew genius. Preface to Geddes
t ran si. of the Pentateuch, fol. t.

54. An attempt towards an approved versn. of the 12 minor prophets, page 5 of preface.

ered by them as a great lawgiver, as is testified by Diodorus Siculus who says, that Moses received his laws from the God *Jao*.[55] His fine form and consummate wisdom are mentioned by Trogus Pompeius,[56] and he takes notice of Moses's success against the Ethiopians, who had invaded the territories of Pharaoh. Trogus was the first of the Latin historians, and attributes the prosperous and flourishing circumstances of the Jewish state to a mixture of justice with religion in their government. He gives a high character of Joseph and mentions his being sold by his brethren to foreign merchants through envy, who carried him into Egypt, where he soon became dear to the king. That Joseph was the first who understood the interpretation of dreams, and foretold a famine many years before it happened, and preserved Egypt, by advising the king to provide stores of corn against the time of need; and that there had been so much experience of the truth of his answers, that they seem to be given rather by God than man.[57]

Artepanus says Moses was commander of the Egyptian forces against the Ethiopians, during a ten years war[58]—yet on this subject we find Moses totally silent, but he does not forget to record his killing the Egyptian.

Numerous, the Pythagorean, says, "That Jannes and Iambres, the chief of the magicians of Egypt, by their sorceries, withstood Moses the leader of the Jews, a man most powerful in his prayers to God."[59] And when speaking expressly of the Hebrew lawgiver, he says, "What is Plato, but Moses conversing in the language of Athens."[60]

Diodorus and Herodotus, take notice of the terrible scourges brought on the Egyptians by Moses.[61] The former, who lived in the time of Julius and Augustus Caesar, and wrote the histories of Egypt, Persia, Syria, &c. also mentions, "That the Troglodites, the indigenous inhabitants of the place, (where Moses crossed the Red Sea) had a tradition from father to son, from their very early and remote ages, that once a division of the sea did happen there; and after leaving the bottom some time, the sea again came back, and raged with great fury."[62] This is the testimony of a heathen historian, not

---

55. Diodorus Siculus in his 1st book says " among the Jews, was Moses who called God by the name of Jao (meaning Jehovah), signifying existence.

56. Justin, lib. 36. chap. 2.

57. Reas. of Christ. 99.

58. Euseb. Pracp. Evang. lib. 9. ch. 27\

59. Plin. Hist. lib. 30. ch. i.

60. Clem. Alex. Strom, lib. 1. page 411.

61. Grot, de Verit. lib. 1.

62. Encyclop. Tit. Red Sea.

writing on the subject of revelation, but merely speaking of the country, the history of which he was writing, and recording the knowledge he had obtained from the natives.

Artepanus mentions a tradition of the manner of the passage of the Israelites through the Red Sea, among the people of Heliopolist[63]—and Tacitus says of the Jews, that they worshipped the Supreme Eternal, immutable Being.[64] Dion Cassius says, that many had written of the God of the Jews, and of the worship that they paid to him[65]—and Varro, the most learned historian among the Romans, much approved the Jewish way of worship, as being free from that idolatry which he could not but dislike in the heathen religion.[66]

The tradition of a seventh day Sabbath among all the heathen nations, could only be derived from the writings of Moses or the teachings of Abraham and his descendants. Clement Alexandrinus, in his Strom V. quotes out of Hessiod, "That the seventh day was sacred." The like out of Homer and Callimachus, to which may be subjoined, what Eusebius has taken out of Aristobulus, lib. 13. ch. 12. "Theophilus Antiochanus to Antelychus, concerning the seventh day, which is distinguished by all men."

Suetonius, in his Tiberius 32d, says, "Diogenes the grammarian, used to dispute at Rhodes on the Sabbath day." Lucian tells us in his Paralogist, "that boys were used to play on the seventh day." Dion Cassius, lib. 33, says, "The day called Saturnus, and the custom of computing time by weeks, was derived from the Egyptians to all mankind." Herodotus, in his second book, tells us, "That the keeping the seventh day was not a new, but a very ancient custom."

Josephus against Appion, about the end of the 2d book, says, "There is no city, Greek or Barbarian, in which the custom of resting on the seventh day, is not preserved, as it is among the Jews." And Philo says, "It is a festival not only celebrated in one city or country, but throughout the whole world."

That there was such a universal destruction by water, as Noah's flood, is confirmed by the concurrent testimony of several of the most ancient writers and nations in the world. That the Egyptians were no strangers to this event, appears from the testimony of Plato, who says, that a certain Egyptian priest recounted to Solon, out of their sacred books, the history of the

---

63. Euseb. Prxp. Evang. lib. 9. ch. 27.
64. Hist. lib. 15.
65. Lib. 37.
66. St. August, de Civ. Dei. lib. 4. ch. 31. Re as. Christ. 100.

universal flood, which happened long before the particular inundation known to the Grecians.

The inhabitants of Heliopolis in Syria, showed a chasm or cleft in the earth in the temple of Juno, which they said had swallowed up the waters of that flood.[67] Herodotus says the Egyptian priests told him, that the sun had four times deviated from his course, having twice risen when he uniformly goes down, and twice gone down when he uniformly rises.[68]

Grotius, in his Treatise on Truth, informs us, "That what Moses says of the origin of the world, is recorded by the Phoenicians and Egyptians. Ovid describes the creation of man and his absolute dominion over the brute creation. Maimonides says, "That the Indians in the east, formerly had the story of Adam and Eve—the tree of knowledge, and the temptation of the serpent; and it is said that the Brahmans and inhabitants of Siam, have them at this day."

Manetho who wrote the history of the Egyptians—Berosus who wrote the Chaldean History—Hesiod among the Greeks; Hecateus, Hellanicus and Ephorus, all unanimously agree, that in the first ages of the world, men lived one thousand years.[69] The account of the ark, the deluge, and those who were saved therein, is also mentioned by Berosus, Plutarch, and Lucian. Berosus was a priest of Belus,[70] and a Babylonian born, but afterwards flourished in the island of Cos. He gives an account of Noah under the name of Xisuthrus, to whom Saturn appeared in a dream, and gave him warning, that on the 15th day of the month Desius, mankind should be destroyed by a flood, and therefore commanded him to build a ship, and having furnished it with provisions, and taken into it fowls and four-footed beasts, to go into it himself, with his friends and nearest relations; this ship was five furlongs in length, and two wide. All this Xisuthrus did, and when the flood came, and began to abate, he let out some birds, which finding no food, nor place to rest on, returned to the ship. After some days he let out the birds again, but they came back, with their feet daubed with mud. In a few days he let them go again, but they did not return, whereby he understood that the earth appeared again above the waters; and so taking down some of the planks of the ship, he saw it rested upon a mountain.[71]

---

67. Univ. Hist. vol. i. page 55.
68. Ant. Univ. Hist. vol. 18, page 207.
69. Burnet's Thco. lib. 2. chap. 4.
70. Joseph, cont. Appion, lib. 1.
71. Univ. Hist.

Eusebius says, that Abydenus made mention of the dove that was sent out to explore the waters. The burmng of Sodom is related by Diodorus, Strabo and Tacitus.

The account of Abraham, Isaac, Jacob, and Joseph, was found in many ancient historians, quoted by Eusebius, and is mentioned in Justin from Trogus Pompeius; and the actions of Moses leading the Israelites out of Egypt, and receiving the two tables of stone from the hands of God, are to be found in many of the same authors, but particularly in the verses which are ascribed to Orpheus, and in the Egyptian histories. Sanchoniathan also mentions many of the facts related by Moses.[72]

In the reign of Darius Hystaspes, about five hundred years before our blessed Saviour, Zoroaster appeared in the world, in whose books are contained many things out of the Old Testament: a great part of the Psalms of David—the history of the Creation and deluge. He mentions Adam and Eve—Abraham, Joseph, Moses, and Solomon. Numenius the Pythagorian, before mentioned, asserts, that the Brachmans of India were not unacquainted with the religion of the Hebrews; and that the laws of the wisest of the heathen nations, were taken from the laws of Moses.[73]

Strabo mentions Moses and the ancient Jews with commendation; he says that many, in honor to the divine majesty, went out of Egypt with Moses, rejecting the worship of the Egyptians and other nations, inasmuch as Moses had instructed them, that God was not to be worshipped by any image; and that he would reveal himself only to the pure and virtuous. He observes, that Moses had great success in the establishment of his government, and the reception of his laws among the neighboring nations—and that his successors for some ages pursued the same methods, being just and truly religious.

Philostorgius says, that the place called by the natives, Clysma, was the place where the Israelites of old, passed over to the other side, without wetting their feet.[74]

Abulfeda, a Mahometan writer of considerable antiquity, says, "Not far from Alkolsum, is the place where Pharaoh and his army were drowned in the sea."[75]

---

72. Stack. Hist. Bib. Introd. xxx.

73. Reason, of Christ, vol. i. 105,106.

All the late discoveries by Sir William Jones, and those recorded by Mr. Maurice, in his Indian Antiquities, confirm the idea.

74. Lib. 3. chap. v. page 489.

75. Shaw's Travels, 349.

Dr. Shaw says, that near Carondal, the natives still preserve a tradition, that a numerous army was formerly drowned near Beden, the same as Clysma.[76]

The names of places which are still preserved in that country, bear some testimony to the truth of the events. Etham is now called Etti, and we still find the wilderness of Sdur and Sin, and the region Paran. Beyond Corondel or Clysma, is a hill called *Gibel al Marah*[77] not far from which is a desert called Sin,[78] and the coast downward seems to have the same name as it had of old, from the bitter waters, with which it still abounds. Elah and Madian also yet remain, and are mentioned by Abulfeda. Below this region are the palm trees, and the twelve wells of water, Diodorus Siculus, mentions the palm grove as it was described by Ariston, who was sent by Ptolemy to descry the coast of Arabia upon the Red Sea.[79]

Here also is still the desert of Faran, the Pharan of Ptolemy, or Paran of the Scriptures. Diodorus further speaks of some rocks or pillars here, graven with some unknown characters, and he gives the reason why this district is so much honored, because all the country round about was parched up with heat, being without water, and without any other trees, that could afford a shade.

Strabo gives a similar account of the Palm Grove and the wells.[80]

In these names we may see the traces of the ancient Marah, as well as the other places mentioned by Moses. The engravings upon the rocks seem still to remain, as they were seen by Monsieur Monconys, some years since, just in this part of the desert, as he was returning from Mount Sinai.[81]

Ariston, Artemidorus, Agatherchides, and Diodorus, who mention these facts, all lived before the Christian era* Even Strabo was but a few years after—and Abulfeda had no temptation to misrepresent what he saw.

We will now proceed to look into other histories and works of learned heathen writers, to see what traces we can find of the great luminous doctrines taught by Moses, as received from God.

Porphyry, the pagan philosopher already mentioned, who lived in the third century, and wrote much against Christianity, as quoted by Eusebi-

---

76. Ibid. fol. 349.
77. Pocock, 156. Shaw, 349.
78. Ibid 350.
79. Lib. 3. page 175.
80. Lib. 16. page 1122.
81. Pocock, 148. Bryant's Plagues of Egypt, 403, 408.

us, says "The way of the Gods is steep and very craggy—the Barbarians found out many of its paths, but the Greeks wandered from them; and those who kept them, spoiled them, but God revealed those hidden ways to the Egyptians, the Phoenicians, Chaldeans; to the Lydians and to the Hebrews." It is well known, that the three first received much of their religious knowledge from Abraham, the father of the Hebrews; from Moses and the Jews. Porphyry adds, "For this reason, Apollo says in an Oracle, the *Chaldeans and Hebrews alone* have got wisdom, purely worshipping the self-begotten king, God."

Chalcidius, in his Timaeus, says, "To this the Hebrews agree, when they say, that God gave to man a soul, by a divine breath, which they call reason, or a rational soul; but to dumb creatures and wild beasts of the forests, one void of reason: the living creatures and beasts being, by the command of God, scattered over the face of the earth, amongst which was the serpent, who by his evil persuasions, deceived the first of mankind."—He mentions Moses by name, and says, "He was the wisest of men, who was enlivened, not by human eloquence, but by divine inspiration." Dionysius Longinus, who lived in the time of the emperor Aurelian, and was the great favourite of Zenobia, the queen of Palmyra, in his book, *of the Sublime*, after saying, "That they who speak of God, ought to take care to represent him as great, pure, and without mixture;" adds, "Thus does he who gave laws to the Jews, who was an extraordinary man, who conceived and spoke worthily of the power of God," when he writes, in the beginning of his laws, "God spake;"what? "Let there be light, and there was light—let there be earth, and it was so."

Among the late discoveries by Europeans, the sacred books of the Chinese, are not the least. Many of them, by the best accounts that can be obtained, were written some hundred years before our Saviour, These books are preserved in several great libraries in Europe, and by the translation given to us by the learned author of the *Philosophical Principles of Natural and Revealed Religion*, we are informed, that the Chinese have five original or canonical books, called *King*, which, in their language, signifies, "a sublime, sacred, immutable doctrine, founded on unshaken principles." These books were looked upon as of very remote antiquity, in the time of Confucius, who lived about six hundred years before our era.

In the book called *Chan-Hai-King*, it is said, "That the sacred mountain Koncalun, was situated in the middle of the world, and all that could be desired, as wondrous trees, marvellous fountains, and flowery shades, were found on that sacred hill, or hidden garden. This mountain is the inferior palace of the sovereign lord, and the animal *Kaiming* guarded the entry." Another book, written by *Hoi-ai-nang-wang*, in speaking of the first earth, says, "This delicious garden, refreshed with zephyrs, and planted with odoriferous trees, was situated in the middle of the mountain, which was the avenue to Heaven. The waters that bedewed it, flowed from a source, called the fountain of immortality. He that drinks of it never dies. From thence flowed four rivers—a golden river betwixt the south and east—a red river betwixt the north and east—a peaceful stream betwixt the south and west— and the river of the Lamb betwixt the north and west. These magnificent floods are the spiritual fountains of the Sovereign Lord, by which he heals the nations, and fructifies all things."

In the book *Chi-King*, it is said, "Heaven placed mankind upon a high mountain, but *Tai-wang* made it fruitless by his fault. *Wenwang*, or the king of peace, endeavoured to render to the mountain its primitive beauty; but *Tai-wang* contradicted and opposed his will. Why did *Tai-wang* plunge us into so many miseries? Our misery has lasted these many ages—the world is lost—vice overflows all, as a mortal poison—we possessed happy, fruitful fields; a woman robbed us of them. All was subject to us—a woman threw us into slavery—she hates innocence, rind loves vice—the wise husband raised up a bulwark of walls; the woman by an ambitious desire of knowledge, demolished them. Our misery did not come from Heaven, but from a woman. She lost human kind—she erred first, and then sinned."

In the book *Y-King*, we have this account of the fall. "The rebellious and perverse dragon, suffers by his pride—his ambition blinded him—he would mount up to Heaven, but he was thrown down upon earth—at first his abode was in the high places, but he forgot himself—he hurt himself, and lost eternal life."

The book *Chu-King*, informs us, "That it is evident, *by the ancient tradition of our fathers*, that *T-chi-y-cou*, or the Beautiful, became deformed. This son of Heaven, was the first author of all revolt; but his rebellion extended at length to all nations, and deluged the world with crimes."

Chan-Kai-King says, "That *Hoangti*, or the Sovereign Lord, ordered a celestial spirit to precipitate T-chi-y-cou into the black valley of misery."And Lopiadds, "That *T-chi-y-cou* having hatched rebellion, went out from the river of the Lamb." And *Koucil-sang* says, "That he is the great impostor or inventor of all evil. He has the face of a man, the body of a serpent, and is all deceit and lies." And by the most modern discoveries made in later times in the East-Indies, by the famous Sir William Jones, in his Asiatic Researches, it clearly appears, that the Hindus have the tradition of the flood in the time of Noah. They also assert, that the evil being, Ahriman, got upon the earth in the form of a serpent, and seduced the first human pair from their allegiance to Ormusd, by persuading them that he himself was the author of all that existed. The man and woman both believing him, became criminal, and thus sin will perpetuate itself till the resurrection.[82]

And Mr. Halhed, who is so justly celebrated for his discoveries in Indian antiquities, has published a commentary on the Veedas, from an old Persian author, wherein it is asserted, that the *Aswammedha Yug*, or the worship by the sacrifice of a horse, does not merely consist in bringing a horse and sacrificing him; but the rite is also to be taken in a mystic signification: the horse so to be sacrificed, is in the place of the sacrificer, and bears his sins into the wilderness, where he is turned adrift, and becomes the expiatory victim of those sins." I need not attempt to show the similitude between this and the scapegoat of Moses, or to prove that it must have been derived from the same source, divine revelation.

Does not all this clearly show, that the Chinese and East-Indians, must have had among them, the tradition of those great events, related with so much precision by Moses, and that they considered them as of divine original.

If we look to the Greeks and Romans, we find their whole mythology founded on like traditions; and whoever carefully and attentively considers the principles that gave rise to their allegorical fables, which in time became the objects of all their religious worship, will plainly see, that they must have taken their rise either from the revelation made to Moses, or the traditions handed down from Abraham, or perhaps from Noah, and carried into all countries at the dispersion of Babel.

This the learned and pious Justin Martyr, in his second apology to the emperor Antoninus Pius, and the senate of Rome, well observes. He asserts, "That all the fables made of, and all the wonders attributed to, Mercury, Bacchus, Hercules, Perseus, Esculapius, and Bellirophon, were only disguises of some ancient traditions concerning the Messiah." As to Ovid and Virgil, it is plain, that the Mosaic account of the creation of the world, gave to the first his whole plan; and the second seems to have had even more than bare tradition: he must have had an intimate knowledge of the predictions

---

82. Extract from the Zendevetter Annual Register for 1762, fol. 227.

contained in the Old Testament, relative to the second coming of Christ, as well as his first; with the belief and expectation of the Jews founded thereon. Hearken to the extraordinary language of this heathen poet, written, just before the advent of the Saviour, and say what else could have given rise to such noble and divine imagery. "The last age sung by the Cumaean Sybil,[83] is come; the great revolution or re-establishment is at hand; justice is going to return upon earth, and the happy reign of Saturn is to be restored—a divine child is to descend from Heaven—so soon as he is born, the iron age will cease, and the golden age will be renewed over all the earth—he will partake of the divine life—see the heroes associated with the Gods, and they shall see him governing the world in peace, by his father's virtue. Then the earth shall produce all things of its own accord : all wars shall cease, and every thing be restored to its primitive felicity. Beloved offspring of the Gods! Great Son of Jupiter! see how the earth—the seas—the Heavens—and the whole universe, rejoice at thy coming."

The testimony of the Magi, inquiring where the king of the Jews was to be born, having seen his star in the east, and therefore they had come to worship him, adds great confirmation to the suggestion, that they must have had the knowledge of, and believed in the Mosaic account of the coming Saviour.

We might continue to enumerate many more great names, both Jews and heathen, who have added their testimony to the authenticity of the books of Moses, with the other sacred and divine scriptures: but this would swell this answer beyond its original design: suffice it to add to the name of Ptolemy Philadelphus, who was a heathen prince of great learning, and a remarkable encourager of the liberal sciences, whose library at Alexandria amounted to four hundred thousand volumes, those of Cyrus and Darius, who desired the prayers and the sacrifices of the Jews, in behalf of themselves and their kingdoms. Alexander the Great, Augustus, Tiberius, and Vitellius, sent victims to be sacrificed at the temple of Jerusalem, as we learn from Josephus and Philo. I will also mention Longinus, the most competent judge of human writings—Tertullian, both pagan and Christian, with a

---

83. The Sybils were said to be a collection of very important predictions and doctrines derived from the ancients, and kept as a religious arcana by the heathen priests. It is very probable, that the original collection, was the substance of traditions, handed down from the patriarchs; and the word Sybil, a corruption of, or mispronunciation of Cabal, which is the Hebrew word for tradition.

thousand others well known to the learned, who ought to be received as indisputable witnesses to a fact of this nature.

To Christians (or even those who barely hold Jesus Christ to have been a moral teacher, of a virtuous, benevolent and amiable character) it is sufficient to establish their faith, and confirm their hope, that their great Lord and Master, as well as his apostles, have given their assent to the truth of these instructive books.

On the whole, then, Moses is handed down to us by antiquity, as the author of these books. The people and nation to which he belonged, and over whom he was ruler and conductor out of Egypt, and whose fathers were personally witnesses of the important events which he relates, have constantly, invariably, unequivocally, and universally acknowledged and revered him as the inspired author of them. This is the testimony of Josephus, the Jewish historian of the first character among them. "We have only twenty-two books, (says he) which comprehend the history of all ages, and merit our belief: *five belong to Moses*, which contain what relates to the origin of man, and the tradition of the several successions and generations down to his death. From the death of Moses to the reign of Artaxerxes, (who was king of Persia after Xerxes) the prophets who succeeded him have, in their books, written what happened in their time.

The other books contain hymns to the praise of God, and precepts for the conduct of human life. What has happened since the time of Artaxerxes, down to our days, has likewise been recorded by the writers thereof; but they have not met with the like credit, because there has not been any certain succession of prophets during that time. And from hence, (says he) it is manifest, what respect and estimation have been paid to the books which complete our canon, since in so long a tract of time, no man has ventured, either to add any thing to them, or diminish or alter any thing in them; since the Jews from their infancy, are accustomed to call them divine institutions; to believe them stedfastly, and upon occasion to lay down their lives in defence of them."[84]

The greatest men of every age and nation since, whether Jews, Christians or heathens, unite their testimony in favor of Moses being the writer of these books, as the word of God, and coming down from him; and our Lord Jesus Christ and his apostles add their attestation. The religious jealousy, the known accuracy, indefatigable care, and curious precision of the

---

84. Joseph, com. Appion.

Jews as a people, not to mention the separation of the ten tribes, by which a violent and lasting opposition and hatred arose between them, so that they became a watch over each other, give peculiar and demonstrative weight to the evidence, as far as it relates to these books having been preserved and handed down to us without important adulterations: and the experience of every serious and attentive believer, in addition to the continued fulfilment of the predictions contained in them even at this day; leaves no reasonable doubt on their minds, with regard to their truth and inspiration.

It is almost four thousand years since they have been written; and never have they been denied to be the work of Moses, as the word of God, till modern times. It is true, as has been already observed, Aben Ezra, a Jew of considerable note, about the year 1200, first supposed that these books had been written in the time of the kings; but then he considered them as inspired writings, let who would be the author of them, and received them as absolute verity. It never entered into his head, to disbelieve the facts recorded in them, or to doubt their being the word or commandments of God.

In the present century, Woolastin, Collins, Tindal, Shaftsbury, aild Bolingbroke, with a number of others, copied Aben Ezra's objections, and without his faith endeavoured to impose them upon the public, as solid objections to the truth and authenticity of the Old Testament. Aben Ezra had been long since fully answered; and now these champions of infidelity, again brought forward a number of pious and learned men, who obviated every colour of argument or proof, and silenced the objections by fair conviction for a time.

But it was not long, before Voltaire, the late king of Prussia, Rousseau, and others, again retailed out these old exceptions, new vamped up, threatening destruction to all the tenets of revelation. The force of truth prevailed against these adversaries, and for a time the enemies to revealed religion, seemed to avoid coming out to public view. Our author has now come forth with the old objections, clothed in a new garb of language, though copied in substance from his predecessors, with much less knowledge of his subject, but more indecent boldness of manner and disrespect, to those who differ from him in opinion.

And are we now, at this period of light and knowledge, under all the advantages of the learned labours of those who have gone before us, to suffer the indigested rhapsodies and unintelligible declamation of a mere pretender to philosophy—one wholly unacquainted, both with the spirit and letter of revelation, to shake our faith founded on the word of God himself, by objections and reasonings that, when carefully looked into, appear not to be founded either on facts or principles, but look more like the ravings of a brain disordered from intemperance or disappointment ?

But is there any thing improbable or unnatural in attributing this work to Moses, as its inspired author, on the evidence adduced for this purpose. From the necessities of mankind, under their then known circumstances, as has already been shown, it cannot justly be denied, but that God must have given some kind of a revelation of himself and his will, with regard to religious worship, and other necessary knowledge, to Adam and the antediluvian patriarchs. Their lives were lengthened out to a great age, perhaps to answer the important purposes of tradition, among others. Tradition was the most natural, probable, and easy mode of conveying down necessary truths received from God, from generation to generation, before letters were known in the world. It is most likely, therefore, that by this means, the few and simple religious principles necessary for man in the infancy of the world, with the attendant history of their creation, and the divine conduct afterwards towards them, were communicated from Adam to Abraham, by the intervention of not more than two or three other persons; and about the same number might have extended it down to Moses.

Methuselah was about 300 years old when Adam died, and therefore not unlikely to be possessed of all Adam's knowledge of those great and interesting events, that had been communicated to him, as the head of his race.

Shem was almost 100 years old when Methuselah died, and therefore might well have been informed by him, as he had been by Adam. Shem lived till Abraham was above 100 years old, who undoubtedly received from him, the necessary instruction in every thing that related to the worship and knowledge of the one everliving and true God, and his dealings with the fathers since the creation, as Abraham was remarkable from his youth, for a faithful attachment to the service of God, in opposition to every species of idolatry.

Abraham lived till Jacob, the son of Isaac, was 16 years old, and might have taught him the leading principles of religion.

Jacob lived till Levi was 67 years old, and undoubtedly gave him all the instruction he could.

Levi lived till Amram, the father of Moses and Aaron, was far advanced in age, and must have furnished him with every information in his power.

It was a prominent feature in Abraham's great character, that he would teach his children, and his children's children after him, whatever he knew of the one true God: it was therefore to be expected, that not only his knowledge in essential matters should be communicated, but that it should be religiously preserved in his family till the time of Moses, so that he might have been an inspired historian, and at the same time have had a general traditional knowledge of the principal truths of revelation from his ancestors. The people also for whom he wrote, must have been tolerable good judges by this means, of the truth of his account of early transactions, according to the tradition they had received, as well as of the evidences of his special divine mission.

I shall now close this part of the subject, with the observations of an author famous in the religious world for his knowledge and piety. "Whatever befel the children $f Israel, either by prophecies, miracles, or the extraordinary appointments of God, according m to the revelations made in the law of Moses, has besides its own proper and intrinsic evidence, the additional proof of all the miracles and prophecies of Moses. So that the proof of the divine authority of Moses's books, is at the same time a proof of all the other books of Scripture, so far as they are in the matter and subject of them, consequent to these.

The Pentateuch, therefore, and the other books of the Scriptures, reciprocally prove each other, like the cause and the effect. The Pentateuch being the cause and foundation of them; and they are the effect and consequence of the Pentateuch, and the fulfilling the several predictions mentioned therein."[85]

I have been the more particular on these first five books of the Bible, because they are the foundation of all the rest; and if our author has perverted the truth with respect to them, and their divine original is well founded, as we presume we have shown to the plainest demonstration; then all his after subtle objections fall to the ground, without further observations, and render a particular answer unnecessary.[86]

If these books of Moses contain a genuine revelation from God, and were inspired by him, together with their account of the dealings of God with the people of the Jews, in consequence of his promises to Abraham, Isaac and

---

85. Reason, of Christ. 188.

86. If the books of Moses were no forgery, we may take it for granted, that none of the other books of the Old Testament, historical or prophetical, are so; because the former being received, no sufficient motive can be imagined for forging any of the rest, if the attempt could have been successful ; nor would the supposition answer any important purpose to unbelievers at this day. Dr. Priestley's Companion, 535.

Jacob, to give them the land of Canaan as an inheritance, while yet tt was in the actual possession of several powerful and warlike nations; and these servants of God, then but a single family of poor men, without riches, power or influence—bringing them out of the land of Egypt with so many undoubted evidences of a divine power—the miraculous support of so large a body of people for forty years in a wilderness—their supernatural protection from the power of the surrounding nations, all forewarned that their design was to invade their country, and to extirpate their whole race—the threatening so punctually executed, of their wandering the space of forty years in the wilderness, till the whole congregation perished there, except Joshua and Caleb—the wonderful and godlike promulgation of the moral and ceremonial law, so full of types and shadows of the promised Saviour or Messiah—and the final actual possession of this very promised land, by driving out all the inhabitants If these are all of divine original, and their authenticity well established, as I conceive they must be in the judgment of every impartial person, who seriously considers them; then it will not require much reasoning to prove the divine original of the whole Bible, as far as is necessary and consistent with the subject matter of these books.[87]

In a word, our author has discovered great inattention to the spirit, as well as language of the sacred books, as also great ignorance of their use and design. It would lead me too far from my purpose, to go into particular answers to all his trifling and profane objections, after the very able answers already given to him by many excellent and learned men, of various denominations.

If satisfaction has been given as to the futility of his objections, as already considered, respecting the divinity of the Pentateuch, or first five books of the Old Testament; his subsequent profane and idle observations will have no weight on the serious and judicious mind. The subject therefore, *for the present*, will be dismissed, with the following observations, as of special importance to every one who reads the sacred volume.

1st. The promises, threatenings, encouragements, examples and prophetic declarations of the books of the Old Testament have been received, in the opinion of the ablest reasoners on the subject, as substantial evidence, *at this late day* of their truth and importance to the children of men.

---

87. Against all this concurring testimony, we find suddenly from Mr. Paine, that the Bible teaches nothing but lies, obscenity, cruelty and injustice. Had he ever read our Saviour's sermon on the mount, in which the great principles of our faith and duty are summed up ? Let us all but read and practise it, and lies, obscenity, cruelty and injustice, and all human wickedness, would be banished from the world. Erskine*s Speech.

2d. The particularity with which these Scriptures mention the times, places, persons, and other minute circumstances of the several facts related therein, add greatly to the force of other testimony adduced in their favor.

3d. By these means all attentive perusers of the sacred volume, have an opportunity of comparing them with the works of contemporary heathen writers, whether historians, naturalists or civilians, so as to furnish themselves with every kind of reasonable evidence in support of a faith, on which their happiness so essentially depends.

4th. A strong and productive source of satisfactory evidence, arises from their recounting so many minute particulars, being the usual conduct of a whole people, immediately and professedly under the Divine direction and protection, from which the agreement, of so many histories, prophecies, commands, and comfortable assurances, scattered through various books, written at such various times, and all under such various circumstances, is preserved not only with themselves, but with each other, however distant in time, or differing in interesting particulars.

5th. The sameness of arrangement and uniformity of system, running through the whole of the sacred Scriptures, both of the Old and New Testaments, show that it is one invariable principle and unity of design, that moves the whole machine of this fallen world, from Adam to the present day, and adds great weight to the evidence of the truth of the divine Scriptures.

6th. By the manner in which the particular and minute historical events of the Jewish people, as the chosen nation of God, are recorded; the evidence in favor of the great truths of revelation, are daily increasing, and will so continue till the second coming of the Lord Jesus, as he has promised.

7th. It is certain, that both Jews and Christians, have undergone the severest persecutions and sufferings, on account of their sacred books, and yet have never been prevailed upon to deliver them up, which shows that they thought them of the highest importance, most genuine and true.

8th. The preservation of the law of Moses, which is the first book, probably, that was ever written in any language, while so many others, more modem, have been lost, shows the great regard paid to it by the Jews, from its first promulgation—the same holds good in a less degree, of most all the other books of the Old Testament, since most of them are older than the most ancient Greek historians; and as the records of all the neighboring nations are lost, we must sup pose those of the Jew s to have been preserved amidst all their captivities and dispersions, from their importance, or from other such cause, as may be an equal evidence of their genuineness and truth.

9th. The great importance of all the sacred books, appears from the many early translations and paraphrases of them—this must have been an effectual means of securing their integrity and purity, if we could suppose any design to corrupt them.

10th. The great religious hatred and animosity which subsisted between the Jews and Samaritans, and between many of the ancient sects of Jews, show of what importance they all thought their sacred books, and led them to watch over one another with a jealous eye—this gives great weight to the evidence of their genuineness and truth.

These indeed are observations borrowed from eminent writers, who have enlarged upon them, with full confirmation of their force and effect, in point of conclusive argument; and ought to have had convictive influence on our author, had he possessed but a tolerable share of modesty, or if truth had been his favorite pursuit.

And now, in the words of Dr. Samuel Chandler to Mr. Collins, the deistical writer of the present century, I shall close with an address to our author— "If he had acted the part of a fair and reasonable adversary, he should have proved a divine revelation, and the prophecies in proof of it, an impossible thing; by showing either that there is no God, or that if there is, he doth not concern himself with the affairs of nations, kingdoms or individuals; or that if he doth, he knows nothing before it comes to pass—or that he hath no wise purposes to answer, by overruling the affairs of the world, and executing the purposes of his own good pleasure—or if he hath, that he cannot discover those purposes to men—or that if he could, there is no wise and kind purpose to be answered by such a revelation—or that if there is, those to whom he has vouchsafed a revelation, could not discover it to others." But our author, by conceding that there is a God, who ought to be worshipped and adored by men—that he has a right, if he please, to make a revelation of himself to men; and of course in such manner as he pleases, and for such purposes as he pleases, has yielded the question, and given up the dispute.

To the above, let me add, as necessary for our author to have shown, that mankind never offended their Creator, by sinning against him; and therefore have never stood in need of reconciliation to an offended God, as the great governor and Lord of all things—or that if they have, that they are able of themselves to atone for such transgression, and therefore never stood in need of a mediator or intercessor—or if they are unable, and stand in such need, that it will be accomplished for them without their own participation, change of temper or disposition; and indeed against their own will, and while opposing every means of it.

Had our author been successful in this proof, then indeed the controversy would be at an end.—But, blessed be the God of Heaven, that while the divine Scriptures remain, wherein life and immortality are brought to light, and Salvation is proclaimed through the name of Jesus Christ, the Son of God, all this is as impossible as to unite sin and holiness.